Money Life$avers:
What Teens Need to Know About Money

by Don W. F. Bell

cartoons
by Randy Rumpf

donwfbell.com

Money Life$avers:
What Teens Need To Know About Money
Copyright © 2014 Don W. F. Bell

Cartoons, Graphics and Illustrations
Copyright © 2014 Don W. F. Bell

All rights reserved. No part of this book may be used or reproduced in any manner whatsoever without written permission from the author, except in the case of brief quotations embodied in critical articles and reviews.

To order additional copies of this title, contact your favorite local bookstore or visit:
www.tbmbooks.com or donwfbell.com.

Printed in the United States of America

The Troy Book Makers
www.troybookmakers.com

ISBN: 978-1-61468-214-1

photo by Lawrence White

To my dear wife, Diane,
without whose inspiration, love, support and editing
this book would not have been possible.

To home school moms and dads for their encouragement
and contributions.

To youth who want to learn about money
so they will have a better chance of achieving their dreams.

To parents, grandparents, mentors and teachers who want
to help today's youth grow up to be happy, financially
independent adults.

Disclaimer

As the field of personal finance and financial literacy is rapidly evolving, some of the information in this book may become obsolete. The author gives no warranty and accepts no responsibility for the accuracy or completeness of the material. Any reliance that users place on the information is, therefore, strictly at their own risk.

The financial information in this book is for educational purposes only and does not constitute financial advice. You are advised to discuss your specific requirements with an independent financial advisor.

> "All the perplexities, confusion and distress in America arise, not from the defects in their constitution or confederation, not from want of honor or virtue, so much as downright ignorance of the nature of coin, credit and circulation…"
>
> – John Quincy Adams, 1829

Personal Finance

The principles and methods that individuals use to acquire and manage income and assets.

Financial Literacy

The ability to use knowledge and skills to manage one's financial resources effectively for lifetime happiness and financial security.

Lifestyle Expectations

In America there is an expectation that every generation will achieve a higher standard of living than the previous generation. Unless the upcoming generation becomes a lot more intelligent about their finances, this may no longer be the case.

Contents

Introduction 1
Money Life$aver Quiz Games 11

$5 QUESTIONS

A Brief History of Money 21
Employment and Income 39
Needs and Wants 53
Smart Spending 61

$10 QUESTIONS

Banking 91
Saving 137
Expenses, Bills & Budgets 159

$20 QUESTIONS

Prepaid Cards 183
Credit 203
Credit Cards 213
Loans 237
Debt 247

Contents

$50 QUESTIONS

Risk 261

Insurance 269

Gambling. 287

Fraud 295

Business 315

Economics. 321

$100 QUESTIONS

Investing. 337

Taxes 373

Money Tips For Teens. 389

Money Tips For Parents 405

Index 431

About the Author 442

> *"The love of money is the root of all evil."*
> — the Bible, Timothy 6:10
>
> *"Lack of money is the root of all evil."*
> — George Bernard Shaw

Introduction

"We are more than what we buy, aren't we?"

Introduction

Financial Literacy: More Important Than Ever

"A fool and his money are soon parted" is a proverb that has been in use since at least 1557, when poet Thomas Tusser wrote a similar phrase in a poem titled "Five Hundred Points of Good Husbandry." The "fool" refers to someone who loses money quickly by being tricked or by spending wastefully. As Tusser's maxim shows, the lack of money smarts – or financial literacy – has plagued people for a very long time.

Even though we have made progress recently in financial education, we still need to do a lot more. The task is made more difficult these days by the volume of financial knowledge a person needs to master in order to function effectively. Add to this the many ways people can lose money either through wasteful spending or fraud and we see how important it is to redouble our efforts to increase financial literacy. Young people in particular need money smarts so they can successfully negotiate the complexities of the modern world of money. If there's any doubt about the need for investment in financial education, consider the following:

- The very nature of money is changing. Currency as we know it (coins and banknotes) is being replaced by a cashless system that uses electronic money, virtual wallets and the Internet. To take advantage of this new money system and not be exploited by it, people need to understand how it works.
- As borrowing money and buying on credit have become more commonplace, many people are now accumulating mountains of debt that will take years to pay off.
- Workers will need more savings and more skills as a cushion against the shocks of today's global economy, which offers less job security and a less predictable income.

Introduction

- The rising cost of college education today often requires students to borrow money. To avoid taking on too much debt, students (and their parents) need to make wise choices about how much to borrow in order to finance their educational investment.

- A comfortable retirement (indeed, any retirement) will be unaffordable for most Americans, unless they learn how to become better savers and investors. Company pensions have been replaced by individual retirement plans that provide less income and less security. In the future, social security and government benefits may be reduced.

- Financial products and services have become increasingly complex.

- Health care costs are rising and health care insurance obtained through employment is often inadequate and unpredictable.

- Advertisers are constantly finding new ways of manipulating consumer emotions, getting people to believe that "wants" are "needs" they can't live without. It's important to develop an awareness of advertising tactics to ensure that purchase decisions are based on real needs and reasoned (objective) criteria rather than on emotional (subjective) appeals.

- Given the overwhelming choice of consumer products and services in today's marketplace, people need to become more informed consumers.

- Con artists are constantly inventing new ways of stealing people's money and identities; phone and Internet scams are widespread. People need to recognize and learn how to avoid becoming victims of fraudulent schemes.

Introduction

Financial literacy is not only vital to each of us individually, it is also essential to the economic stability and vitality of our country. Financially literate citizens are more likely to be self-sufficient and less dependent on government-funded economic assistance. They will also be more discerning consumers and will demand higher-quality products and services. This, in turn, will encourage competition and innovation in the marketplace. And these informed people will incur less debt, save more money and have resources left to invest in building a healthier, stronger national economy.

The "Happiness Economy"

Today's media continually bombard us with images of the rich and famous, suggesting that we should all seek to achieve their extravagant lifestyle. If only we'd buy this car, that dream home, that electronic gadget, that diamond necklace, those designer shoes….we'd be just like them. And the more wonderful things we own – according to the ads we see everywhere – the happier we'll be. But are all these things truly the stuff of a happy life?

If we subscribe to this materialist dream, we'll need more and more money to be happy. From there, it's only a short step to the belief that money itself is the main goal in life. But is this belief based on fact? Do we really need pots and pots of gold to be happy? Perhaps not. Isn't it more valuable to be healthy, respected and excited about your life?

Maybe there's another way to think of money. Maybe you can see it simply as a tool for maximizing your happiness. This approach to managing money can be referred to as the **"*happiness economy.*"**

Introduction

Still, while we may not need millions to be happy, we do need a certain amount to sustain ourselves and also pursue our dreams. In the United States, the "magic number" is thought to be an annual income of about $75,000 (2012 dollars). Researchers at Princeton University found in a recent study that up to a point, higher household incomes are, indeed, associated with a better outlook on life. Interestingly, though, the beneficial effects of money tapered off entirely after the $75,000 mark.

The big question for each one of us is: just how much money do we really need to be happy? For starters, we all need enough monetary resources for the basics of life – food, shelter, clothing. We also need a solid education and health care. For a few people, the basics are all they need to be happy, but for most of us, there's more to life.

In determining how much is enough, look hard at yourself and decide what is central to your own personal happiness. Generally speaking, your happiness will depend on how well you engage your own personal talents, passions and values and how well you manage your money to accomplish your dreams.

Your **talents and passions** are unique. To be truly happy, you need to build on your talents and pursue those things you find most fun and exciting. Maybe you have an aptitude for math, love science and want to be an astrophysicist. Maybe you are musical and want to play trumpet in a symphony orchestra. Maybe you are a people person and aspire to become a social worker here in the United States or in the developing world. Maybe you just love car mechanics, gardening, cooking, painting …. the possibilities are endless.

Introduction

Besides your personal talents and passions, there is the more elusive matter of **personal values.** To be truly happy, you need to live your life in accordance with the values you believe to be most important. You absorb values from your family, friends, teachers and social and religious organizations, as well as from the cultural environment in which you live. Words that express values include: honesty, loyalty, charity, truthfulness and helpfulness.

Often you act on your values by contributing time and money to good causes. Research has shown that most of us derive more happiness from spending our "extra" money n others rather than on ourselves.

Knowing who you are in terms of talents, passions and values is not enough, however. We all need a strategy for accomplishing our dreams, and that strategy almost always involves money. Unfortunately, when it comes to managing money, we seldom think or act with a view to the future, and this short-term focus is one of the greatest obstacles to realizing our dreams. Every day we are tempted to spend money on things we may not need or even really want. In this way, we may fritter away our funds and jeopardize our long-term happiness.

The best antidote to this behavior is learning how to manage money effectively. This, coupled with a set of realistic, personal goals, can lead to a happy life.

> *"Choosing to pursue the four basic values of faith, family, community and work is the surest path to happiness."*
> — Arthur C. Brooks, social scientist and author

Introduction

Learning About Money the Hard Way

Most of us learn about money the hard way by making mistakes. We pick up just enough knowledge to survive, but rarely enough to thrive. In school we learn basic arithmetic that we can apply to money transactions. We go with our parents to the store and learn how to buy small items with our allowance. Maybe someone gives us some money to put in a savings account. Later we may take on a part-time job, start spending our own earned money, open up a checking account and get a credit card.

Still later we go off to work and, if we're lucky, take home enough to start investing some of our earnings. But rarely have we taken the time to seriously study and discuss how best to manage our money. In our increasingly complex financial world, this haphazard approach is clearly not sufficient to ensure that we will lead a happy life and avoid expensive, painful errors.

If we don't learn enough about managing money, we may find ourselves in a ton of trouble with our dreams drifting further and further away.

There are many pitfalls:

- We may start relying on credit cards to cover basic expenses. When we don't pay our credit card balance (what we owe the credit card company) in full every month, we incur finance charges that could grow into a large debt.
- We may take on a high-interest loan for college, a car or a house only to discover that we can't handle the costs.
- We may be victimized by a scam, give away personal information and lose money through no fault of our own.
- After a car accident we may find that our insurance is insufficient and we're liable for thousands of dollars in damages.

Introduction

- We may be lured into gambling or investing our money in some risky, money-losing enterprise.
- We may develop unrealistic expectations about our future, our earning power and how much stuff we can afford to buy. Unrealistic expectations eventually clash with reality, leading to disillusionment, disappointment, frustration and anger.

One or any combination of these troubles can scuttle our dreams, impair our health, destroy cherished relationships and even lead to irreversible poverty.

Even with some degree of money smarts, we may run into unanticipated financial difficulties that can put our dreams and happiness at risk. We may experience trouble finding a job, or lose the one we have. To be employable, we may need to borrow money for more education. We may suffer a costly health crisis. In any of these situations, the more we know about money, the better off we'll be.

The Fun Way To Learn About Money

It's no fun learning about money in the "school of hard knocks," but it may not be much more fun learning about the subject in a lecture or a book. In fact, it might be downright boring. For most folks, facts about money, banks, credit cards and the like don't just jump off the pages of a book and grab their attention. They don't say, "Wow! Am I ever glad I learned that financial fact! That's so cool! What a lifesaver!"

So, how to make a potentially dull subject – personal finance – engaging and fun? Why not reverse the standard teaching approach and ask questions first before presenting content? In this way the reader's interest is immediately piqued and they're primed to absorb the explanation. That's how this book is organized.

Introduction

The question and answer (or "guess and learn") approach is similar to many popular TV games shows. It's an excellent way to build knowledge. When you choose a correct answer to a challenging question, you get positive reinforcement for what you already know. And even when your answer is wrong, there is the stimulation from getting immediate feedback and learning something new.

A special feature of this book is that it can be used to play individual or group games. As with TV quiz games, participants in group games enjoy the excitement of competing with each other and the pleasure of sometimes winning. In this lively context, learning is inevitable (even if no one wins a million dollars).

Readers can work their way through the book one chapter at a time, or they can use the table of contents or index to zero in on a topic about which they would like to learn more. In some instances, they may find they know more than they thought; in others, they may find they know less. But, since this is not a final exam, there should be no stress – it should be fun!

Lifelong Financial Learning

Of course, reading this book is just the start of a lifelong learning process. The financial world is in constant flux. Today, for instance, we are moving away from currency. The nature of money transactions in the 21st century will be very different from what they were in the 20th century. We will need to stay current with this changing financial sphere.

For young people, time is on their side. If they learn the basics of effective money management, keep abreast of new developments and create long-term goals, they will have a good chance of maintaining a comfortable standard of living, realizing their dreams and living a happy life.

Introduction

How This Book Is Organized

This book contains over four hundred quiz questions arranged in five levels - $5, $10, $20, $50 and $100. Generally, the higher the dollar level, the more difficult the question. For each $ level, quiz questions are presented on odd-numbered pages and correct answers and relevant content on even-numbered pages.

To add some fun to the learning experience, this book also offers entertaining cartoons, quotations and money trivia. These items effectively reinforce important financial concepts.

The book concludes with a compendium of essential money management advice in the form of tips for teens and parents.

The book's content is based mainly on two resources:

- the *National Standards in K-12 Personal Finance Education* (developed by the Jump$tart Coalition for Personal Financial Literacy – jumpstart.org) and
- *Money As You Grow – 20 Things Kids Need to Know to Live Financially Smart Lives* (developed by the President's Advisory Council on Financial Capability – moneyasyougrow.org).

Money Life$avers integrates material found in the resources above and elsewhere. It is a handy reference guide to the financial terms and concepts considered most important for young people to understand.

> *"Go confidently in the direction of your dreams. Live the life you have imagined."*
> — Henry David Thoreau

Money Life$aver Quiz Games

"Our money-smart teen contestants are awesome! They're on their way to winning the $10,000 jackpot!"

> *"A game can easily be made fascinating enough to put over the dullest facts."*
>
> — A.M. Mood and R.D. Specht,
> "Gaming as a Technique of Analysis"

QUICK ONE-PERSON QUIZZES

Object: to have fun learning about money with little concern for selecting correct answers.

- Browse the table of contents or index to find a topic that interests you, or flip through the book quickly, looking for something that grabs your attention.
- Turn to a page of questions. Try answering one question. (Note: More than one answer may be correct. Pick all correct answers.)
- Turn to the following answer page, check your answers(s) against the correct answer(s) and read the accompanying explanation.
- Continue with the next question on the previous page or return to the table of contents or index to find another topic that interests you.

RULES FOR AN INDIVIDUAL QUIZ GAME

Object: to have fun learning about money while trying to improve your score every time you play the game.

Setup for an Individual Game:

- Make a copy of the Money Life$aver Score Card (see end of this chapter). If using play money, collect play money from another game (e.g., Monopoly) with $5, $10, $20, $50 and $100 denominations.
- Pick one of the five levels of play ($5 through $100).
- Decide how to end the game – either after a preset number of questions have been answered (e.g., 10) OR a preset period of time limit has elapsed (e.g., 20 minutes).

Money Life$aver Quiz Games

Playing the Game

1. Turn to a page of questions at the appropriate $ level. Select a question you have not answered before.
2. Write the letter(s) for the correct answer(s) (e.g., a,b,c...) on the back of the score card or on a separate sheet of paper. (Note: More than one answer may be correct.)
3. Turn to the following answer page, check your answer(s) against the correct answer(s) and read the accompanying explanation. (Note: When multiple answers to a question are correct, you must have selected ALL the correct answers for your response to be considered "correct.")
4. Do one of the following:

- *If your response is correct,* put a check (v) in a box in the appropriate $ column on your copy of the score card. *If the game is using play money,* collect the quiz question $ amount in play money
- *If your response is incorrect,* put an X in a box in the appropriate $ column on your copy of the score card.

5. Repeat actions 1-4 until you have completed your preset number of questions or time period.
6. After the last turn enter your final score on the score card.

Winning

Play the game again with a new copy of the score card using the same criteria for ending the game (i.e., a preset number of questions or a fixed time period). If you improved your score, you win!

Money Life$aver Quiz Games

RULES FOR A GROUP MONEY QUIZ GAME

Friends, family members or students playing a group game may enjoy pretending they are on a TV quiz game show.

Object: to have fun playing the game while trying to attain the highest score using the Money Life$aver Score Card, or alternatively, trying to accumulate the most play money.

Setup for a Group Game:

1. Players must decide on the following game conditions:

- *Questioner* – who will ask the questions – a non-player (e.g., a parent or teacher) OR individual players (taking turns in the role of questioner).

- *Difficulty levels* – which *one* of the five difficulty levels ($5, $10, $20, $50 or $100) will be played.

- *Penalties* – whether players will be penalized for incorrect answers, e.g., for an incorrect answer to a $5 question, the player subtracts $5 from his/her score card or play money. (A player cannot have a negative score. The lowest score is zero.)

- *Play Money* – whether play money will be used in the game.

- *Game Ending* – whether the game ends after a preset number of rounds has been played (e.g., 20) OR a preset period of time to play has elapsed (e.g., 20 minutes).

2. Make a copy of the Question Log and copies of the Money Life$aver Score Card for every player (see end of chapter). Players choose a player number and write their name and player number on their score card.

3. If players decide to use play money, collect play money in $5, $10, $20, $50 and $100 denominations from another game (e.g., Monopoly) and store in a "game bank" (e.g. a small box).

Money Life$aver Quiz Games

Playing the Game

Clockwise play. Play always proceeds in a clockwise direction around the circle of players. When group members are taking turns asking the questions, the questioner is always the person to the left of the player whose turn it is.

Player 1 starts the game.

On your turn:

1. The Questioner asks you a quiz question (at the appropriate $ level) that has not been asked before in this game.

2. You may ask to see the question, but may not, of course, look at the answer(s).

3. You must answer the question, even if you are unsure of the correct response(s). Write the letters for the correct answer(s) (e.g., a,b,c…) on the back of your scorecard or on a separate sheet of paper. (Note: More than one answer may be correct.)

4. The Questioner reads the answer and the explanation.

5. The Questioner checks your response, declares it correct or incorrect and records the result (e.g., $5-22 √ or $5-22 X) in the player's column in the Question Log. (Note: When multiple answers to a question are correct, you must have selected ALL the correct answers.)

6. If the game uses play money and the answer is correct, the Questioner awards the player the quiz question $ amount in play money. If the answer is incorrect and there is a penalty for wrong answers, the player pays the game bank the quiz question $ amount in play money.

7. Document your response and current score on your score card.
- *If your response is correct,* put a check mark (√) in a box in the appropriate row and $ column on your score card.

- Calculate your current score (add the current quiz question $ amount to your previous score in the Current Score column) and enter the new score in the Current Score column.
- *If your response is incorrect,* put an X in a box in the appropriate row and $ column on your score card.
- If there is no penalty for wrong answers, carry your current score down to the next line.
- If there is a penalty for wrong answers, subtract the quiz question $ amount from the last current score and enter the result in the Current Score column. A score can never be less than zero.

Play then passes to the player on your left.

Ending the Game:

- Conclude the game when the preset number of rounds has been played OR the preset time period has elapsed. (Note: If the time period elapses somewhere in the middle of the last round, continue playing until every player has had their turn on that round.)
- Players enter their final score at the bottom of their score cards.

Winning the Game:

The player with the highest score and the most play money (if used) wins.

Game Variation: Playing More Than One Difficulty Level

Before the game begins, players agree on which difficulty levels ($5 - $100) are to be played during the game and who gets to decide the difficulty level of each question asked (i.e., the questioner or the current player).

Money Life$aver Question Log

After each player's turn, the Questioner notes the $ level, question # and result (i.e., "√" for a correct response or an "X" for an incorrect response) within a box in the appropriate column. Example: $5-22 √ or $5-22 X

Round	Player 1	Player 2	Player 3	Player 4
1				
2				
3				
4				
5				
6				
7				
8				
9				
10				
11				
12				
13				
14				
15				
16				
17				
18				
19				
20				

Money Life$aver Score Card

Player# _____ Name: _____

After your turn, put a "√" for a correct response or an "X" for an incorrect response in the appropriate $ column box. Calculate and enter your score in the Current Score column.

Turn	$5	$10	$20	$50	$100	Current Score
1						
2						
3						
4						
5						
6						
7						
8						
9						
10						
11						
12						
13						
14						
15						
16						
17						
18						
19						
20						

Final Score $ _____

A PARENT / TEACHER / MENTOR GUIDE

If you're a parent, teacher or mentor, you can use the quizzes in this book to add excitement to the learning process.

- Browse the table of contents or index to find a topic you want your student(s) to learn more about.
- Present a quiz question orally, on paper, or on a whiteboard, projection screen, or computer screen.
- Ask students which answer(s) they think are correct and why.
- Display the correct answer(s). Read and discuss the explanatory notes.
- If you are a parent, you can use this occasion to start a dialogue with your child about how this topic relates to your family finances.
- Optional: have students keep track of how many questions they answered correctly using the Money Life$aver Score Card.
- Optional: offer rewards for correct answers. The rewards could be an object or activity that is known to motivate the player or group of players.

Parents, teachers and mentors may be more comfortable presenting the content first and then following up with quiz questions. For material that is almost entirely new to students, this approach is certainly acceptable.

When conducting a group game, the Question Log can be used to identify topics that are giving students difficulty.

A Brief History of Money

Other Words for Money

Many colorful terms are used to denote money. Some have to do, understandably, with food such as bread, dough, gravy, clams and bones. Other money terms and slang include: cash, chips, frogskins, lolly, moolah, bucks, greenbacks, shrapnel, loot, riches, treasure, folding stuff, wad, wherewithal, wonga and on and on.

How the Dollar Sign ($) Came to Be

According to the Oxford Dictionary, the $ symbol came from the handwritten "ps,", which was an abbreviation for "peso" in old Spanish American books. The symbol as we know it first appeared in the 1770s in manuscript documents of English-Americans who were doing business with Spanish-Americans. It started to appear in print after 1800.

Origin of the Word "Dollar"

The word "dollar" comes from a Flemish or Low German word "daler" (in German "taler" or "thaler"), which was short for Joachimstaler. This was a coin that came from the silver mines of Joachimstal in what is now the Czech Republic. The term ultimately became associated with a coin that circulated in the Spanish-American and British North American colonies at the time of the Revolutionary War. It became the name used for a unit of United States currency (paper money and coins) in the late 1700s.

A Brief History of Money $5

Question 1. **A method of exchanging goods or services directly without money:**

a. sell
b. consign
c. loan
d. auction
e. barter

"I want one hundred chickens for this bear."

> *"In societies of low civilization, there is no money."*
> — Herbert Spencer

$5   A Brief History of Money

***Answer 1.* e – Barter.** In very early times it is thought hunter-gatherer societies had a form of exchange that involved the sharing of valuable goods amongst all the members of the community. When someone came home empty-handed after a day of hunting and gathering, for instance, other members of the group would give him food without any expectation of immediate or even future reimbursement. They might have done this out of pure sympathy (anyone can have a bad day) or to achieve some status, but they also could have done this to ensure the survival of the group as a whole.

As humankind evolved, people turned to farming, and the practice of barter became more prevalent. Barter is the direct exchange of one good or service for another. No money or other such medium is involved. If the farmer down the way had something you needed or wanted (say, a basket of olives), you would try to find something he needed that was of an equivalent value (a bag of barley, perhaps) and you would make an exchange. Today, individuals, organizations and governments still find barter more advantageous than money in certain circumstances.

However, the bartering process was problematical. What if two people just couldn't agree on the value of some items they wanted to exchange? What if a farmer wanted to barter something big and heavy - a load of watermelons, for instance - but had no way of transporting them? What if you wanted a cow but had nothing to exchange until your crop of apples ripened? With everyone trying to acquire and unload all kinds of stuff, a farmer could end up involved in a series of trades just to obtain the one basket of yams he wanted in the first place. All this was awkward and time-consuming. People needed a better way of exchanging goods that would eliminate these problems.

A Brief History of Money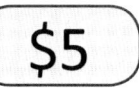

Question 2. **Before coins and paper money, some of the commodities people used as money to trade goods were:**

a. fur
b. shells
c. beans
d. tea
e. sharks' teeth

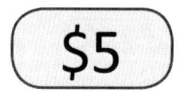

A Brief History of Money

***Answer 2.* a,b,c,d,e – Commodity money.** To overcome problems with the practice of barter, people went in search of items that could be used as a common medium of exchange or "money." Just about anything can be used for money, as long as everyone agrees to use the same item.

In ancient China, they decided to use cowry (snail) shells as money. Farmer A could go to the market with a supply of shells and buy a cow from Farmer B who in turn could use the shells to buy a new spade. These shells weren't valuable in and of themselves but they were easy to find, carry and exchange.

More often the items used as money were valuable in some way. Sometimes they were beautiful and rare, like feathers or sharks' teeth. Sometimes they were useful such as salt, rice, tools, nails, furs, or tea. These latter items are referred to as "commodities", which are basic things that many people need or want to sustain or improve their lives. They are: (1) products that are the same regardless of where they come from or who produces them such as rice and (2) products that hold the same value for everyone such as salt.

Many commodities were easy to measure out and trade such as rice. But throughout history, cattle have been used as a medium of exchange, as well. Whatever your commodity money was, though, you could use it to buy just about anything you wanted – if beans were being used as money, you could hand over five bags of beans to buy a special cooking pot or a basket of peaches.

Today, we still have commodity markets, but for everyday exchange of goods, commodity money just didn't work out that well. Carrying heavy bags of salt, for instance, was laborious and some agricultural products, such as seeds, were difficult to preserve – they would rot and lose their value.

A Brief History of Money $5

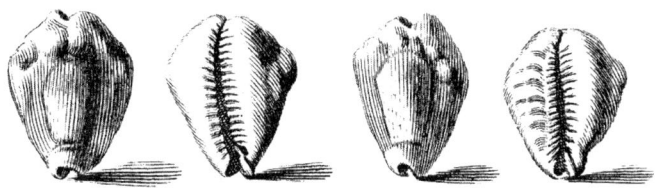

Cowry shells used as money – eighth to sixth century BCE

Question 3. Coins made from gold, silver and copper became a popular form of money because:

a. Gold, silver and copper were considered to be valuable materials
b. Gold, silver and copper are hard to fake with less valuable materials
c. Gold, silver and copper are soft enough to shape into coins
d. Coins are hard to lose
e. Coins can be made in standard weights and imprinted with recognizable symbols, e.g., the image of a king

$5   A Brief History of Money

Answer 3. **a,b,c,e – Coins.** Commodity money mainly consisted of agricultural products, which could be bulky and difficult to use as a medium of exchange. People needed a more efficient way to pay for the goods they wanted. This is when they started to use raw forms of gold, silver and copper for money. These metals were rare and therefore considered valuable. They were also durable and hard to fake – there's nothing else quite like gold, silver or copper. Plus, small lumps of these metals were fairly easy to carry and use in making calculations.

Nonetheless, despite all their good properties, lumps of the rare metals posed problems. Storekeepers had to keep scales to weigh them in order to estimate their value, and customers often didn't trust the scales.

Around the seventh century BCE, the King of Lydia (part of modern-day Turkey) came upon a solution. He invented coins, the first in the Western world. Using a mixture of gold and silver, the Lydians made bean-shaped coins in standard weights with an imprint of the king's personal seal. This gave people confidence in the value of the coin. As the practice of making standardized coins spread throughout the ancient world, rulers marked their money with a variety of recognizable symbols, including animals and mythical beings. Since coins were given a certain value, it became easier for people to determine the cost of the items they wanted to buy and sell.

However, just as with commodity money, coins had drawbacks. They were heavy to carry and slippery and could easily fall out of a pocket. Plus, pickpockets lurked in public places ready to steal them from you. Once coins were gone, there was no way to reclaim their value. Today we still exchange coins, but the metals have little value; they are now simply tokens representing a certain value.

***Question 4.* A banknote is:**

a. the same as a letter of credit

b. a form of credit

c. banker's notes about accounts

d. a debt

e. a slip of paper that could be exchanged for silver or gold coins held in a bank or other safe location

***Question 5.* A letter of credit is a form of representative money that is:**

a. an early form of traveler's checks

b. a safe alternative to carrying lots of coins and paper money

c. a slip of paper that could be exchanged for silver or gold coins at a foreign bank

d. a letter from a friend saying you are worthy of credit

This is one of the earliest-known coins. It was made during the 7th century B.C. in the kingdom of Lydia (now Turkey). Weighed lumps of electrum (a mixture of gold and silver) were stamped (minted) with images of lions and bulls to confirm their weight and value.

Answer 4. **e – Representative money: banknotes.**
Representative money differs from commodity money in that it is not, in and of itself, valuable; it is merely a token of value. Banknotes are an early example of this form of money. They came into being as a way for people to safeguard their coins against loss or theft and to make business transactions easier. People began to leave their coins with a monastery, goldsmith or bank in exchange for a slip of paper on which was written the value of the coins that were being held. The slip of paper was easier to carry but less attractive to thieves. It could be passed from one person to another in the course of buying and selling goods with the understanding that at any time anyone could turn in the banknote for the coins. Of course, it was still possible to lose a banknote and with it any opportunity to reclaim the coins.

Answer 5. **a,b,c – Representative money: letters of credit.** In Italy during the 12th and 13th centuries, influential families began to set up banks, and gradually a network of banks spread throughout Europe. These banks greatly facilitated commerce. All over Europe at that time, markets were springing up. Merchants traveled from one city to another buying and selling wares in these markets. But travel was risky in those days; robbers on the open highway frequently pounced on people to steal their coins. So instead of carrying these tempting items, a merchant would get a letter of credit in his name from his hometown banker (see page 32 for an example). With the letter in hand and proof of identity, the merchant could go to another banker in a faraway city and exchange the letter for coins. This was an early form of a traveler's check. (A more complex form of letters of credit is still used today, especially in international trade.)

A Brief History of Money $5

One of the most famous examples of representative money was the old British Pound bill, or so-called Pound Sterling. The Bank of England guaranteed that the bearer of the bill could exchange it for an actual pound of sterling silver. The 1896 U.S. note (below) could be exchanged for five U.S. dollars' worth of silver.

This bank note image is from the National Numismatic Collection at the Smithsonian Institution.

"Electricity Presenting Light To The World" is an extraordinary banknote. A winged female, "Electricity", holds an electric lamp aloft high over America. To her left, Jupiter holds in one hand the lightning that powers the lamp and with his other hand, pulls on reins of lightning to restrain his horses. Fame sits at Electricity's feet, trumpeting her achievement to the world. To Electricity's right is a bald eagle, standing guard over the Western Hemisphere. Behind the eagle, with the United States Capitol in the background, is Peace with one hand upraised beside a dove. This remarkable blend of legend, patriotism and beauty came together to create a note widely regarded to be the most beautiful currency in United States history.

$5   A Brief History of Money

> Smith Bros & Co.
> CIRCULAR LETTER of CREDIT
> No. B24609
>
> New York, March 25. 1916
>
> Gentlemen:
>
> We request that you will have the goodness to furnish Jerrod Ball the bearer, whose signature is at foot, with any funds he may require to the extent of £500=(say Five Hundred pounds Sterling) against his drafts upon Messrs SMITH BROS. & CO. LONDON: each draft must bear the number (No B24609) of this letter, and we engage that the same shall meet due honor. Whatever sums Mr. Ball may take up you will please endorse on the back of this circular letter which is to continue in force till March 25. 1899 from the present date.
>
> We are respectfully, Gentlemen,
> Your obedient servants
> Smith Bros & Co.
>
> THE SIGNATURE OF
> Jerrod Ball
>
> To Messieurs
> the bankers mentioned on
> the 2d page of this Letter of Credit

Letters of credit (such as the example above) are a form of representative money and, together with banknotes, are the forerunners of our modern paper money.

A Brief History of Money $5

Question 6. **Fiat money is:**

a. money backed by gold reserves
b. money not backed by gold or silver reserves
c. money given value by government decree
d. a form of money the United States adopted in 1776

Question 7. **The year the United States switched to fiat money:**

a. 1851
b. 1901
c. 1931
d. 1971
e. 2001

Question 8. **The invention of currency (coins and paper money) made it easier to:**

a. trade goods
b. store money
c. transport money
d. collect taxes
e. counterfeit money

"Back in my day you could cash in your dollars for gold. Now a dollar is worth whatever the government and people think it's worth. But don't worry kid, you can still buy stuff with it."

Answer 6. **b,c – Fiat money.** Fiat money refers to money that is not backed by reserves of a certain commodity, usually gold or silver. The money itself is given value by government fiat (Latin for "let it be done") or decree. Without government guaranteeing the value of our bank notes, they would just be pretty pieces of paper with pictures of dead presidents.

Governments throughout history have often switched from representative money to fiat money in times of need (e.g., war) either by simply printing the paper money they needed or by ceasing to exchange paper money for gold or silver.

Answer 7. **d – Change from representative to fiat money.** In 1971, the United States switched from representative to fiat money. At the same time many countries in the developed world fixed their currencies to the American dollar, thereby changing their currency from representative to fiat-based money as well.

Answer 8. **a,b,c,d,e – Advantages of currency.** Coins and paper money are referred to collectively as currency. The invention of currency made it easier to store money, transport money and trade goods. It also made it easier for governments to collect taxes. On the down side, paper money was easier to fake (counterfeit).

Virtual Currencies

Virtual currencies (such as bitcoins) can be used just like dollars when doing electronic money transactions. The value of a bitcoin derives from the limited supply of "virtual" coins and the agreement among users that the "coins" constitute real currency. Bitcoins can sometimes be cheaper to use than regular currencies, as there are fewer "transaction fees." However, as bitcoins are not regulated or backed by a government, they are less secure and less stable than traditional currencies.

A Brief History of Money $5

Question 9. **Counterfeit money is:**

a. the same as play money

b. fake money that looks like real money

c. illegal to create or use

d. not harmful to anyone

A Brief History of Money

***Answer 9.* b,c – Counterfeit money.** Counterfeit money is fake money produced without the legal sanction of a state or government. It so closely resembles an official form of currency that many people mistake it for real money. Governments are continually working to design new bills with special security features, such as holograms, to foil counterfeiters.

It's a crime to counterfeit money. Not so very long ago the penalty for counterfeiting was death. "To Counterfeit is Death" was printed on American money in the early days of the republic. Government authorities eventually detect and confiscate counterfeit money, but not before people get hurt. Individuals and companies that unknowingly accept counterfeit money do not receive any compensation for their loss.

During the Civil War, one third of United States money was counterfeit. President Lincoln created the United States Secret Service to go after the counterfeiters. Counterfeiting was not only the realm of small criminals but was used by nations at war to destabilize the economy of opponents. Britain did this during the American Revolutionary War, as did Nazi Germany during World War II.

"Virtual" Wallets – Another Way To Pay

"Virtual" wallets are now appearing in the marketplace. They allow individuals and businesses to transfer funds electronically. Some of the things you can do with a virtual wallet: send or receive online payments; purchase or sell goods and services; make or receive donations; exchange cash with someone. You can download a virtual wallet application to your smartphone and link it to your bank account or credit card. Then you can use your smartphone to make purchases at stores that have the capacity to process your virtual wallet transactions. One of the most popular "virtual wallets" today is PayPal.

A Brief History of Money

Question 10. **Electronic money:**

a. can be used in the same way as other forms of currency
b. is the newest form of money
c. is widely used today
d. does not exist in physical form
e. is totally secure

Question 11. **Money can be:**

a. any metal circulating as a medium of exchange
b. paper money such as government banknotes
c. electronic money
d. anything generally accepted as payment for goods and services

Answer 10. **a,b,c,d – Electronic money.** This is the newest form of money. Terms for electronic money include e-currency, virtual currency and cyber currency. Electronic money exists only in banking computer systems, not in any physical or tangible form.

In the United States, amazingly, only a small portion of the currency in circulation is in the form of dollar bills and coins. Every day more and more people receive their paychecks through direct deposit, move money from one place to another with electronic fund transfers (EFTs) and spend money using credit and debit cards. While we still find physical money convenient in certain situations – buying an ice cream cone or dropping a donation in the Salvation Army pot – its use has been diminishing.

There are two types of electronic money: identified e-money and anonymous e-money (digital cash). Identified e-money is associated with a person and contains data revealing that person's identity. Identified e-money allows banks to track money as it moves electronically through the economy. Anonymous e-money (e.g., bitcoins) works just like real currency. Once it is taken from an account, it can be spent or given away without leaving any record of transactions. As with earlier forms of money, security remains an issue with all types of electronic money.

Answer 11. **a,b,c,d – Money today.** Money can be just about anything that a group of people agrees to use as payment for goods and services. Today, you could probably find all of the following forms of money in use somewhere in the world: commodities such as rice, wheat, etc.; coins made of valuable or common metals; paper money backed by gold or simply deemed by a government to be of a certain value; electronic currency.

Employment and Income

Employment and Income

Salary

The word "salary" goes back to the Latin word that originally denoted an "'allowance given to a Roman soldier for buying salt" or "salarium". Unlike today, salt was once a highly valued commodity. Wars were even fought over it. The old Latin word eventually broadened out to mean "fixed periodic payment made for work done" and passed in this sense via the Anglo-Norman word "salarie" into English.

Source: Dictionary of Word Origins, John Ayto

Lifelong Learning

We now live in a hypercompetitive world where technology and globalization are changing the very nature of work. A middle-class lifestyle is no longer achievable by simple hard work and a basic education. Low-skill jobs that pay well are gone. To survive and thrive in this new work world, workers need to engage in lifelong learning, constantly upgrading their skills to a higher level. They need to apply all the passion, curiosity and creativity they can muster to remain employable and stand out from the herd.

Education and Unemployment Rates

The unemployment rate in 2012 was:
- 12% for high school dropouts
- 8.8% for high school graduates
- 6.6% for those with two years of college
- 4.1% for people with four years of college

Question 12. **To get something you want or need that costs money:**

a. ask for it
b. take it
c. wish for it
d. pay for it with your own money
e. save money for it

Question 13. **To earn money:**

a. ask for it
b. wish for it
c. borrow it from family and friends
d. do work that pays money
e. withdraw cash from an ATM machine

Question 14. **A person who is earning income working for a company on a regular basis is called:**

a. a volunteer
b. a contract worker
c. a temporary worker
d. a migrant worker
e. an employee

Question 15. **Term(s) for money you earn by working:**

a. wages
b. salary
c. income
d. pay
e. grant

$5 — Employment and Income

Answer 12. **d,e – Paying for things you need or want.** Once in a while you may be lucky enough to receive a gift, but usually you will have to pay with your own money for something you need or want. Sometimes you may even have to save for a while to purchase an expensive item.

Answer 13. **d – Working to earn money.** While there are other legal ways to acquire money (trading stocks, bequests from a relative's will), for the most part you will need to work to earn money for yourself.

Answer 14. **e – Employee.** An employee is a person who is hired to do work for an employer (another person or a business) on a regular basis. An employee performs specific duties in return for payment. Employers control when, where and how an employee is to perform the work.

Answer 15. **a,b,c,d – Words for money earned by working.** There are several words used to refer to money that you earn by working, each with a slightly different meaning. They include: pay, wage, salary, income.

"The jobs of the 21st century are becoming more specialized and more technical, demanding more advanced skills."

— Margaret Spelling,
former United States Secretary of Education

Question 16. **Word(s) used to describe an employee's pay as determined by multiplying an hourly rate by the number of hours worked:**

a. salary
b. paycheck
c. bonus
d. commission
e. wage

Question 17. **Word(s) used to describe the sum of money an employee receives for doing a particular job usually over the course of a year:**

a. salary
b. paycheck
c. bonus
d. commission
e. wage

Question 18. **Word(s) for additional money given to an employee for superior on-the-job performance:**

a. wages
b. salary
c. refund
d. perk
e. bonus

Question 19. **Payment that an employee receives for selling goods or services, often based on a percentage of sales made or on a fixed amount per sale:**

a. commission
b. profit
c. bonus
d. salary
e. tips

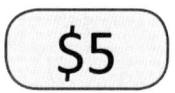 Employment and Income

Answer 16. **e – Wage.** A wage is based on the number of hours worked. The employee is paid for the number of hours worked multiplied by an hourly rate, e.g., $15 per hour x 15 hours = $225.

Answer 17. **a – Salary.** The word "salary" refers to an annual fixed sum of money an employee is paid for a particular job, regardless of the number of hours worked. Normally, the employee receives a portion of that salary on a regular basis during the course of a year (weekly, biweekly or monthly).

Answer 18. **e – Bonus:** additional money, over and above an employee's usual pay, given in recognition of superior on-the-job performance.

Answer 19. **a – Commission:** money received by an employee for services performed. Commissions are based on a percentage of sales made or a fixed amount per sale.

Employment and Income

Question 20. **Some ways of acquiring income:**

a. earning money from working
b. selling goods at a profit
c. earning interest on savings
d. receiving dividends from investments
e. printing money

Question 21. **Which of the following can be considered income?**

a. allowance
b. cash tips from a job
c. gift money
d. customer rewards and discounts
e. lottery winnings

Question 22. **Wage or salary before deductions for taxes and other purposes:**

a. take-home pay
b. gross pay
c. earned income
d. unearned income
e. compensation

Question 23. **Examples of "earned income:"**

a. earnings from employment
b. sales commissions
c. tips
d. interest from a savings account
e. dividends from investments

$5   Employment and Income

***Answer 20.* a,b,c,d – Income.** Income is literally money coming into your life. In addition to receiving money in exchange for the work you do, you can obtain income by:
- selling goods, property or investments at a profit
- earning interest on savings
- receiving dividends from investments

***Answer 21.* a,b,c,e – Other examples of income.** At certain times in your life, you can rely for income on an allowance or cash tips from a job. Other potential income sources – gift money and lottery winnings, for example – are always less reliable.

***Answer 22.* b – Gross Pay:** wage/salary before deductions for taxes and other purposes.

***Answer 23.* a,b,c – Earned income:** all the taxable income you receive from working, including wages, salary and tips. *Unearned income* is money that wasn't obtained by working such as interest income earned in your savings account, dividends from stocks you own, pensions, social security, unemployment benefits, lottery winnings and investment returns.

Employment and Income

Question 24. **Gross wage or salary minus deductions (e.g., for taxes, health care premiums and retirement savings) is:**

a. take-home pay
b. gross pay
c. earned income
d. unearned income

Question 25. **Personal income minus personal taxes equals:**

a. gross pay
b. earned income
c. unearned income
d. discretionary income
e. disposable income

Question 26. **Spending money available after paying for food, clothing and shelter:**

a. gross pay
b. earned income
c. unearned income
d. discretionary income
e. disposable income

Question 27. **The term "compensation" encompasses which of the following:**

a. payment for work performed
b. merit pay increases
c. cost-of-living increases
d. gambling debts
e. noncash rewards for work performed

 Employment and Income

Answer 24. **a – Take-home pay:** gross pay or salary (plus bonuses), minus deductions (for taxes, health insurance, Social Security, Medicare, and retirement savings). Your paycheck stub shows all these figures. New employees are often shocked by the difference between their salary and their take-home pay.

Answer 25. **e – Disposable income:** gross personal income minus deductions for taxes. This amount does not include voluntary retirement contributions and transportation deductions.

Answer 26. **d – Discretionary income:** the amount of a person's income that is available for spending after taking care of taxes and essentials such as food, clothing and shelter.

Answer 27. **a,b,c,e – Employee compensation.** This term refers to everything an employee can expect to receive from an employer in return for work or services performed. Compensation includes wages or salaries and merit and cost-of-living (COLA) increases, as well as an array of possible benefits including payment to injured or unemployed workers or their dependents. When deciding whether or not to take a job, consider the full compensation package, not just the gross pay.

Employment and Income

Question 28. **In addition to a wage or salary, some jobs offer other benefits, such as:**

a. health insurance
b. life insurance
c. retirement plans
d. dental insurance
e. sick leave

Question 29. When working a part-time job, you generally:

a. work fewer than 35 hours per week
b. are paid on an hourly basis
c. receive health insurance benefits
d. have vacation and paid holidays
e. receive sick-time benefits

Question 30. **Advantages of having a part-time job while in school include:**

a. earning money
b. gaining business experience
c. learning about managing money
d. improving grades
e. saving money

Question 31. **Risks of having a part-time job while in school include:**

a. lower grades
b. fatigue and sickness
c. reduced options to take desired or needed classes
d. less time for fun with friends and family
e. transportation costs

 Employment and Income

Answer 28. **a,b,c,d,e – Employee benefits:** forms of value, often non-monetary, that an employee receives from an employer in addition to wages or a salary. Benefits can be: job training, paid vacation and sick days, maternity leave, child care assistance, life insurance, subsidized meals and retirement plans. Benefits may also include health, dental, or life insurance, but employees are often required to pay for part of this insurance coverage.

Job-related benefits mandated by government include: Social Security, Medicare, unemployment insurance and workmen's compensation insurance.

Answer 29. **a,b – Part-time work.** Part-time work is a form of employment that involves working fewer hours per week than a full-time job, usually less than 35 hours per week. In most cases part-time employees are paid on an hourly basis (in other words they receive a wage, not a salary) and have limited or no company benefits such as health insurance, vacation time, sick time, paid holidays and unemployment compensation.

Answer 30. **a,b,c,e – Advantages of a part-time job while in school.** Provided it doesn't interfere with your school work, a part-time job is a good way to earn money, gain experience in business and learn about managing money.

Answer 31. **a,b,c,d,e – Risks of a part-time job while in school.** If a job requires you to work too many hours, you might not get enough sleep. This could cause you to become sick and your grades could suffer. You might also not be able to take maximum advantage of class offerings at your school due to your work schedule. Plus you would likely have less leisure time to spend with friends and family or to pursue special interests. These are all trade-offs you must consider when deciding whether or not to take a job while in school.

Employment and Income $5

Question 32. **People with a career typically:**

a. invest time and money in education beyond high school
b. need minimal training
c. pick work that suits their interests and talents
d. enjoy going to work
e. are happier and healthier than those working at jobs

Question 33. **Generally, people with more skills, knowledge, experience and education earn more.**

a. true
b. false

Question 34. **How much more money can a college graduate earn than a high school graduate?**

a. no more
b. about the same
c. about 20% more
d. about 70% more
e. about 100% more

"I don't consider all the pizza I can eat to be a job benefits package."

Employment and Income

***Answer 32.* a,c,d,e – A career is a lot more than a job.** A career entails long term commitment to a line of work; a job often involves a short term arrangement. For a career, an individual typically needs to invest time and money in education beyond high school and throughout their working lives. This is usually not the case for someone working at a "job", which often requires only minimal training. People on a certain career path choose work that suits their interests and talents. As a result, they enjoy going to work every day and tend to be happier and healthier than those who find themselves doing work that isn't engaging or challenging. It is possible, of course, that your chosen career is one that doesn't provide sufficient income. In this instance, a job will make it possible for you to pursue your passions while keeping bread on the table.

***Answer 33.* a – Education and income.** Generally, the more skills, knowledge, experience and education you have, the more money you can earn.

***Answer 34.* d – Earning capacity.** A college graduate earns about 70% more than a worker with only a high school diploma.

> *"Has it been a lot of work? Not really.*
> *It's only work if you'd rather be doing something else."*
> — the late Pauline Phillips,
> on her career as newspaper columnist "Dear Abby"

Needs and Wants

Needs and Wants

> *"You can't always get what you want,*
> *But if you try sometimes well you might find,*
> *You get what you need..."*
> — the Rolling Stones
> "You Can't Always Get What You Want"

Needs vs. Wants

There's a difference between things you want and things you need. Distinguishing between needs and wants is an important life skill. It's usually not possible to spend less on your needs without endangering your health or safety. However, you can save a lot of money by spending less on your wants. Plus, having a lot of stuff doesn't necessarily lead to happiness. In fact, just the opposite could end up being true.

Kids who don't understand the difference between needs and wants risk developing a constant consumer craving that inevitably leaves them feeling disappointed and dissatisfied.

> *"Earth provides enough for every man's need, but not every man's greed."*
> — Mahatma Gandhi

Question 35. **Basic needs include:**

a. food
b. water
c. shelter
d. car
e. warm clothing in winter

Question 36. **A paying job is a need, because it allows people to provide for their own basic needs and not be dependent on others.**

a. true
b. false

Question 37. **Job-related needs include:**

a. bus fare, bike or car to travel to work
b. work clothes
c. tools and machines required for your job
d. an instrument (if you are a professional musician)
e. prepared food

Question 38. **Safety-related needs include:**

a. a helmet when riding a bicycle or motorcycle
b. a life preserver when boating
c. a seat belt when driving
d. work gloves when handling household chemicals
e. sun block and sun-protective clothing

Question 39. **A want is:**

a. something you can't live without
b. something you can live without
c. something you'd like to buy but don't need
d. something you need to earn a living
e. something you need to keep you safe

$5 Needs and Wants

Answer 35. **a,b,c,e – Basic needs:** things you can't live without, including food, water, shelter and basic clothing. A car may or may not be a necessity. If you require a car to get to work or go to the grocery store, it's a need. Otherwise it's probably just an expensive toy.

Answer 36. **a – Need for employment.** To provide for your own basic needs and not be dependent on others or the government, you need a paying job.

Answer 37. **a,b,c,e – Job-related needs.** You need transportation to get to work. Thus, bus fare, a bike or car may be a need. You may need special clothes for work. You may also need certain tools, machines or perhaps a musical instrument. You, of course, need food, but most often a packed lunch will suffice. Restaurant meals, fast food, soda and snacks from vending machines are all luxuries.

Answer 38. a,b,c,d,e – Safety-related needs. At work, you may be involved in dangerous activities that require safety equipment (e.g., construction boots, masks and hats). Employers may supply such things, but if they don't, employees must obtain safety gear for themselves. At home and at play, personal safety-related needs include:

- a helmet for riding a bicycle or motorcycle
- a seat belt when driving
- work gloves when handling household chemicals
- sun block and sun-protective clothing
- a life preserver when boating

Answer 39. **b,c – Wants.** A want is something you desire but can live without. Lots of things we'd like to buy are wants, not needs.

Needs and Wants $5

Question 40. **Examples of wants:**

a. snack foods
b. sporting goods
c. video games
d. electronic equipment such as smartphones
e. warm clothes to wear during cold weather

Question 41. **Examples of nonessential spending:**

a. buying fresh food to eat
b. renting an apartment
c. purchasing designer clothes
d. going to the movies
e. eating out

Question 42. **When you have only a small amount of money and you need to buy food for yourself and a birthday present for your friend, which store should you go to first?**

a. toy store
b. sporting goods store
c. grocery store
d. electronics store
e. clothing store

Question 43. **A good way to save money is to spend less money on:**

a. needs
b. wants

$5 — Needs and Wants

***Answer 40.* a,b,c,d – Examples of wants:**
- sporting goods such as skis, skates, bikes
- video games, toys
- electronic equipment - smartphones, TVs
- snack foods - chips, soda, candy, ice cream
- eating out at restaurants

In areas that have cold weather, warm clothes are a need not a want.

***Answer 41.* c,d,e – Examples of nonessential spending.** We all need to spend money on certain essentials like fresh food, basic clothing and shelter. It is not essential, however, to spend money on designer clothes, a night out at the movies, or dinner in a restaurant.

***Answer 42.* c – Spend money on needs first.** If you spend money on your wants first, you may not have enough money left to pay for all your needs. For example, if you need to buy food and also want to buy a present for your friend, go to the grocery store first, buy essential items, then use the money you have left over to purchase a present. (After all, when it comes to gifts, it's truly the thought that counts.)

***Answer 43.* b – A good way to save money.** You shouldn't scrimp on your needs, because this may put your health or safety at risk. To save money, spend less on your wants.

Needs and Wants

Question 44. **If your current clothes are adequate, which statement is more correct?**

a. You need to buy new clothes.
b. You want to buy new clothes.

"Dude. You want the Nikes and you want the Reeboks. The decision is simple. You need both."

Question 45. **Because you won't always have enough money to buy everything you want, you need to:**

a. have a credit card
b. borrow money from family and friends
c. set spending priorities
d. forget about making "dream" purchases
e. carefully consider how to allocate your money

$5 — Needs and Wants

Answer 44. **b – New clothes are usually a want.** You may want to buy new clothes; but as long as your current clothes are in good condition and serve to keep you comfortable and presentable every day, you don't need to buy anything new. New designer jeans or sneakers are wants, not needs.

Answer 45. **c,e – Money to spend is limited.** Because you don't have an unlimited amount of money, you can't always buy everything you want. You have to set priorities, take care of needs first and carefully consider how you dispense with the rest of your money. Sometimes you'll have to forego a "dream" purchase until you've saved enough money to buy it.

Opportunity Cost / Trade-offs

You don't have an endless amount of money, time and energy, do you? It's important to carefully consider how you spend these limited resources. Every choice you make is an opportuntity lost to do something else with these resources.

If you spend too much money on clothes and food now, you may limit your opportunity to save money for important medium-term goals (e.g., college) and long-term goals (e.g., retirement) in the future.

If you drop out of high school or college now, you may lose the opportunity to earn a higher income later in life.

Opportunity cost is the value of the possible alternatives you give up when making one choice instead of another (also known as trade-offs).

Smart Spending

Smart Spending

> ### *Impulsive Spending vs. Smart Spending*
> It's easy to spend money. Impulsive spending happens when you buy something on the spot in response to advertising or peer pressure without any thought. Smart spending involves patience and analysis - asking yourself questions before making a purchase. Knowing how to be a smart spender is essential to managing your money well.

> "Beware of little expenses; a small leak will sink a great ship."
> — Benjamin Franklin

> "I was part of that strange race of people aptly described as spending their lives doing things they detest, to make money they don't want, to buy things they don't need, to impress people they don't like."
> — Emile Gauvreau, American author (1891-1956)

> "Intuitively, we know that the best stuff in life isn't stuff at all, and that relationships, experiences and meaningful work are the staples of a happy life"
> — Graham Hill, British racing driver (1929-1975)

Smart Spending $5

BEFORE MAKING PURCHASE

Question 46. **Important questions to ask before making a purchase:**

a. What will my friends think of this purchase?
b. Do I really need this or do I just want it?
c. Do I need this to do my job?
d. Do I need this to stay healthy and safe?
e. Can I borrow money for this purchase?

Question 47. **Setting spending priorities involves:**

a. buying something you want first
b. making a list of needs and wants
c. setting wants aside and considering needs first
d. weighing benefits of spending money on one need vs. another
e. ranking needs from most important to least important

Question 48. **After determining that they really need to buy something, smart shoppers:**

a. buy the item with their credit card right away and worry about paying the bill later
b. decide if they can afford to buy it right now
c. wait until they've saved enough money to buy it outright
d. borrow money from a friend so they can get it right away
e. wait for a sale

Question 49. **Things smart shoppers do ahead of time:**

a. research a product they want to buy
b. rely exclusively on their own common sense when making purchase decisions
c. review the product in consumer magazines and websites
d. talk to friends who have purchased similar products
e. try out but don't immediately buy a possible purchase

$5 — Smart Spending

***Answer 46.* b,c,d – Important questions to ask before making a purchase.** Do I really need this or just want it? If it's something you need to do your job right now or to stay healthy and safe, the answer is "yes". If it's just something that would be fun to have but you don't have much money, the answer is "no". You'd be better off saving the money.

***Answer 47.* b,c,d,e – Setting spending priorities.** Out in the "marketplace", you will spend more wisely if you have created a spending plan in advance. First, make a list of your needs and wants. Set aside your wants for now and weigh the relative benefits of spending money on one need vs. another. List your needs from most to least important. This list is the basis for your spending priorities.

***Answer 48.* b,c,e – Smart shoppers wait.** After you've determined that you really need something, the next thing to do is decide whether you can afford to buy it right now. You may need to wait and save up for it. By waiting and scanning the newspapers for sales, you may be able to find exactly what you want at a better price or perhaps locate a similar, but less expensive, alternative. Buying used might be one possibility – people are always holding garage and estate sales – but this requires time and care in order to find what you really want.

***Answer 49.* a,c,d,e – Smart shoppers do their research.** Smart shoppers prepare by doing research on a product they want to buy – reviewing consumer magazines and websites, talking to friends and family who have purchased similar products, and trying out products at a store (without immediately making a purchase).

Smart Spending

Question 50. **Ways of finding information on a product:**

a. information on the package
b. the product web site
c. advertising
d. publications and websites of consumer groups
e. price comparison web sites

Question 51. **Advertising:**

a. may not help you make a smart spending decision
b. can create a desire for a product you may not need
c. tries to persuade you to buy products and services
d. sometimes gives misleading or false information
e. always tells you all you need to know about a product

Question 52. **When you need to make a purchase that costs a lot of money (e.g., a computer), you should:**

a. Save time shopping - just buy the first item you see.

b. Save money - buy the least expensive product you can find.

c. Research products, comparing quality, features, price and warranty.

d. Do research on customer satisfaction with products you may consider buying.

e. Wait until the product goes on sale.

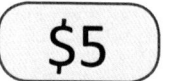 Smart Spending

***Answer 50.** a,b,c,d,e* – **Find unbiased product information.** Although plenty of information is available about most consumer products, not all information is accurate. Smart shoppers use multiple avenues to find product information. To varying degrees, claims on packages, on product websites and in advertisements can provide some clues about a product, but the best sources of facts are the publications and websites of independent consumer groups. Price comparison websites can also be useful.

***Answer 51.** a,b,c,d* – **Advertising awareness.** You cannot rely on advertising to help you make smart spending decisions. Advertisers are in the business of selling things. They strive to create a desire in you for a product or service and to persuade you to buy it. They don't usually tell you all you need to know to make an informed decision and may even give misleading or downright false information.

> *"Advertising is the art of convincing people to spend money they don't have for something they don't need."*
>
> — Will Rogers

***Answer 52.** c,d,e* – **Making a big purchase.** Whenever you buy a product you are taking a risk. The more costly the product, the bigger the risk. You risk wasting your money on a poor quality product that is missing certain features you need. So don't just jump at the first product you see or buy something because it's the least expensive. To get the best value for your money on a pricey item, it's important to do your research and bide your time. Research products, comparing quality, features, price and warranty. Do research on customer satisfaction with items you are considering. Once you've selected the best product, wait for it to go on sale.

Smart Spending

Question 53. **Comparison shopping involves comparing new/used products for:**

a. price
b. quality
c. features
d. reliability/durability ratings
e. guarantees and warranties

Question 54. **You want to buy a big item like a new TV, but you don't have enough money right now. A money-smart response is to:**

a. Borrow the money from your friends or family.
b. Put it on your credit card.
c. Wait for a cash infusion (gift, bonus, etc.).
d. Make it a savings goal.
e. Put it on a layaway plan.

> ***Benefits of Buying Used or Refurbished Products***
>
> *Used or refurbished products can cost a lot less money. Reusing them can be good for the environment, too. Buyers should be careful, though, because compared to new products, used or refurbished products can emit more pollutants, use more energy or contain toxic elements that are now outlawed. Before buying such a product, carefully examine it for defects and ask the seller a lot of questions to determine how it was cared for in the past and what has been done to refurbish it (replacement parts, new paint etc.). Often such products cannot be returned and do not carry a warranty.*

$5 — Smart Spending

***Answer 53.* a,b,c,d,e – Comparison shopping.** Before making a purchase, smart shoppers look at a variety of potential products, examining them for:

- price
- quality
- features
- reliability/durability ratings
- guarantees and warranties

***Answer 54.* d,e – Saving for a big purchase.** When you don't have enough money right now to purchase something big that you need, you should make it a savings goal and regularly put aside a fixed amount of money towards the purchase of the item. You can also put an item on layaway if it's just what you need but you don't have the money at present. (*Layaway* is a payment plan in which a buyer reserves an article of merchandise by placing a deposit on it with a retailer. When the buyer finishes paying for the article, he/she can take it home.)

Warranty

A written guarantee from the manufacturer or distributor that specifies the conditions under which a product can be returned, replaced or repaired.

More Money-Saving Tips

You can find more tips on saving money on gifts, entertainment, used cars, vacations and hobbies at donwfbell.com.

Smart Spending

WHEN MAKING A PURCHASE

Question 55. **Which of the following statements are false:**

a. Name brand products are always of better quality than generic products.
b. Newer-model products are always of better quality than older-model or used products.
c. Price is always the most important factor.
d. The most expensive product is always the highest in quality.
e. You always save money when you buy something on sale.

Question 56. **When making a purchase:**

a. Thoroughly inspect the item for flaws or damage.
b. Always assume the stated price is fixed and non-negotiable.
c. Find out what the return policy is.
d. Count your change if you paid with cash.
e. Keep the receipt, instructions and packaging.

Question 57. **Ways to pay for purchases include:**

a. cash
b. check
c. debit card
d. credit card
e. demonetized currency

Be Systematic About Purchase Decisions

- *Gather and evaluate relevant consumer information.*
- *Consider the costs and benefits of various alternatives.*
- *Consider consumer repair information, including how easy an item is to fix and whether you can fix it yourself.*

Smart Spending

Answer 55. **a,b,c,d,e – False notions.** The main thing to keep in mind when shopping is to seek out the best price on a product that fits your particular needs. Many people have false notions that interfere with achieving this objective. False notions include:

- You'll always get better quality in a named brand or newer-model than in a generic, older-model or used product.
- Price is the most important factor. (In fact, it's only one.)
- It's always best to buy the most expensive product. (Expensive products are not always the highest in quality or suited to your needs.)
- It's always best to pay as little as possible. (A cheap product may break sooner and lack a guarantee.)
- You always save money when you buy something on sale.

Answer 56. **a,c,d,e – Things to remember when making a purchase.** Even after you've done your research and decided what to buy, you need to take a few precautionary steps:

- Inspect the item thoroughly at the store for flaws/damage before purchasing.
- If the product is a floor sample or flawed in any way, ask the merchant for a discount.
- Find out what the return policy is.
- Count your change if you pay with cash.
- Check your receipt for accuracy.
- Keep the receipt, instructions and packaging.

Answer 57. **a,b,c,d – Ways to pay.** It used to be that cash was the only way to pay, but today there are many payment options:

- cash, check, debit or "gift" card
- credit card (subject to limits on how much can be charged)
- Supplemental Nutrition Assistance Program or SNAP card (formerly "food stamps", subject to income eligibility requirements and certain restrictions on purchases)

Smart Spending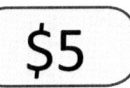

Question 58. You are at greater risk of spending beyond your means when you pay with a credit card than when you pay with cash because:

a. You don't see money disappearing immediately from your wallet.

b. The pain of payment is deferred until later.

c. There are no limits on how much you can spend with a credit card.

d. It's easy for you to go right on buying stuff you can't afford until you finally reach your credit limit.

e. You can buy all kinds of things online without realizing how much you've actually spent until the credit card bill arrives.

Question 59. Which payment method can be the most costly?

a. cash
b. check
c. debit card
d. prepaid card
e. credit card

Just Say "No" to Extended Warranties

When buying electronics or appliances, you will often be asked if you want an extended warranty. Most products are unlikely to need repair during the extended warranty period and the cost of repairing the item may be similar to or less than the cost of the warranty. If you are concerned about the possibility of products failing, be your own insurance company. Set up a small emergency fund to help pay for repairs or replacements.

***Answer 58.* a,b,d,e – Paying with a credit card versus cash.**
You're at greater risk of spending beyond your means when you pay with a credit card than with cash. If you pay with cash, you notice your wallet getting thinner and thinner, and when it's empty, you have to stop buying. But with a credit card, the pain of payment is deferred until later, so you can go right on buying stuff. This is especially easy to do when shopping on the Internet. On the day your credit card bill arrives, you may find you've overspent and don't have enough money to pay what's due. Then it's panic time!

***Answer 59.* e – Credit card purchases may be more costly than you think.** Paying with a credit card can be the most costly form of payment. If you don't pay your credit card balance (what you owe the credit card company) in full every month, you will incur fees and interest charges. You are, in effect, borrowing money and paying for the privilege.

For example, if you have a credit card balance of $1000 and only make the minimum payments (e.g., $25 a month), it could take you 5 years to pay off the debt and cost you $538 in interest charges (assuming an 18% interest rate). To estimate the cost of credit, use a credit calculator, e.g., practicalmoneyskills.com/wizards/credit/.

It's safer to pay with a bank debit card (a "pay now" card), because you're using money that's currently in your bank account. (You could, of course, overdraw your account.) It's even safer to pay with a prepaid debit card that has been "loaded" with money in advance. As you buy things, the purchase price of each item is subtracted from the card's balance until there's no money left, so there's no chance of spending into oblivion.

Smart Spending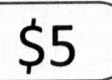

Question 60. **To find the best deal on standard grocery store items choose:**

a. the item with the largest box
b. a brand you know is popular
c. the generic store brand
d. the item on sale or store special
e. the item with the lowest unit cost

Question 61. **Buying in bulk is always the best value:**

a. true
b. false

Question 62. **A "smart spender" responds to a big sale by:**

a. planning to spend big
b. making dream purchases on credit
c. staying home to avoid spending too much
d. purchasing only needs
e. buying inexpensive, fun little things

Sales/Specials - Not Always a Good Deal

Just because something is on sale, doesn't mean you should buy it. If you need it, then it may be a good deal; but if you don't need it, you're just wasting your money.

Smart Spending

***Answer 60.* e – Groceries and unit prices.** The "unit price" (or "unit cost") tells you the cost of a product per a certain unit of measure such as an ounce, pound, liter, kilogram, etc. Many stores, including grocery stores and pharmacies, show the "unit price" on the store shelf next to the purchase price of an item (not on the product itself). However, in some instances you may have to calculate the unit price yourself. Do this by dividing the total cost of each item you are considering (e.g., a box of cereal) by the measure being used (e.g., ounces). Comparing unit costs is one of the best ways to find the best buy. Blindly choosing the largest size, popular brand or generic store brand isn't smart shopping.

Unit price comparison example: What is the best buy? A 10-ounce box of Crispy Kernels cereal at $2.00, or a 15-ounce box of Crackly Crunch at $4,00?

$2.00 ÷ 10 ounces = $.20 (unit price)

$4.00 ÷ 15 ounces = $.26 (unit price)

Common wisdom would say the bigger, 15-ounce box would be the better buy, but in this instance the smaller box is the better value.

***Answer 61.* b – Bulk buying.** You don't always save money by buying in bulk. Check the unit prices for what you want to buy; the larger quantity may not always be cheaper. Also, decide if you would be buying more of a certain product than you need, especially if it's perishable or you don't have sufficient space to store it.

***Answer 62.* d – Smart spenders at big sales.** A smart spender responds to a big sale by going purposefully to purchase only what he or she really needs.

Smart Spending $5

Question 63. **High-pressure sales pitches with purchase deadlines do not help you make money-smart decisions:**

a. true
b. false

Question 64. **If you buy a sale item on the spot without much forethought, you may shortchange yourself on:**

a. quality
b. specific features you really want in a product
c. a product guarantee or warranty
d. the ability to return the product
e. having time to comparison shop

Question 65. **Buying a product on sale is worthwhile when:**

a. You really need the product.
b. You can afford to buy it.
c. The quality of the product is such that it will last.
d. You can return the product later if you don't want or need it.
e. You think it would sell in a garage sale.

> *"Luxury:*
> *the lust for comfort,*
> *that stealthy thing that enters the house as a guest,*
> *and then becomes a host,*
> *and then a master."*
> — Kahlil Gibran

Smart Spending

***Answer 63.* a – High-pressure sales pitches and bargaining.**
Be skeptical of high-pressure sales pitches with purchase deadlines. Salespeople are paid to make sales and you can't count on them to help you make informed, rational decisions. Find out for yourself which product is the best value for you! If a salesperson is open to bargaining, you could try to negotiate a better price for yourself. This may be possible with certain types of products such as antiques. In informal settings, like garage sales, you may also be able to negotiate a better deal.

***Answer 64.* a,b,c,d,e – Shortchanging yourself on sale items.**
You're in the mall and you see a sign that says "special" or "big sale." You had no intention of shopping for the advertised items, but you are attracted by the signs. You enter the store and buy an item on the spot without thinking. In such cases, you may have shortchanged yourself on quality, features, a product guarantee or warranty, the ability to return the product and the time to comparison shop.

***Answer 65.* a,b,c,d – When is it worthwhile to buy sale items?**
It usually makes sense to buy a sale item after you've given it some advance thought and know:

- It is something that you need and has the features you want.
- You can afford to buy the product without borrowing money.
- The product is of good quality; it is made to last.
- The product can be returned later if you change your mind.
- The price is competitive.
- The item is on sale only for a short while.
- The item is a "closeout" (the item may be discontinued and the supply is limited) and/or the price will go up soon.

Smart Spending

Question 66. **Peer pressure can lead to:**

a. saving money for your future goals

b. buying "cool" clothes or trendy gear just to impress friends

c. spending money you can't afford to spend

d. doing things you really don't want to do

e. making up your own mind about what you really want to buy

Question 67. **When pressured by friends to spend money you don't want to spend, it's money-smart to just say:**

a. "No, I can't afford that."
b. "No, I don't buy on credit."
c. "I'd rather make up my own mind."
d. "OK. You're right, I should buy that."
e. "No, I need to save my money for other things."

"Shirley! You shop at the Bargain Barn?!"

***Answer 66.* b,c,d – Peer pressure.** Members of a peer group are usually similar in age, socioeconomic background, occupation and interests. Individuals have a strong inclination to conform to the standards of their peer group, so it's easy for the group to induce them to spend money unwisely and engage in actions they might otherwise avoid. Because you want to impress your peers, you may buy "cool" clothes and other trendy gear even though you don't really want or can't afford these things. The truth is, good friends will like you for who you are, not for what you have, and real friends won't try to make you do things you don't want to do.

***Answer 67.* a,b,c,e – Resisting peer pressure.** You don't have to give in to pressure from your friends to spend money when you don't want to. If you can stand your ground, you may even help your friends make wise decisions. When you're feeling pressured, it's a good idea to have responses in mind for those times such as:

- "No, I can't afford that."
- "No, I don't buy on credit."
- "I need to think about it for a while."
- "I'd rather make up my own mind, thanks."
- "I really need to save my money for other things."

Point of sale (POS)

Point of sale (POS) is the location where a spending transaction occurs. When customers make purchases at a store cash register, point of sale software keeps track of sales, inventory and customer information.

Smart Spending

Question 68. **Buying something on a whim without thinking about needs, goals or consequences is:**

a. going for broke
b. rational purchasing
c. budget buying
d. seeking instant gratification
e. impulse buying

Question 69. **An impulsive purchase can be triggered by:**

a. an attractive display
b. an appealing ad
c. a familiar brand name or label
d. a desire to improve your mood when you're feeling down
e. a desire to gain favor with your friends

"You're not falling for that old sales gimmick are you?"

Answer 68. d,e – **Impulse buying:** giving in to the desire for instant gratification and buying something on a whim without thinking about needs, goals or consequences. Most of the time this is not "smart spending."

There are some rare occasions when you can justify an impulse purchase, such as when you're on vacation in a faraway place that you are not likely to visit again. You see a beautiful piece of craft work at a reasonable price, fall in love with it and believe it would give you pleasure for years to come. In such an instance, an impulse buy can be worthwhile.

Answer 69. a,b,c,d,e – **Triggers for impulse buying.**
Sometimes we purchase a product and bring it home only to start wondering what on earth possessed us to buy the thing. Probably one or more triggers caused us to act impulsively. These include:

- an attractive product or display
- an appealing ad
- a familiar brand name or label
- a desire to improve your mood when you're feeling down
- a desire to gain favor with your peers
- acting on a recommendation of a friend without considering other factors

> *"What I'm always trying to say to the consumer is: buy less, choose well, make it last."*
>
> — Vivienne Westwood, an English fashion designer and businesswoman

Smart Spending

Question 70. **When you make an impulsive purchase, you risk acquiring a product that:**

a. you don't need or want
b. lacks key features you want
c. is inferior in quality compared to other products
d. has no guarantee or warranty
e. costs too much

Question 71. **You can reduce the risk of buying on impulse by:**

a. developing a budget before shopping
b. limiting the amount of cash you take shopping
c. refraining from using a credit card to make purchases
d. taking a "time-out" before making a purchase
e. staying home when you're tired, hungry or otherwise stressed out

"I bought this @*!! parrot on impulse.
PLEASE take him back. He's driving me nuts."

Answer 70. **a,b,c,d,e – Impulsive purchases are risky.** You may belatedly realize after making an impulsive purchase that you:

- bought something you don't need or want
- bought a product that lacks key features you want
- bought an inferior quality product
- bought a product with no guarantee, warranty or return option
- paid too much money for a product
- bought a product you can't afford

Answer 71. **a,b,c,d,e – Reducing the risk of buying on impulse.** You don't need to feel out of control. There are ways to protect yourself from the risk of buying on impulse. They include:

- knowing what you really need to buy
- developing a budget before shopping
- limiting the cash you take shopping
- leaving your credit card at home
- taking a "time out" before making a purchase
- pledging before setting off to shop that you won't make a "consolation" purchase if you don't find what you want
- staying home when you're tired, hungry or otherwise stressed out

> *If you feel out of control when you go shopping, you may have a problem. You can get help from a counselor or a support group, such as Debtors Anonymous.*

Smart Spending

Question 72. **Waiting until the time is right to obtain something you really want:**

a. delaying gratification

b. recklessness

c. negligence

d. procrastination

e. oversight

Question 73. **Advantages of delaying a purchase:**

a. You may decide later you don't need the product.

b. You can shop around for a lower price.

c. The price may drop if the product goes on sale.

d. You can consider better ways to spend your money.

e. You may miss out on a sale.

Question 74. **Signs of "shopoholism" or compulsive shopping:**

a. buying more things than are needed

b. spending money within a budget

c. spending to soothe feelings of anger or sadness

d. juggling multiple credit card accounts to accommodate spending

e. having arguments about money with family members

***Answer 72.* a – Delaying gratification:** waiting until the time is right to obtain something you really want, i.e., exercising self-control or willpower. Delaying gratification gives you more options for how to spend your money. It often entails resisting the urge to buy a product on credit (essentially borrowing money) and opting to wait until you can pay the full cost.

***Answer 73.* a,b,c,d – Advantages of delaying a purchase.** In delaying a purchase, you give yourself time to:

- calm down about a potential purchase that seems exciting
- decide whether you really need the product
- shop around for a lower price and/or a better product
- watch for sales when the price of the product may drop
- consider better ways to spend your money.

***Answer 74.* a,c,d,e – Compulsive shopping (shopoholism)** Compulsive shoppers can't control their spending. They continue buying despite destructive consequences. This behavior is chronic (continuous) and is considered to be a form of addiction. It may have a genetic basis. Some people seem more prone to this addiction than others.

Signs of a shopping addiction include: buying more things than needed; feeling high (euphoric) when shopping; feeling guilty about a spending spree; thinking about money all the time; shopping to sooth feelings of anger, depression or loneliness; juggling multiple credit cards to accommodate spending; hiding secret credit cards and purchases from family members; lying about shopping expenditures; spending more money than earned; and spending into serious debt. This behavior can seriously impair relationships with family members and friends.

Smart Spending

Question 75. **A spendthrift is:**

a. a compulsive shopper
b. a troubled person who spends money profusely and wastefully
c. a thrifty person who saves every penny
d. a person who has spent all their prosperity
e. a person who is cautious about spending

Question 76. **Ways to prevent shopping binges:**
a. Use cash, don't pay for purchases with a credit card.
b. Surf the web looking for sales.
c. Make a shopping list and buy only what's on the list.
d. Have just one credit card and use it only for emergencies.
e. Avoid discount warehouses.

"Sorry I'm late. Macy's was having a sale.
I stood outside for three hours just to test my willpower!"

Answer 75. **a,b,d – A spendthrift.** This colorful term is used to describe a compulsive shopper. A spendthrift is a troubled person who spends money profusely and wastefully. "Money burns a hole in their pockets" and they're likely to "shop till they drop". The word comes from an obsolete sense of the word "thrift" which meant prosperity rather than frugality (or thrift). So a "spendthrift" is one who has spent their prosperity.

Answer 76. **a,c,d,e – Preventing shopping binges.** Almost everyone overdoes it on shopping once in a while, especially during the holiday season, but this doesn't mean they've become a shopaholic. To prevent bad habits from taking hold, follow these guidelines:

- Make a shopping list and buy only what is on the list.
- Use cash, check, or a debit card instead of a credit card.
- Keep just one credit card and only use it for emergencies.
- Avoid discount warehouses.
- Window-shop after stores have closed.
- Don't watch TV shopping channels.
- Avoid shopping online or phoning in catalog orders.
- Take a walk or exercise when the urge to shop arises.

> *You can fall into a lot of financial trouble by:*
>
> - *trying to "keep up with the Joneses" (buying everything your friends and neighbors have)*
> - *buying the latest gear just because it's the latest*
> - *spending all your money as soon as you receive it*
> - *spending regularly on little things ($1.00 here on soda, $1 there on snacks - it all adds up)*
> - *buying on impulse without thinking in advance*

Smart Spending $5

AFTER MAKING A PURCHASE

Question 77. **A store's return policy tells you:**

a. the place in a store where returns are handled
b. how to find the store's location on a map
c. under what conditions a product can be returned
d. how often shoppers return to the store
e. what the discount is for return customers

Question 78. **What to do after you purchase an item:**

a. Review the receipt.
b. Check the product to make sure it is in good condition.
c. Try not to damage the packaging.
d. Keep the product safe from damage/theft in case you need to return it.
e. Return the product as soon as you realize it's not in good condition or you don't want it.

"Sorry about the defect in your skateboard, but the return period is over."

Answer 77. **c – Store return policies.** A store's return policy tells you under what conditions a product can be returned for replacement, refund or store credit. Stores are becoming more strict about their return policies. Before you buy a product, find out the store's policy, because sometimes you can only receive a credit, not a refund. When a store gives you a refund on your credit card, it may not show up on your card's balance for 3 to 5 business days.

Answer 78. **a,b,c,d,e – After the purchase.** Often we make purchases only to find out afterwards that something isn't quite right. Maybe a product doesn't work, maybe the clerk forgot to put it in the bag, maybe the clerk charged you for something you didn't buy. This is why it's so important to keep the receipt. Here's what to do when you come home from the store or receive an item from an online merchant:

- Review your receipt. (A receipt shows where and when you made a purchase, along with the purchase price and taxes paid.)
- Make sure you weren't charged for something you didn't intend to buy.
- Make sure you return home with all the products you bought. (You may have left one at the check out.)
- Check the product you purchased in a store or online to make sure it's in good condition.
- Try not to damage packaging so it can be ret.
- Keep the product and packaging safe from damage in case you decide to return it.
- Return the product as soon as you realize it's not in good condition or you don't want it. (Don't wait. The merchant's return period may expire before you realize it and then you'll be out of luck.)

CONSUMER PROTECTION

Question 79. **A letter to the seller or manufacturer documenting a product problem and stating the desired solution:**

a. a request for a recall
b. a compensation request
c. a bad-product report
d. a request for a refund
e. a complaint letter

Question 80. **Consumer protection laws and organizations are designed to:**

a. protect the rights of consumers
b. encourage the free flow of information in the marketplace
c. require disclosure of detailed and truthful information
d. prevent fraudulent or unfair business practices
e. protect consumers from spending too much money

> ***Consumer Financial Protection Bureau (CFPB)***
>
> *"Our mission is to make markets for consumer financial products and services work for Americans — whether they are applying for a mortgage, choosing among credit cards, or using any number of other consumer financial products...Above all, this means ensuring that consumers receive all the information they need to make the financial decisions they believe are best for themselves and their families—that prices are clear up front, that risks are visible and that nothing is buried in fine print. In a market that works, consumers should be able to make direct comparisons among products and no provider should be able to use unfair, deceptive, or abusive practices."*
>
> *For more information, go to: consumerfinance.gov.*

Answer 79. e – Complaint letter. If you are unhappy with a product or service, you can write a complaint letter to the seller or manufacturer documenting the problem and requesting a replacement or refund.

Answer 80. a,b,c,d – Consumer protection laws. Consumer protection laws provide for government oversight of the marketplace with the aim of protecting consumers' rights. The laws encourage the free flow of information in the marketplace and require businesses to disclose detailed and truthful information about their products, particularly when safety or public health is concerned (e.g., children's equipment, power tools, food). The laws also prevent businesses from engaging in fraud or using other practices to gain unfair advantage over competitors. Nonprofit consumer organizations use these laws to help consumers make better choices and get assistance with their complaints.

The Federal Trade Commission's Consumer Protection Laws

The Federal Trade Commission (FTC) is a United States government consumer protection agency. The FTC's Bureau of Consumer Protection works for the consumer to prevent fraud, deception and unfair business practices in the marketplace.

The Bureau:

- *enhances consumer confidence by enforcing federal laws that protect consumers*
- *empowers consumers with free information to help them exercise their rights and spot and avoid fraud and deception*
- *wants to hear from consumers who need information or want to file a complaint about fraud or identity theft*

For more information go to: www.ftc.gov/bcp

Banking

Banking

"I used to hide my money under my mattress. Now I keep it in a bank account. I sleep better knowing it can't be lost, stolen or destroyed."

Banking $10

Question 1. **A bank offers financial services such as:**

a. checking accounts
b. savings accounts
c. mortgages
d. payday loans
e. credit scores

Question 2. **A bank is a good place to:**

a. meet people
b. keep money safe
c. buy stuff
d. store valuables (e.g., coin collections, jewelry)
e. buy gold

Question 3. **A bank is a financial institution where you can:**

a. deposit money
b. withdraw money
c. borrow money
d. save money
e. earn interest on your money

Question 4. **Credit unions differ from banks in that:**

a. Members are part owners.
b. Credit unions are nonprofits.
c. Members must belong to a union.
d. Members must have a good credit rating.
e. Members can make loans to themselves.

Question 5. **Banks and credit unions make money by:**

a. charging interest for loans
b. gambling with other people's money
c. buying and selling houses
d. printing more money
e. charging fees for banking services

$10   Banking

Answer 1. **a,b,c – Financial services offered by banks.** Services that banks offer include checking and savings accounts and car and home loans (mortgages).

Answer 2. **b,d – Banks: safe and secure.** A bank is a secure place to keep your money and your valuables. You can store important documents and valuables, such as jewelry and coin collections, in a *safe deposit box* (also called a *safety deposit box*) usually held within a larger safe or vault at a bank. When you purchase a box, you are given a key and you are the only one who has access to the box.

Answer 3. **a,b,c,d,e – Common banking services.** When you have a bank account you can:

- deposit money
- withdraw money
- borrow money to make large purchases (e.g., cars, houses)
- save money
- earn interest on your money

Answer 4. **a,b – Credit Union:** a financial institution, similar to a bank, that provides the same types of services. Unlike banks, credit unions are nonprofit and their members are part owners (shareholders) of the institution. Generally speaking, credit unions see themselves as more community-oriented, caring more about serving people than making profits.

Answer 5. **a,e – Earning their profit.** Banks and credit unions make money by charging interest on loans and fees for managing checking and saving accounts.

Banking $10

Question 6. **A bank keeps track of your money in:**

a. a big piggy bank
b. a safe deposit box
c. a vault
d. a safe
e. an account

Question 7. **To open a bank account, you need to provide identification(ID), such as a:**

a. current passport
b. bus pass or travel card
c. birth certificate
d. student ID card
e. driver's license

Question 8. **An account commonly used for paying bills:**

a. a savings account
b. an investment account
c. a checking account
d. a credit card account

Question 9. **A written promise to pay someone money from your bank account is:**

a. a promissory note
b. an IOU
c. a receipt
d. a check
e. a certificate of deposit

Question 10. **It's not OK to write a check using:**

a. red ink
b. black ink
c. blue ink
d. a pencil
e. a felt-tip pen.

$10   Banking

Answer 6. **e – Account:** an arrangement you make with a financial institution (e.g., bank or credit union) to hold and keep track of your money. The most common types of accounts are checking and savings accounts.

Answer 7. **a,c,e – Opening a bank account.** To open a bank account, you need a government-issued identity document (e.g., a driver's license, passport, birth certificate) that proves you are who you say you are.

Answer 8. **c – Checking account.** A checking account facilitates money transactions, allowing customers to deposit and withdraw their money more or less at will. A checking account is used for writing checks to pay bills. It is not set up for the purpose of saving money, so a customer would not typically earn any interest on such an account.

Answer 9. **d – Check:** a written promise you make to pay someone (the payee named on the check) a stated amount of money that will be taken from your checking account.

Answer 10. **d – Writing checks.** Checks must be written in ink not pencil, because a check written in pencil could be easily altered.

IOU (abbreviated from the phrase "I owe you")

An IOU is an informal document acknowledging a debt, usually specifying the debtor (the person who owes money), the amount owed, and sometimes the creditor (the person who is owed money). IOUs may be signed or carry distinguishing marks or designs to ensure authenticity.

Banking $10

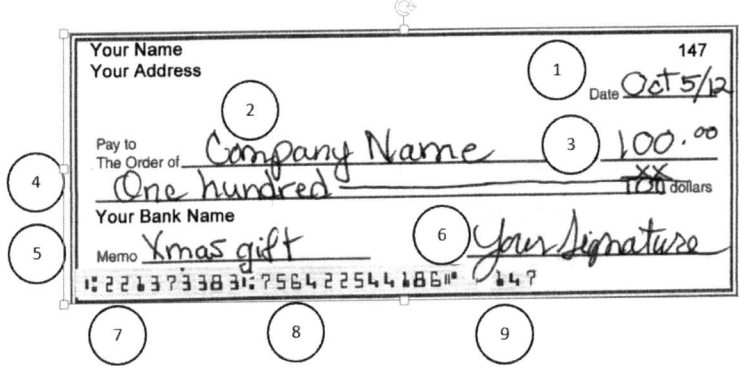

Check: a written promise you make to pay someone a stated amount of money from your checking account

Important information (numbers 1-9) on a check.

1. The date the check is written.
2. The payee's name (a person or company).
3. The amount payable in numerals.
4. The amount payable written in words followed by a line drawn through the space ending with cents written as a fraction.
5. Memo: the reason for writing the check.
6. Signature of bank account owner.
7. The bank routing number or routing transit number (RTN) – a nine digit number (begins and ends with |:)used to identify a financial institution.
8. Bank account number.
9. Check number.

The RTN and bank account number are required when transferring money between accounts at different banks.

Banking

NUMBER OR CODE	DATE	TRANSACTION DESCRIPTION	PAYMENT, FEE WITHDRAWAL (-)		FEE	DEPOSIT, CREDIT (+)	$ 1225 00
100	7/13	Kitty Kare	50 00				50 00
							1175 00
101	7/14	Dr. Amos annual checkup	25 00				25 00
							1150 00
102	7/15	Top Notch Grocery	105 00				105 00
							1045 00
103	7/16	Dress Smart party outfit	70 00				70 00
							975 00
104	7/16	Strength Builders membership fee	150 00				150 00
							825 00
105	7/18	Shoes for You sneakers	80 00				80 00
							745 00
106	7/20	Burger Bistro lunch out	20 00				20 00
							725 00
	7/20	Check deposit				300 00	300 00
							1025 00

Checkbook register: a small book where you keep a record of the checks you write, your cash withdrawals, your deposits, any charges the bank makes and your current account balance.

Important information (numbers 1-6) to record in your checkbook register.

1. Check number.
2. Date
3. Transaction description
4. Payment amounts
5. Cash withdrawals
6. Deposits
7. Balance

Balance refers to the amount of money currently in your account.

Banking $10

Question 11. **When you put money into your bank account, you are making a:**

a. debit
b. withdrawal
c. payment
d. transfer
e. deposit

Question 12. **A deposit should show up in your bank account within:**

a. a half day
b. 1 business day
c. 2 business days
d. 5 business days
e. 7 business days

Question 13. **The fastest, simplest and safest way to deposit a paycheck into your bank account is to:**

a. arrange for direct deposit
b. go directly to the bank and deposit it
c. put it in a lock box
d. put it in your checkbook register
e. cash it and put the cash in your wallet

Question 14. **Other ways of depositing money into your bank account:**

a. Mail a check with a deposit slip to your bank.
b. Make a deposit at an ATM.
c. Transfer money electronically from another account.
d. Give your money to a friend to take to the bank.
e. Deposit checks using your smartphone.

 Banking

Answer 11. **e – Deposit.** When you make a deposit, you are putting money into a checking or savings account.

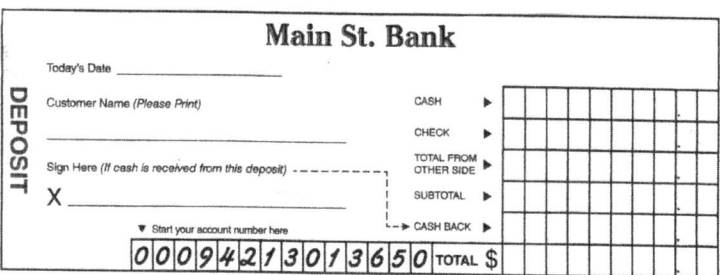

Deposit Slip – indicates the bank account and kind of funds (cash, checks) being deposited.

Answer 12. **c – Deposit lag time.** It can take up to 2 business days for a deposit to be added to your account.

Answer 13. **a – Direct deposit.** You can authorize your employer to deposit your paycheck electronically (directly) into your bank account. No cash or checks change hands. This option is the fastest, simplest and safest way to make deposits.

Answer 14. **a,b,c,e – Other ways to make a deposit.** In addition to in-person and direct deposits, you can:

- Mail endorsed checks along with a deposit slip to your bank. (Note that it is not safe to send cash by mail.)
- Make a deposit at an ATM.
- Transfer money electronically from one account to another account.
- Deposit checks with your smartphone by taking a photo of the check and sending it to your bank via the Internet.

Banking $10

Question 15. **When you deposit a check at a bank in person you need to:**

a. fill out a deposit slip
b. endorse your check
c. provide identification (ID)
d. show your debit card
e. talk to your banker

Question 16. **When you take cash out of a bank account, you are making a:**

a. deposit
b. withdrawal
c. payment
d. transfer
e. deduction

Question 17. **To withdraw cash from your bank in person, you must provide:**

a. a completed withdrawal slip
b. a check made out to "Cash" with your signature on the back
c. your bank statement
d. a note asking for cash
e. your identification (ID)

Question 18. **The word "balance" can mean an amount of money:**

a. in a checking account
b. in a savings account
c. owed on a credit card
d. owed on a loan
e. in an investment account

 Banking

Answer 15. **a,b,c – Making a deposit in person.** To do this, you must provide the teller with a completed deposit slip, the check (endorsed on the back with your account number and signature underneath) and identification (ID).

Answer 16. **b – Withdrawal.** When you make a withdrawal from your checking or savings account, you are subtracting money from your account balance.

Answer 17. **a,b,e – Withdrawing cash in person.** Provide the teller with ID and either:

- a completed withdrawal slip (a paper form that includes the account number, the date, the amount, your signature) or
- a check made out to "Cash" or your name with your signature on the back

Answer 18. **a,b,c,d,e – Balance.** The amount of money in your checking, savings or investment account. Balance can also mean the amount of money you owe on a credit card or loan.

"I'm sorry sir. We don't accept notes asking for cash. You'll have to fill out a withdrawal slip."

Banking $10

Question 19. **Before writing a check, you should know:**

a. the balance in your savings account
b. the balance owing on your credit card
c. the balance in your checking account
d. the balance owing on your car loan
e. the balance remaining on your debit card

Question 20. **Ways to check your current bank balance:**

a. Review your monthly bank statement.
b. Phone your bank.
c. View your account balance online.
d. Print a balance receipt at a cash machine.
e. Consult your up-to-date checkbook register.

Question 21. **A checkbook register is a small book where you can keep a record of:**

a. the checks you write
b. your cash withdrawals
c. your credit card balance
d. your deposits
e. bank charges

Question 22. **It is important to keep your checkbook register up-to-date. Otherwise, you could:**

a. forget the date, payee and amount of checks you have written
b. forget the amount of cash withdrawals and deposits you have made
c. bounce checks
d. lower your credit score
e. incur overdraft fees

Answer 19. **c – Always know your balance.** Before writing a check, always know the balance (the amount of money) in your checking account; otherwise, you may not have enough money to cover the check and you could be charged an overdraft fee.

Answer 20. **a,b,c,d,e – Checking your bank balance.** Here are some ways to check your bank balance:

- Review your monthly bank statement.
- Phone (or possibly text) your bank.
- View your account balance online.
- Print a balance receipt at a cash machine.
- Consult your up-to-date checkbook register.

Answer 21. **a,b,d,e – Checkbook register:** a small book where you keep a record of the checks you write, your cash withdrawals, your deposits, any charges the bank makes and your current account balance. Although banks do not require you to keep a checkbook register, there are many good reasons to do so. (See example on page 98.)

Answer 22. **a,b,c,e – Keep your checkbook register up-to-date.** It is important to make an entry in your checkbook register every time you write a check, withdraw cash or make a deposit (see page 98). Otherwise, you could easily forget the transaction date, payee (for checks) and amount you've deposited or withdrawn from your account. Without this information, you won't know how much money is in your checking account, which could lead you to bounce checks and thus incur overdraft fees. At the end of the month you will need all this information to balance your checkbook and verify that your records match the bank's records. (See page 108 for directions on balancing a checkbook.)

Banking $10

Question 23. **A monthly summary from your bank of your financial transactions:**

a. a loan
b. a mortgage
c. a statement
d. a bill
e. a debt

Question 24. **Who balances your checkbook?**

a. you
b. the bank
c. the teller
d. your parents
e. your stockbroker

Question 25. **You need to balance your checkbook monthly to find out:**

a. what the current balance is in your savings account

b. what fees were charged by the bank

c. which checks are still outstanding (not cashed yet)

d. whether you forgot to include any checks or deposits in your checkbook register

e. whether the bank statement is accurate

Banking

Answer 23. **c – Statement:** a summary from a bank of all financial transactions occurring over a given period of time (usually a month) in an account. For a checking account, the statement shows all deposits, withdrawals and bank charges.

	FIRST DREAM BANK 100 Pot 'of Gold Blvd. Greenback, NR		Checking Account Statement Page : 1 of 1		
	Silver Dollar 111 Happy Lane, Anytown, USA	check#	Statement period 2012-11-22 to 2012-12-21		Account No. 005-123-456

Date	Description	Ref.	Withdrawals	Deposits	Balance
2003-10-08	Previous balance				0.55
2003-10-14	Payroll Deposit - HOTEL			694.81	695.36
2003-10-14	Web Bill Payment - MASTERCARD	9685	200.00		495.36
2003-10-16	ATM Withdrawal - INTERAC	3990	21.25		474.11
2003-10-16	Fees - Interac		1.50		472.61
2003-10-20	Interac Purchase - ELECTRONICS	1975	2.99		469.62
2003-10-21	Web Bill Payment - AMEX	3314	300.00		169.62
2003-10-22	ATM Withdrawal - FIRST BANK	0064	100.00		69.62
2003-10-23	Interac Purchase - SUPERMARKET	1559	29.08		40.54
2003-10-24	Interac Refund - ELECTRONICS	1975		2.99	43.53
2003-10-27	Telephone Bill Payment - VISA	2475	6.77		36.76
2003-10-28	Payroll Deposit - HOTEL			694.81	731.57
2003-10-30	Web Funds Transfer - From SAVINGS	2620		50.00	781.57

Answer 24. **a – It's up to you.** You are responsible for balancing your checkbook. No one else has all the information necessary to do this.

Answer 25. **b,c,d,e – Benefits of a balanced checkbook.** Balancing your checkbook once a month will keep you aware of your financial situation, including:

- what fees were charged by the bank
- which checks are still outstanding (not cashed yet)
- whether you forgot to include any checks or deposits in your checkbook register
- whether the bank statement is accurate (i.e., whether it includes all transactions)
- how much money you have in your account so you don't risk overdrawing your account and paying a fee

Banking $10

Question 26. To update the balance in your checkbook:

a. Be sure you have entered in your checkbook register all the checks written and deposits made, then calculate the balance.

b. Subtract all the service fees shown in the bank statement.

c. Add interest earned in your savings account.

d. Add future direct deposits.

e. Add future direct withdrawals.

Question 27. To update the balance on your bank statement:

a. Write down your bank statement balance.

b. Add deposits not reported yet.

c. Subtract checks not reported yet.

d. Subtract cash withdrawals not reported yet.

e. Add unreported interest.

Question 28. Examples of high-liquidity assets (things that can be quickly converted to cash):

a. money in a checking account

b. money in a savings account

c. real estate (a house or property)

d. stocks

e. gold

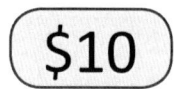 Banking

Answer 26. **a,b – Updating your checkbook balance.** Follow these steps.

1. Be sure you have entered all the checks written and deposits made. Calculate the current balance.

2. Add up all the service fees shown on your bank statement and subtract this total from the balance in your checkbook register.

Example:
Checkbook balance	$704
Service fees	- $3
Updated checkbook balance	$701

Answer 27: **a,b,c,d – Updating your bank statement balance.** Follow these steps.

1. Write down the bank statement balance.

2. Add or subtract recent transactions that do not appear yet on your bank statement, e.g., your recent deposits, checks and cash withdrawals.

Example:
Bank statement balance	$750
Add deposits (not on statement)	+$100
Subtract total of checks (not on statement)	- $49
Subtract cash withdrawals (not on statement)	- $100
Updated bank statement balance	$701

(The updated checkbook and statement balances should be equal.)

Answer 28: **a,b,d,e – Liquidity:** the quality of an asset that permits it to be quickly converted to cash. Because money in a checking or savings account is easily converted to cash, a checking account has high liquidity. Stocks and gold also have high liquidity. Real estate (a house or other property) has low liquidity, as it may take a long time to sell and convert to cash.

Question 29. **Advantages of checking accounts:**

a. low liquidity

b. high liquidity

c. low-risk

d. high-risk

e. high interest rate

Question 30. **If you have overdrawn your account:**

a. Your credit card payment is overdue.

b. You have spent more money than your credit card limit.

c. Your bank balance is less than zero.

d. You will probably have to pay an overdraft fee.

e. You still owe money to the payees on bounced checks.

Question 31. **A check labeled non-sufficient funds (NSF) is also called:**

a. a bad check

b. a bounced check

c. a cold check

d. a rubber check

e. a hot check

Banking

Answer 29: **b,c – Advantages of checking accounts.** Checking accounts have high liquidity (you can easily convert deposits to cash). Another advantage is low-risk. Money in United States bank accounts is insured against bank failure up to $250,000 by the Federal Deposit Insurance Corporation (FDIC).

Answer 30: **c,d,e – Overdrawing an account.** When you write a check for an amount greater than what you have in your checking account (the balance), you are deemed to have insufficient funds (also referred to as "non-sufficient funds" – NSF). You have overdrawn your account. The result is that the bank rejects the check, refuses to give money to the payee and charges you an overdraft fee (e.g., $35).

Answer 31: **a,b,c,d,e – Bad check lingo.** NSF checks are also referred to as: bad checks, dishonored checks, bounced checks, cold checks, rubber checks or hot checks.

"$35 for my boomeranged check? That hurts!"

Question 32. Disadvantages of checking accounts:

a. usually, a minimum balance must be maintained
b. high-risk
c. lack of acceptance by many merchants
d. low liquidity
e. low or no interest earned

Question 33. A money order is a financial instrument that is:

a. more trusted than a personal check
b. used to deposit funds in a bank account
c. purchased at a post office, grocery store or bank
d. used in place of a check
e. less trusted than a personal check

Question 34. A bank or credit union deposit account that pays you interest and allows withdrawals:

a. checking account
b. savings account
c. investment account
d. credit account
e. debit account

Question 35. Generally, money in a savings account is used to:

a. pay for unexpected financial emergencies
b. save for short-term spending goals
c. buy investments that serve long-term goals
d. pay day-to-day expenses
e. pay down debt

Answer 32: **a,c,e – Disadvantages of checking accounts.** Checking accounts earn low interest (or none) and usually require a minimum balance to avoid fees. Also, many merchants are unwilling to accept personal checks, even if you provide ample ID.

Answer 33: **a,c,d – Money order:** a financial instrument that allows the individual named on the order to receive a specified amount of cash on demand. Money orders are used by people who do not have checking accounts. One of the main benefits of a money order is that it is more trusted than a personal check, because it is prepaid. Money orders can be obtained at many locations, including a post office, grocery store or bank. A small fee may be required.

Answer 34: **b – Savings account:** a type of deposit account held by a bank or credit union that pays a small amount of interest. With a savings account, you may be required to maintain a minimum balance (e.g., $25), but you usually can withdraw cash at any time.

Answer 35: **a,b,c – Purpose of a savings account.** Generally, the purpose of a savings account is to set aside money for unexpected financial emergencies and short- and long-term goals (e.g., a car, a vacation). A secondary purpose is to earn some interest on savings. Maintaining a savings account is an important part of smart money management. (To understand more about money management and moving money around, see page 124.)

Banking $10

Question 36. **Advantages of savings accounts:**

a. safe
b. low-risk
c. high liquidity
d. high interest rate
e. a good place to store money for spending goals and "rainy day" emergencies

Question 37. **You don't have to pay tax on the interest you earn on a savings account:**
a. true
b. false

Question 38. **Disadvantages of savings accounts:**

a. require a larger initial deposit than a checking account
b. limit the number of checks per month
c. limit the number of transfers and withdrawals
d. don't earn interest
e. risk of losing money if the bank goes bust

> ### The Federal Deposit Insurance Corporation (FDIC)
>
> *It used to be that when people heard rumors that a bank was failing, they would run to the bank to withdraw their money before the bank went bankrupt. As most of the bank's money was out on loan, the more money people withdrew, the more likely the bank was to fail. To prevent these panic "runs" on banks and to protect depositors, the federal government started the FDIC in 1933. The FDIC insures deposits in United States banks up to $250,000 per account. In the recent Great Recession of 2008-2009, a couple of hundred banks failed, but because of the FDIC's guarantee, no depositor lost money.*

Banking

***Answer 36:* a,b,c,e – Advantages of a savings account.** Some of the advantages of savings accounts are:

- *Safe place to store your money* – Money held in a savings account can't be stolen, lost or destroyed by accident. Plus you are less likely to spend this money frivolously.
- *Low-risk* – Money in a savings account is insured against bank failure up to $250,000 by the Federal Deposit Insurance Corporation (FDIC).
- *High liquidity* – Money in a savings account is available immediately for financial emergencies and short- and long-term spending goals.
- *Guaranteed rate of return (interest)* – Money in a savings account earns a small amount of interest each month. The interest is calculated as a percentage of your deposit, e.g., 3% on a $100 deposit.

***Answer 37:* b – Taxes on interest earned.** You must pay income tax on savings account interest.

***Answer 38:* a,b,c – Disadvantages of savings accounts.** These accounts may require a larger initial deposit than a checking account and may place limits on check-writing, transfers and withdrawals. Also, they may not allow for cash withdrawals using an ATM card.

> "I used to be a banker, but then I lost interest."
> — Anonymous

Banking $10

Question 39. **A machine that links you electronically to your bank account:**

a. automatic time machine

b. automatic banking machine

c. automatic teller machine

d. automatic lottery terminal

e. slot machine

Question 40. **You can get electronic access to your bank account using a specially encoded :**

a. passkey

b. business card

c. card key

d. ATM card

e. address card

Question 41. **What does the acronym PIN stand for?**

a. personal information number

b. private information number

c. professional information number

d. private investment number

e. personal identification number

$10 Banking

Answer 39: c – **Automatic teller machine (ATM).** This type of "cash machine" takes the place of a bank teller. ATMs are linked to an interbank computer network. Using an ATM, a customer can connect to his or her financial institution to perform such transactions as withdrawing cash from a bank account or making a deposit. Typically you pay no transaction fee when using an ATM owned by your bank; you do pay a fee if the machine is owned by a third party.

Answer 40: d – **ATM Card:** a plastic card issued by the bank where you hold your checking account. It shows your name, account number and bank logo on the front. An encoded chip or magnetic stripe on the back of the card holds a unique number that identifies you as a bank customer. The card allows you to access your checking account electronically via an ATM. ATM cards operate over interbank networks, such as STAR and Cirrus. (Credit card companies do not issue ATM cards, so you will not see their logo on ATM cards.)

ATM cards can be used only to withdraw cash or make deposits, not to make purchases. When you use an ATM card, money is deducted immediately from your checking account and the transaction is posted to your account.

Answer 41: e – **PIN:** stands for "personal identification number." This is a secret number that a customer creates to use in accessing his/her money accounts, usually at an ATM.

Banking $10

Question 42. **To get cash from an ATM machine you need:**

a. an ATM card

b. a wallet

c. a PIN

d. a store card

e. a withdrawal slip

Question 43. **It is possible to make deposits in your bank account at an ATM:**

a. true

b. false

Question 44: **Another way to use an ATM card:**

a. check a bank account balance

b. buy investments

c. make an online purchase

d. borrow money

e. buy a car

> "Happiness lies not in the mere possession of money; it lies in the joy of achievement, in the thrill of creative effort."
> — Franklin D. Roosevelt

$10 Banking

Answer 42: **a,c – Getting cash from an ATM.** To obtain cash from an ATM, you need both your ATM card and a PIN. Swipe your card or slide it into the machine and enter your personal identification number (PIN). Select "Withdrawal" and choose the account that holds your money. Select or type in the amount that you wish to take out of the account and confirm the transaction.

Answer 43: **a – Making deposits at an ATM.** To make a deposit at an ATM, you will also need your ATM card and PIN. Small deposits are best. (Always make large deposits in person at your bank.) It may take several days for the full amount of your deposit to be available to you. At the machine:

1. Choose the on-screen option for deposits and the account into which you want to put your deposit.
2. Enter the amount of your deposit.
3. Make your deposit. (Some banks will require you to use deposit envelopes and slips along with your cash or checks.)
4. Wait for the ATM to confirm your deposit and then take your receipt

Answer 44: **a – Checking your bank balance.** You can use an ATM card at an ATM machine to check your account balance. You cannot use an ATM card to borrow money or make purchases of any kind.

Banking $10

ATM ADVICE

Question 45. **Other than yourself, who should know your PIN (Personal Identification Number)?**

a. bank staff

b. a trusted personal friend

c. family members

d. someone helping you use an ATM

e. no one

Question 46. **Ways to keep your PIN safe:**

a. Write it on a piece of paper and hide it in your wallet.

b. Never give out your PIN in response to email or telephone requests.

c. Choose a PIN password that is not obvious.

d. Write your PIN on the back of your ATM card.

e. If you suspect fraudulent activity, report it to the bank and police and change your PIN immediately.

Question 47. **If you have more than one ATM card, it's best to have just one PIN:**

a. true

b. false

Banking

Answer 45: **e – Don't share your PIN.** Only you need to know this number.

Answer 46: **b,c,e – Other ways to keep your PIN safe:**
- Don't write it on a piece of paper that you hide in your wallet.
- Never give your PIN in response to email/phone requests.
- Choose a PIN that's easy to remember but not one that can be associated with you personally – don't use your initials, your birthday or your social security number. Also avoid easy-to-guess passwords (e.g.,1234).
- If you suspect fraudulent activity, report it to the bank and police and change your PIN immediately.

Answer 47: **b – Separate PINs for each card.** If you have more than one ATM card, it is advisable to create different PINs for each.

Question 48., which type of card is directly connected to your checking account?

a. store card
b. prepaid card
c. credit card
d. debit card
e. gift card

Question 49. A debit card can be described as:

a. a "pay before" card

b. a "pay now" card

c. a "pay later" card

d. a "pay whenever" card

e. an "electronic check"

Question 50. A good way for a teen to gain experience managing money without much risk is to:

a. borrow money from a friend to buy a car

b. open a joint checking account with his/her parents

c. buy lottery tickets every week

d. use a credit card

e. play poker for money with friends

Question 51. Debit cards can be used like ATM cards to withdraw money from your checking account via an ATM:

a. true

b. false

$10   Banking

Answer 48: **d – Debit card** (also known as a bank card or check card): a type of card that is directly connected to your checking account. It can be used to withdraw or deposit money (similar to an ATM card). It can also be used to make purchases (similar to a credit card). Because of their versatility, debit cards are much more common than ATM cards. Debit cards show the card holder's name, account number, bank logo and the word "debit" on the front. They also show the logos of a major credit card company, such as VISA or Mastercard, as well as interbank networks. Transactions are processed over credit card and interbank computer networks. As with other cards, there's a magnetic stripe on the back that holds a unique bank customer number. (So-called "pre-paid" debit cards look similar to debit cards but have different properties – see page 190).

Answer 49: **b,e – "Pay Now" Card.** A debit card acts like an electronic check. When you use it to make a purchase, the money comes out of your bank account almost immediately, as opposed to a credit card ("pay later card") which allows you make payment days or weeks later.

Answer 50: **b – A first step toward financial independence.** A teen and his or her parents can decide to open a joint checking account that comes with a debit card. In this way, a teen can gain experience handling money without much risk while parents can set rules and monitor their teen's transactions.

Answer 51: **a – Getting cash with a debit card.** A debit card can function like an ATM card, that is, you can use it at an ATM to withdraw money from your checking account. To do this, you swipe your card, select "debit" and enter your PIN. You can also get cash back when making a purchase with a debit card.

Banking $10

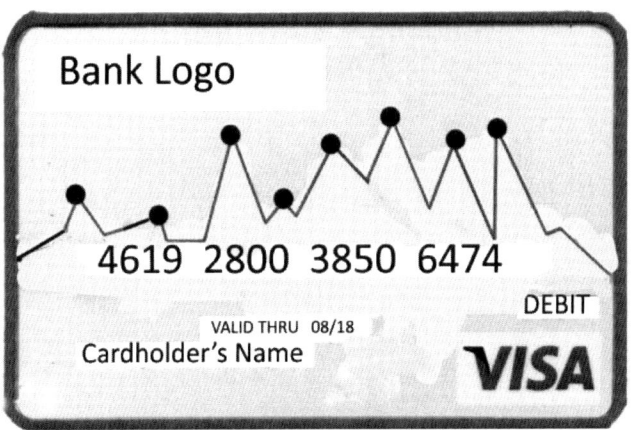

On the front of a debit card is the issuing bank logo, the card number, the expiry date, the card holder's name and the credit card payment network logo (e.g., Visa)

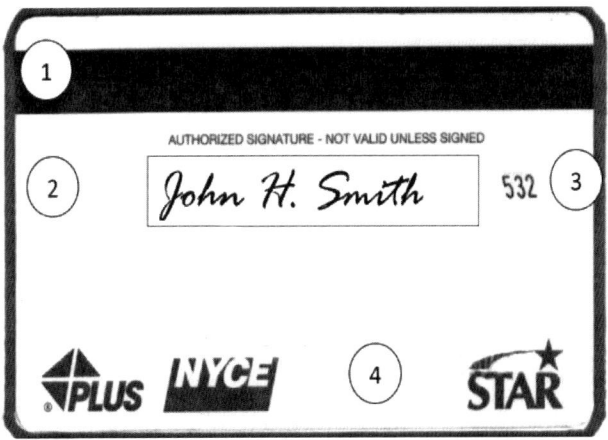

On the back of a debit card is: **1.** a magnetic stripe that contains encoded information that validates the card when it is run through a card reader, **2.** the card holder's signature, **3.** a 3-digit security code (often asked for by merchants) that helps prevent fraud, **4.** logos of interbank networks that can be used by this card.

$10   Banking

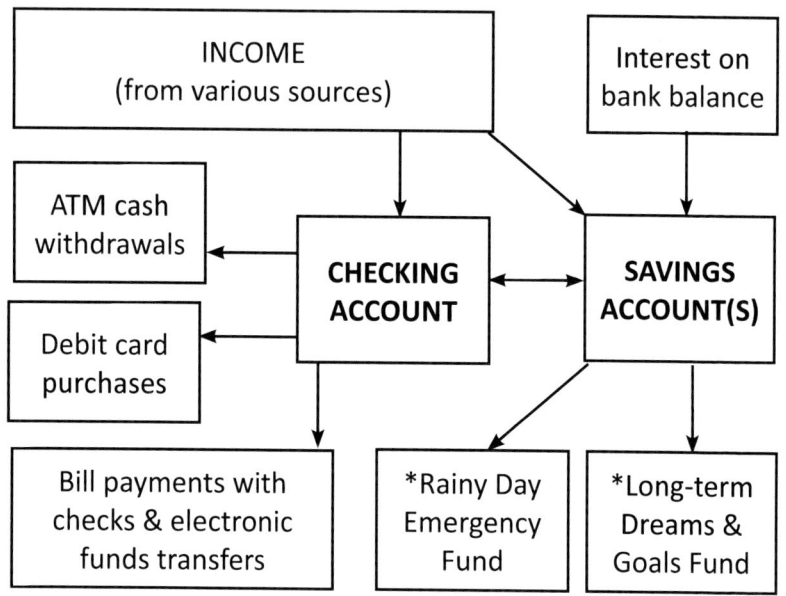

Money Management Basics

The chart above shows how money flows in and out of checking and savings accounts. It's your job to manage the flow. A certain percentage of income (e.g., 10-20%) is put into the savings account and the remainder goes into a checking account. Money in the savings account earns interest while steadily accumulating there. It can be used later for unexpected financial emergencies and short- and long-term goals (e.g., a car, a vacation). Money can easily be moved between the checking and savings accounts. The Rainy Day Emergency Fund and Long Term Dreams & Goals Fund can be separate savings accounts or sub-accounts within one savings account. Cash can be withdrawn from the checking account at an ATM or by getting cash back when making a purchase using the debit card. The checking account is used for paying everyday bills, expenses and credit card balances with checks and electronic funds transfers.

Banking $10

Question 52. **A debit card can be used to:**

a. withdraw cash from an ATM
b. make a store purchase
c. get cash back when making a store purchase
d. make purchases online
e. borrow money

Question 53. **Advantages of a debit card:**

a. allows you to borrow money instantly
b. easier to acquire than a credit card
c. more secure than cash or checks
d. more widely accepted than checks
e. may be used to obtain cash

Answer 52: **a,b,c,d – Other ways to use a debit card.** In addition to using a debit card to withdraw cash from an ATM, you can:

- make a store purchase (use the card as you would a credit card and sign for the purchase)
- get cash back when making a store purchase (use the card as a debit card and enter your PIN number instead of signing)
- buy online (though not advised as there is less fraud protection than for a credit card)

Answer 53: **b,c,d,e – Advantages of debit cards.** Some advantages of debit cards:

- **easier to acquire than a credit card.** Some people cannot obtain a regular credit card, because credit card companies do not consider them to be good risks.
- **more secure than cash or checks.** There is better fraud protection for debit cards than for cash or checks.
- **more widely accepted.** Merchants prefer card payments to personal checks.
- **allows for "free" cash.** Cardholders can obtain cash for no extra charge when they use their bank's ATMs. (Credit card companies, on the other hand, charge interest and higher fees for cash advances.)
- **cash back.** Cardholders can also obtain cash when making a purchase.
- **debt protection.** As you cannot borrow money using a debit card, you are less likely to overspend and go into debt.

Banking $10

Question 54. **Activities that take money directly out of your checking account:**

a. a cash withdrawal from an ATM

b. using a credit card to make a purchase

c. using a debit card to make a purchase

d. paying a bill with a check

e. direct debit, e.g., requesting your bank to regularly withdraw money from your checking account to pay a bill

Question 55. **When using an ATM, take precautions:**

a. Make sure no one can see the PIN you enter.

b. Beware of thieves who try to distract you.

c. Count the cash you withdraw before moving away from the ATM.

d. Quickly put away your cash.

e. Print and keep a receipt.

Question 56. **Disadvantages of debit cards:**

a. If you need a large amount of money for a financial emergency, you are limited to the amount in your account.

b. You can't use your debit card to improve your credit score.

c. There is a danger of overdrafts.

d. There are many fees.

e. There is less protection from consumer fraud than credit cards

***Answer 54.* a,c,d,e – Direct withdrawal methods.** These activities directly remove money from a bank account:

- a cash withdrawal from an ATM/cash machine
- a cash withdrawal from your bank in person
- using a debit card to make a purchase
- paying a bill with a check
- requesting your bank to regularly withdraw money to pay bills, e.g., your car payment

***Answer 55.* a,b,d,e – Taking precautions at an ATM.** Here are some general precautions:

- Try to use an ATM in a secure space that you can access preferably through a locked door.
- Use an ATM in a familiar, well-trafficked, well-lit area.
- Get out your card before you approach the ATM.
- Always check to be sure no one is looking over your shoulder to decipher your PIN ("shoulder surfing") as you enter it on the ATM keypad.
- Avoid being distracted while using an ATM, especially if the machine is not in a secure space. A criminal could snatch your card and money while you are distracted. (If someone makes you uncomfortable, cancel your transaction, leave the machine and contact your bank to make sure the transaction was cancelled.)
- Don't stand in front of the machine and count your money. First, make sure you have removed all the cash from the machine along with your card and the receipt. Then quickly put everything in a secure place in your wallet where would-be thieves can't see it.
- Keep your receipt until you record your withdrawal in your check register.

Banking - Answers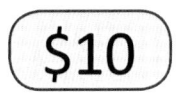

***Answer 56.* a,b,c,d,e – Disadvantages of debit cards.** Here are some of the main disadvantages:

- **Limited amount of money for big emergencies.** The amount of money available to you with a debit card is limited to the amount in your checking account. (With a credit card, you can usually borrow a large amount for an emergency.)
- **Not all merchants accept debit cards.**
- **Credit score not improved.** When you use a debit card, you are simply spending money from your checking account. This will not help build up your credit score (see page 206).
- **Danger of overdraft.** If you don't keep your checkbook register absolutely up-to-date when making debit card purchases and other withdrawals, you could be in danger of exceeding the balance in your account (overdraft).
- **Many fees.** Banks charge a variety of fees for debit card use. They apply a charge almost every time a card is used. They may also charge a monthly service fee. If the account balance drops below a minimum level or the account is overdrawn, the bank may charge still another fee.
- **Disputed charges more difficult to resolve.** With a credit card, you can dispute a charge before actually paying it. With a debit card, you can only dispute a charge after you've paid it. Since merchants already have your money, they have less incentive to resolve a dispute.
- **Less protection from consumer fraud.** Your debit card information could be used by unscrupulous individuals if your card is stolen or you purchase something via the phone or Internet. Potentially, you could lose all the money in your account.

Banking

You Could Lose All Your Money!

Report unauthorized use of your debit card immediately! Your chance of losing all your money increases the longer you wait to contact your bank about unauthorized/fraudulent use of your debit card (unlike a credit card where your loss is limited to $50). You may not learn about a problem until you receive a statement from your bank, and then it takes time to resolve the matter. So, even after you contact your bank, checks you write to pay your bills could bounce. What a mess!

When you are trying to resolve unauthorized use of your debit card, be sure to keep a record of the date(s) you phone the card issuer. Also, follow up every phone call with a letter--and keep a copy of every letter.

Timing of Reporting Unauthorized Use	*Maximum Loss*
Within 2 days of unauthorized use	*$50*
From 3-60 days after unauthorized use	*$500*
More than 60 days after unauthorized use	*All the money in your account*

Question 57. **Online banking:**

a. allows you to conduct financial transactions on a secure website

b. allows you to access your bank accounts from a computer or smartphone

c. requires you to preregister for the online service

d. requires you to create an online account and password

e. is safer than banking in person

Question 58. **Common online banking activities:**

a. view account balances

b. download bank statements

c. make bill and credit card payments

d. transfer funds between accounts that are linked

e. fill out loan applications

Question 59. **Ways to manage your bank account:**

a. visit your bank in person

b. use the mail

c. use your phone

d. use an ATM

e. use the Internet

***Answer 57.* a,b,c,d – Online banking:**

- allows you to conduct financial transactions on a secure website
- allows you to access your bank accounts using a computer or smartphone
- requires you to preregister for the online service
- requires setting up an online account and password
- is faster than banking in person, but less safe because it is easier for thieves to commit fraud online

***Answer 58.* a,b,c,d,e – Common banking activities.** With online banking, you can:

- view account balances and recent transactions
- download bank statements
- make bill and credit card payments
- transfer funds between accounts that are linked
- buy or sell investments
- fill out loan applications
- view images of paid checks
- order check books

***Answer 59.* *a,b,c,d,e* – Bank account management.** You can manage your bank account in many ways. You can:

- visit your bank in person
- deposit checks by mail
- use a standard phone to conduct bank transactions
- use an ATM machine to withdraw cash, make deposits and check your balance
- access your account on a home computer
- use a mobile device (smartphone or tablet) connected to the Internet to conduct bank transactions

Banking $10

Question 60. **The electronic exchange or transfer of money from one account to another without the physical movement of cash is referred to as:**

a. FTE – Funds Transfer Exchange

b. IT$ – Internet Transfer

c. E-Transfer

d. ETF – Easy Transfer of Funds

e. EFT – Electronic Funds Transfer

Question 61. **Examples of electronic funds transfers:**

a. cardholder-initiated transactions where a cardholder makes use of a payment card

b. direct deposit of employee payroll payments by an employer

c. electronic bill payments

d. night deposits at bank

e. wire transfers

> ### *Mobile Banking with a Smartphone*
>
> *Using a mobile device, such as a smartphone, for financial transactions will become increasingly common in the future.*
>
> *Using your smartphone, you will be able to:*
> - *monitor account balances and activity*
> - *transfer money*
> - *make purchases and pay bills*
> - *make deposits*

$10 Banking

Answer 60. e – Electronic funds transfer (EFT): the term used to describe the exchange or transfer of money from one account to another without the physical movement of cash. Such transfers may be done within a single financial institution or across multiple institutions via an interbank computer system.

***Answer 61. a,b,c,e –* Examples of EFT:**

- cardholder-initiated transactions, where a cardholder makes use of a payment card, such as a debit card or credit card
- direct deposit of employee payroll payments by an employer
- electronic bill payments
- wire transfer (see below)

A "night deposit" is a physical, not an electronic transaction. Merchants deposit their daily cash, checks and credit card slips in a bank drop box outside of banking hours.

Wire Transfer

A wire transfer is money transferred electronically from one person or institution to another. A wire transfer can be made from one bank account to another bank account or through an exchange of cash at a cash office such as Western Union. Wire transfers originated in the 19th century and were sent via telegraph messages. As telegraphs were transmitted over wires, the transmissions came to be known as wire transfers.

Banking $10

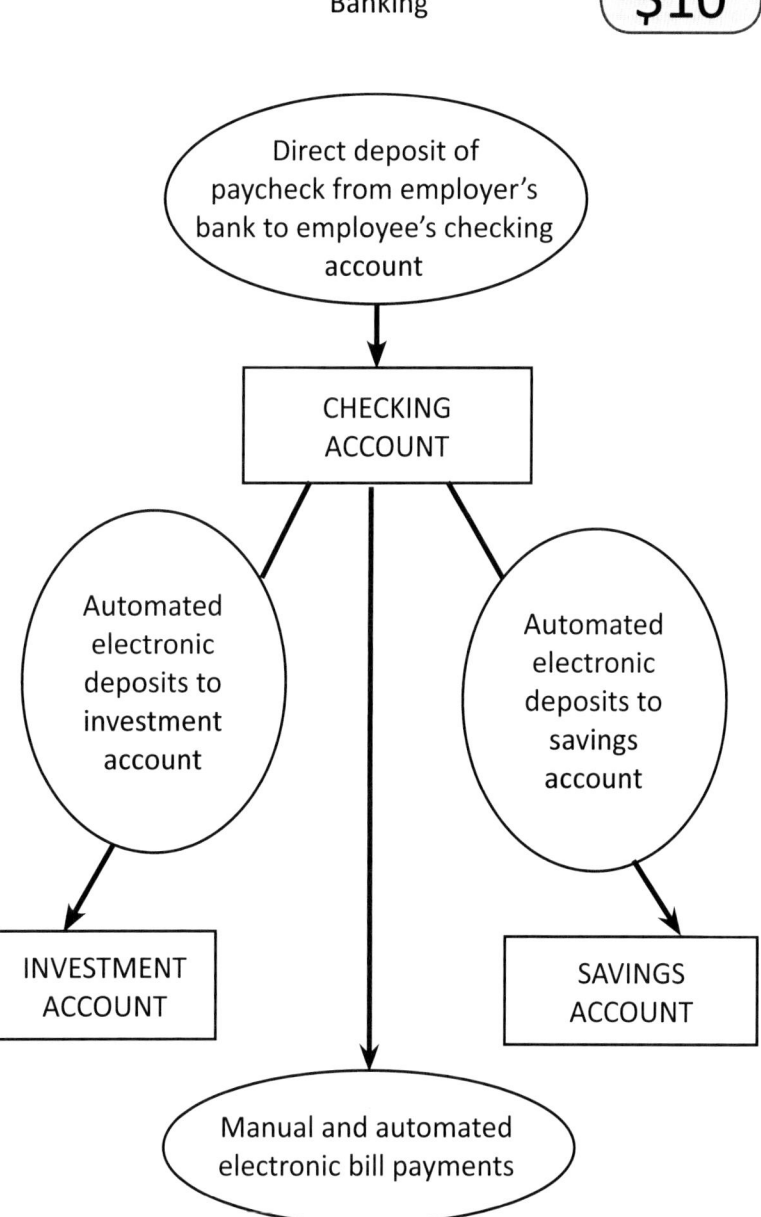

Examples of Electronic Funds Transfers (EFT)

 Banking

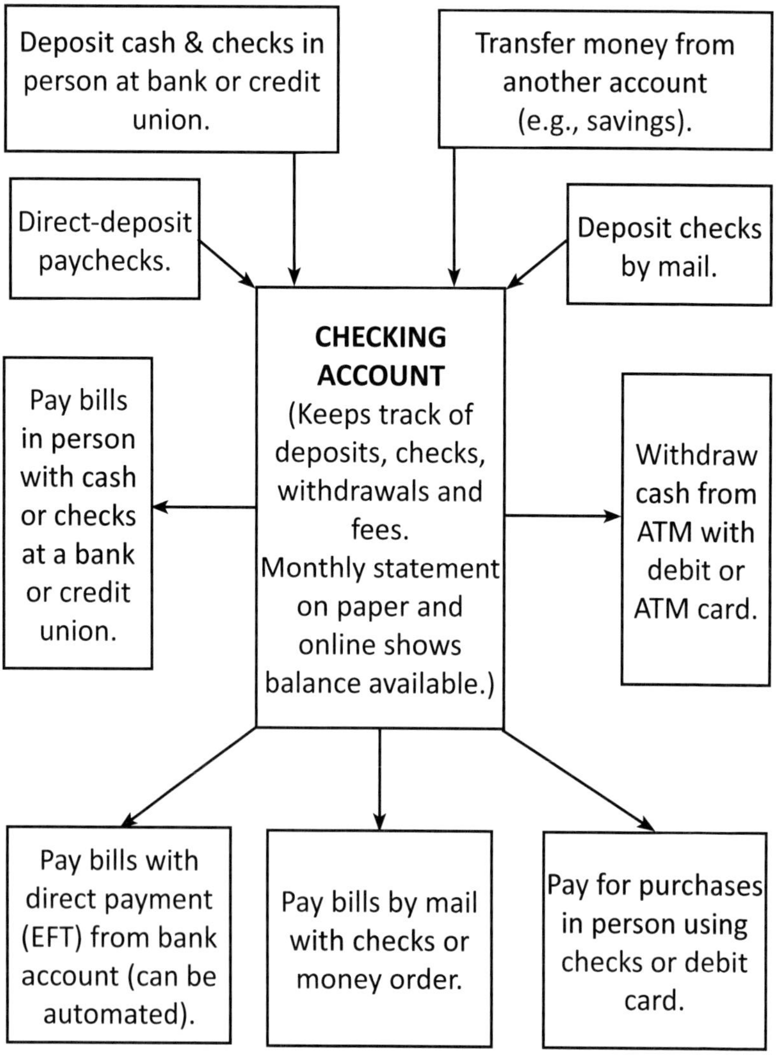

```
┌─────────────────────────┐      ┌─────────────────────────┐
│ Deposit cash & checks in│      │ Transfer money from     │
│ person at bank or credit│      │ another account         │
│ union.                  │      │ (e.g., savings).        │
└───────────┬─────────────┘      └───────────┬─────────────┘
                │                                │
┌──────────────┐│                                │┌──────────────┐
│Direct-deposit││                                ││Deposit checks│
│ paychecks.   ││                                ││  by mail.    │
└──────┬───────┘│                                │└───────┬──────┘
       │        ▼                                ▼        │
       │   ┌──────────────────────────────────────┐       │
       │   │           CHECKING ACCOUNT           │       │
┌──────▼─┐ │      (Keeps track of deposits,       │ ┌─────▼──────┐
│Pay bills│ │      checks, withdrawals and fees.  │ │ Withdraw   │
│in person│►│      Monthly statement on paper     │►│ cash from  │
│with cash│ │      and online shows balance       │ │ ATM with   │
│or checks│ │      available.)                    │ │ debit or   │
│at a bank│ └──────────────────────────────────────┘ │ ATM card.  │
│or credit│        │         │         │             └────────────┘
│union.   │        ▼         ▼         ▼
└─────────┘
┌───────────────┐ ┌───────────────┐ ┌───────────────┐
│Pay bills with │ │Pay bills by   │ │Pay for        │
│direct payment │ │mail with      │ │purchases in   │
│(EFT) from bank│ │checks or      │ │person using   │
│account (can be│ │money order.   │ │checks or      │
│automated).    │ │               │ │debit card.    │
└───────────────┘ └───────────────┘ └───────────────┘
```

Understanding the big picture of how a checking account works is crucial for managing your everyday finances efficiently. This flowchart illustrates what you've learned in this chapter about how you can use a checking account.

Saving

"If you never remember another thing I say, remember this – spend less than you earn and save at least 10% of your money. That's the secret to having a happy, financially secure life."

Today's Youth Are Into Money

Today's youth think that making money, having money and spending money are cool. They need to learn that saving money, investing money and donating money are cool, too.

Let's Revive the Old-Fashioned Value of Saving

Sadly, the idea of economizing, saving and waiting until you can actually afford to pay for something has become old-fashioned. Kids (and adult kids) today are encouraged by banks, creditors and advertisers to believe that they can have whatever they want right now. Waiting and saving are just too hard, too boring. But there's a big price to pay for this impatience. Many are now deeply in debt. When we borrow to buy, we pay a lot more in the long run. To keep our heads above water, we need to revive the old-fashioned value of saving.

Truth in Savings Act

A federal law that requires financial institutions to disclose specific information about the terms and costs of interest-earning accounts — such as annual percentage yield (APY) — and certain other financial services.

Saving $10

Question 62. **Saving is the practice of:**

a. buying things on sale
b. never spending any of your money
c. putting some money aside for future use
d. buying some unusual thing on impulse because you might need it in the future
e. saving every cent

Question 63. **Some good reasons to save money:**

a. to expand your options in life
b. to achieve long-term goals
c. to pay for something special like a big trip
d. to protect yourself in case of a financial emergency
e. to donate to a favorite charity

Question 64. **Your savings allow you to:**

a. enjoy your daily life without the fear of running out of money
b. feel free to buy whatever you want whenever you want
c. make a large, important purchase without worry
d. feel confident because you have "money in the bank" to achieve your important life goals
e. experience less stress during financial emergencies

Question 65. **One of the hardest things to do in life is to:**

a. give money away

b. buy gifts

c. save money

d. borrow money

e. spend money

$10   Saving

***Answer 62.* c – Saving.** Saving is the practice of putting some money aside for future use. Keeping every last cent you have is hoarding, not saving.

***Answer 63.* a,b,c,d,e – Why save?** There are many specific reasons to save money, but overall, when you save you are expanding your options in life. Instead of just getting by, you are building up resources that will allow you to:

- achieve long-term goals, such as a college education
- pay for special things once in a while, such as going on a big trip or buying something you really want
- protect yourself from disaster should you experience a financial emergency that could plunge you into debt
- help out your community by donating to a favorite charity, such as a local food bank or animal rescue organization

***Answer 64.* a,c,d,e – The emotional rewards of saving.** Your savings allow you to:
- enjoy your daily life and pay for your basic needs without the fear of running short of money
- make a large, important purchase without worrying about going into debt
- feel confident because you have "money in the bank" to achieve your important life goals
- experience less stress during financial emergencies, because you have a monetary "cushion" to see you through

***Answer 65.* c – Saving can be hard to do.** Spending money is one of the easiest things in life to do. Saving money, on the other hand, is one of the hardest. However, if you keep track of how you spend your money, you'll find it easier to save.

Saving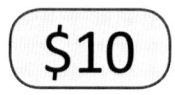

***Question 66.* Typical excuses for not saving:**

a. I'm young. I have plenty of time later on to save.
b. I don't have much money. When I'm making more, I'll start saving.
c. I have more important things to spend my money on right now.
d. I don't have the willpower to save.
e. Money isn't important to me.

***Question 67.* Habits that keep people from saving:**

a. eating out, buying take-out food, buying snacks
b. going on shopping sprees
c. collecting store coupons
d. shopping a lot online
e. hanging out at the mall

"It's not that I'm bad at saving, it's just that I'm good at shopping."

Saving

Answer 66. **a,b,c,d,e – Typical excuses for not saving.**
Excuses can take many forms and they are often a cover for not mustering the willpower to save for important goals. Being young, not having much money or not caring about money are not good excuses in themselves for not saving. If you have taken care of your basic needs and don't have debt to repay, then you should be able to save some money. Often, you can start saving money simply by reducing your spending on wants.

Answer 67. **a,b,d,e - Habits that keep people from saving.**
Here are some habits that may limit one's ability to save:

- eating out, buying take-out food, buying snacks
- going on shopping sprees (impulse buying)
- shopping a lot online – it's too easy to click and buy
- hanging out at the mall – too many temptations to spend money

Saving $10

Question 68. Helpful habits for savers. Here are some habits that help people save:

a. saving 10-20% of all income in a savings account

b. hanging out at malls and cruising for sales

c. ignoring advertising

d. buying products on layaway

e. keeping a record of expenses

Question 69. The "pay yourself first" principle:

a. Spend money on yourself first, before paying bills.

b. Spend money on yourself before treating friends.

c. Buy what you want first, before saving or investing.

d. Put part of your paycheck in savings and investments before paying bills or buying anything.

e. Buy what you need before paying bills.

"I used to spend every penny I got. Now, whenever I get some money, *I pay myself first*, that is, I save some of it before I ever spend a nickel."

$10 Saving

***Answer 68.* a,c,d,e – Helpful habits for savers.** Here are some habits that can help you save money:

- saving 10-20% of all income in a savings account (Money in a savings account is harder to spend than cash or money in a checking account.)
- paying bills and credit card balances promptly to avoid late-payment fees
- trimming unnecessary expenses and buying only what you need
- resisting the urge to buy goods without thinking when caught up in the excitement of a sale
- ignoring advertising
- buying products on a layaway plan instead of paying with credit card and incurring interest charges (Layaway: after you put down a deposit, the store holds a product for you until you have paid the full price. See page 68.)
- keeping a record of expenses

***Answer 69.* d – The "pay yourself first" principle.** Save some money from your paycheck before paying bills or buying anything, even if it's only a small amount. You might think that paying your bills is the very first thing you should do, but if you always do this, you may never put money aside as savings. There's one exception to this rule – you should first pay down any debt that is costing you a lot of money in interest payments.

Saving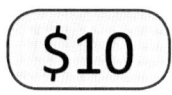

Question 70. **If you regularly save small amounts of money, you will eventually accumulate a large amount of money.**

a. true
b. false

Question 71. **A good saving habit is:**

a. Save only when you have lots of money.

b. Keep your money safe under a mattress.

c. Wait till you have a job to save money.

d. Buy what you want, then save what's left.

e. Save 10% of your money first, before spending.

Question 72. **Buying something on sale is always a good way to save money:**

a. true
b. false

Origins of Piggy Bank

The piggy bank originated in a type of jar used during the Middle Ages. These jars were called "pygg" jars after the form of clay (pygg) from which they were made. Pygg jars were used to store all kinds of household items, including money. Over time, people began to refer to the jars as "pygg banks." The term has no connection whatsoever to pigs. At some point, people saw the humor in the similarity between the two words – pygg and pig – and started making the jars in the shape of pigs.

 Saving

Answer 70. **a – Saving small amounts.** If you regularly save small amounts of money in a savings account, you will eventually accumulate a large amount. For example, if you saved $1 a day, in five years you could have more than $2,100 in savings (assuming your money earned 5% interest per year).

Answer 71. **e – The 10% saving rule.** It's simple. Whenever you acquire some money, save 10% of it first, before you spend a cent.

Answer 72. **b – Buying at sales is not always saving.** You often hear people say they've saved a bundle by buying something at a big sale. If they truly needed an item, they may have indeed saved a bit. More often than not, however, they didn't need the item and would have done better avoiding the sale and putting the money in their savings account. And even if they did need the item, they might have been able to find it somewhere else for less if they'd done some research before buying.

Saving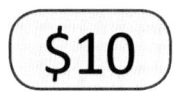

Question 73. **If you want to buy an expensive item, but you don't have enough money to pay the full right price now, the "money smart" thing to do is:**

a. Just keep wishing for it until it comes your way.
b. Ask your parents to buy it for you.
c. Ask your friends to loan you money.
d. Buy the item on your credit card.
e. Save up enough money to buy it.

Question 74. **Setting savings goals is a good thing to do.** Goals help you to:

a. avoid frivolous spending
b. put aside money on a routine basis
c. live within your means and stay out of debt
d. buy whatever you want
e. accumulate funds for a large purchase or expenditure in the future

Question 75. **How to achieve savings goals:**

a. rely on your bank to keep track of your savings activities
b. write down your savings goals
c. assume that your savings goals will be realized automatically
d. refer regularly to your list of savings goals
e. report your progress in saving to an "accountability buddy"

Question 76. **Which of these is the best way to state a savings goal?**

a. I will start saving money for a school trip.

b. I will save all my change for a school trip.

c. I will save $5 a week for a school trip.

d. I will save $5 a week until I have the $100 I need for the trip.

Saving

Answer 73. **e – Buy without borrowing.** If you want something but don't have enough money to pay for it right now, the adult thing to do is to just keep saving until you have enough to pay the full purchase price. If you borrow money to make the purchase now, you'll probably have to pay interest on the loan.

Answer 74. a,b,c,e – **Why setting savings goals is a good thing.** Without savings goals, it's very difficult to resist all the temptations that come your way. As a result, you may fritter away all your money and never achieve your dreams. Savings goals constantly remind you to:

- avoid frivolous spending
- put aside money on a routine basis
- live within your means and stay out of debt
- accumulate funds for a large purchase or expenditure

Answer 75. b,d,e – **How to Achieve Savings Goals.** You can't go on auto pilot when striving to achieve your savings goals. First, you need to write them down. Then you must refer to them regularly and check your bank statements to see how well you're doing (every month). From time to time it may be necessary to update your goals as your life circumstances change. For some people, it may be helpful to report your progress to an "accountability buddy" who can help you stay on target.

Answer 76. **d – Goal statements.** The best way of stating savings goals is to specify:

- the total goal amount
- an incremental savings amount (e.g., $10)
- a payment schedule (e.g., weekly)
- an overall time frame (e.g., 20 weeks)

For example: "I want to save $100 for the school trip, so I will save $5 a week for 20 weeks to reach my goal."

Saving

Question 77. **When you receive income, the top three "money smart" priorities to do are:**

a. spending money on wants
b. paying down debt
c. saving money for specific goals
d. spending money on needs
e. giving money away

Question 78. **A "rainy day" fund is money set aside for:**

a. living expenses in case of job loss
b. an emergency car repair
c. a health crisis
d. entertainment on a rainy day
e. replacing an important piece of broken equipment, e.g., a computer or refrigerator

"I'm singin' in the rain,
Just singin' in the rain,
My 'Rainy Day Fund'
Makes me happy again!"

***Answer 77.* b,c,d – The top three priorities.** When you receive income, the top three "money smart" things to do are to:

1. Pay down debit.
2. Set some money aside in savings.
3. Spend money on needs/pay your bills.

Once you've done these three things, in the order presented, you're free to spend the rest of your money on other things.

***Answer 78.* a,b,c,e - A "rainy day" fund:** money set aside to pay for expenses resulting from an unexpected event. Losing your job is one of the most difficult unexpected events. But if you have set aside some money for emergencies, you may be able to cover basic living expenses during a period of unemployment. Without any savings, you could be forced to borrow money just to get by.

Other examples of unexpected events that could cost you money:

- Your car breaks down and needs expensive repairs.
- You become seriously sick or injured and incur big medical bills.
- Your refrigerator "dies" and needs to be replaced.
- The computer you use for school or work crashes and needs to be replaced.

> "A banker is a fellow who lends you his umbrella when the sun is shining, but wants it back the minute it begins to rain."
>
> — Mark Twain

Saving $10

Question 79. **Whenever an unexpected windfall (e.g., a large sum of money) comes your way, you should first:**

a. have a big party with your friends

b. buy all the stuff you've ever wanted

c. take your time deciding how to make the best use of the money

d. tell all your friends

e. consult a trustworthy financial advisor to help you plan how to use your money

 Saving

Answer 79. **c,e – Windfall:** unexpected and unearned good fortune, often a large financial gain. Examples include: gift money, a pay bonus, prize money, lottery winnings or an inheritance. Never count on receiving a windfall, but if you should be so lucky, take your time deciding how to make the best use of it. Don't succumb to an all-too-common pitfall and spend every cent. (Sadly, some big lottery winners go bankrupt within a few years.)

First, try to keep your good luck quiet. Tell as few people as possible. You don't want "friends" coming after you for money or treating you differently than before. Consult a trustworthy financial advisor to help you plan how to use your money to further your long-term goals.

"What to do with your windfall? First, pay off all debts and expenses. Second, set aside money for 'rainy days' and long-term goals such as college, a car, a house and retirement. Then, if you have anything left, you can treat yourself to something special."

Saving $10

Question 80. **Put your savings in a safe place, such as:**

a. a lockbox at home
b. a savings account at a bank
c. a secret hiding place in your backyard
d. a hiding place in your wallet
e. your locker at school

Question 81. **Advantages of keeping your savings in a savings account:**

a. Your money will earn interest.
b. You can save money for special goals.
c. You won't have money to spend on gifts later.
d. You'll have money readily available for financial emergencies.
e. You won't be able to take out the money when you need it.

Question 82. **A certificate of deposit (CD) is:**

a. a receipt for a savings account deposit
b. a receipt for a checking account deposit
c. a time-limited deposit that pays interest
d. a certificate for buying a music CD online
e. a receipt for adding money to a money card

Question 83. **Where will your money grow the fastest?**

a. in a piggy bank
b. in a checking account
c. in a savings account
d. in a certificate of deposit
e. in a credit card account

Saving

***Answer 80.* a,b – Where to put your savings?** Put your savings in a safe place where you can keep track of it. When you first start saving, it's OK to put your money in a piggy bank or lockbox at home, but it's always safer in a savings account at a bank. Some people put money in a special savings account for a particular purpose or long-term goal, e.g., to buy a car, to have money for college. Putting money in a savings account is an easy way to make money, because you will earn interest on your original deposit. In other words, your money will be "working" for you.

***Answer 81.* a,b,d – Advantages of a savings account.** (See also page 114) Some advantages include:
- Your money will earn interest.
- You are less likely to spend that money frivolously.
- You can accumulate money for a special goal (e.g., a car).
- You can take out your money whenever you need it (e.g., a financial emergency).
- Your money can't be lost or stolen.
- You can easily keep track of your money by checking your balance anytime on the phone or online.

***Answer 82.* c – Certificate of Deposit (CD).** A CD is a special type of deposit in a bank. It is different from a savings account in that it has a specific, fixed term (often monthly, three months, six months, or one to five years), and usually a fixed interest rate. It is intended that the CD be held until maturity, at which time the money may be withdrawn together with the accrued interest.

***Answer 83.* d – Advantages/Disadvantages of CD's.** CDs earn more interest than savings accounts. The main disadvantage is that your money is less accessible. If you cash in your CD before the term is complete, you must pay a penalty.

Saving $10

Question 84. **Excessively accumulating money while avoiding spending or investing is called:**

a. hedging
b. stockpiling
c. stashing
d. saving
e. hoarding

Question 85. **People who excessively stockpile their money at home:**

a. risk losing it
b. may endanger their health by not spending money on basic needs
c. aren't earning interest on their money
d. aren't using their money to reach goals
e. aren't using their money to enjoy their lives to the fullest

"Your Majesty, hoarding your money isn't doing anybody any good. Why not give it to the peasants so they can plant crops. Then with the harvest, we can all have a feast."

Saving

Answer 84. **e – Hoarding:** excessively accumulating money and not spending or investing any of it. Hoarding is not the same as saving. Saving has a purpose: to make more money and accumulate funds for something you need or want.

Answer 85. **a,b,c,d,e – Hoarding money is not money-smart:**

- Money hoarded at home is not safe; coins and bills can be lost, destroyed or stolen. Once you have accumulated enough money to fill a piggy bank, jar or lockbox, it's time to put it in a safer place, e.g., a bank account.
- You may endanger your well-being by not spending money on your needs.
- Your money is unemployed – it's not earning interest and not being used to help you reach your goals.
- Your money is not helping you, your family and your friends enjoy life.

Beware of Overspending on Hobbies and Collections

It's fun to have hobbies and build a collection of favorite objects (e.g., coins, teddy bears, musical instruments, etc.). However, if the impulse to spend money on hobbies and collections is unchecked, it could be a money-wasting form of hoarding. You need to carefully consider every purchase; otherwise, you could end up buying a lot of things you really can't afford, don't have time to enjoy, or don't have space for.

> "Compound interest is the eighth wonder of the world. He who understands it, earns it ... he who doesn't ... pays it."
>
> — Albert Einstein

Saving

Simple vs. Compound Interest

Imagine you had an amazing opportunity to invest $100 at an interest rate of 50% a year. (Wow!)

If the investment earned simple interest, then your investment would grow by $50 (50% of your original investment or principal) every year. Looking at the solid line on the chart below, you see that you would start year 2 with a total of $150, year 3 with $200, year 4 with $250...etc. At the beginning of year 10 you would have a total of $550.

However, if you could earn compound interest, your investment would grow much faster. Your money would be earning 50% interest on the original principal plus 50% on the sum of all the subsequent years' interest earnings. Looking at the dotted line on the chart below, you see that you would start year 2 with a total of $150, year 3 with $225, year 4 with $338...etc. At the beginning of year 10, you would have a total of $3,844. (Experiment with various compound interest scenarios at: investor.gov/tools/calculators/compound-interest-calculator.)

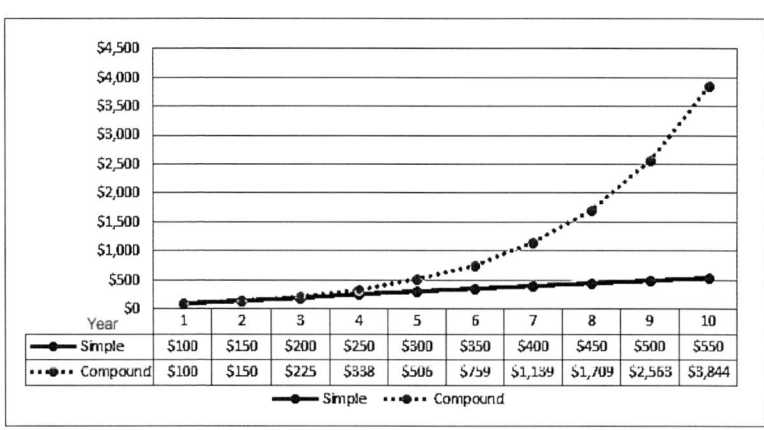

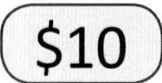

Saving

Saving Takes Grit

Saving – foregoing the pleasure of spending in the present for the benefits of a long-term goal in the future requires grit, perseverance, passion, mental toughness and courage.

"Savings represent much more than mere money value. They are the proof that the saver is worth something in himself. Any fool can waste; any fool can muddle; but it takes something more of a man to save and the more he saves the more of a man he makes of himself. Waste and extravagance unsettle a man's mind for every crisis; thrift, which means some form of self-restraint, steadies it."

— Rudyard Kipling

Nest Egg

A "nest egg" is a sum of money saved or invested for one specific purpose, e.g., education, a house, retirement, even entertainment (vacations and cruises). The money in the nest egg should be used only for the purpose you saved it for.

Good Money Management

For an illustration of good money management, see page 124.

Expenses, Bills & Budgets

Expenses, Bills and Budgets

Budget – A Tool for Making Dreams Come True

Many people would rather do anything than create a budget. They see it as a tedious and somewhat mystifying exercise that involves pulling numbers out of thin air.

In fact, a budget is a cool tool for achieving your dreams faster. There are clear, straightforward steps to take in creating a budget and the more you do it, the better you become. Don't think of budget-making as boring and baffling; think of it, instead, as a process that will help you get what you really want out of life.

Along the way, you can pick specific saving targets (e.g., money for a tech toy, clothing item, car, trip, college degree). And with a budget in place, you will be better able to eliminate unnecessary expenses and achieve your dreams more quickly.

Expenses, Bills and Budgets $10

Question 86. **Money you spend on basic goods and services to sustain you and your family:**

a. sum
b. balance
c. price
d. debit
e. expenses

Question 87. **Many expenses are for basic needs, such as:**

a. food
b. housing
c. utilities (electricity, heat, phone, etc.)
d. transportation (bicycle, car, taxi, public transit)
e. smartphone service

Question 88. **Utilities (household services considered to be necessities) include:**

a. electricity
b. water
c. heat
d. Internet
e. cable TV

Question 89. **Fixed expenses are those that:**

a. are paid only once
b. vary depending on usage
c. fluctuate with the market
d. cost the same each month
e. are fixed to a bank account

Question 90. **Expenses that change from month to month:**

a. fixed expenses
b. variable expenses
c. credit card expenses
d. debit card expenses
e. loans

$10 Expenses, Bills and Budgets

Answer 86. **e – Expenses:** money you pay out for goods and services that help to sustain you and your family. These include costs that are fixed and those that are variable.

Answer 87. **a,b,c,d – Basic needs.** Many family expenses fall into the realm of basic needs, including food, housing, utilities (electricity, heat, phone, etc.), clothing and transportation (e.g., bicycle, car, public transit). For general communication, emergencies and personal security, a basic phone has become a need in today's world. Internet access at home, at school or a library is also considered a basic need, as it connects people to other people and important information (e.g., job listings). A smartphone (which costs more because you must pay for Internet access as well as phone service) is not a basic need because Internet access is available through other devices.

Answer 88. **a,b,c,d – Utilities –** a collective term referring to a number of household services, including electricity, water, heating/cooling, telephone and Internet, for which you and your family must pay. The government often regulates these services. Cable TV is also a service, but it's not a necessity. You can easily live without it.

Answer 89. **d – Fixed expenses –** expenses that cost the same amount each month. Rent and car payments are examples of fixed expenses.

Answer 90. **b – Variable expenses –** expenses that change from month to month. Your food, clothing and entertainment expenses are variable.

> *"Expenditures rise to meet income."*
> — Cyril Northcote Parkinson's Second Law

Expenses, Bills and Budgets $10

Question 91. **Money you pay a landlord for an apartment:**

a. bill

b. mortgage

c. rent

d. security deposit

e. collateral

Question 92. **A contract you sign when you rent an apartment:**

a. mortgage

b. lease

c. bill

d. loan

e. security deposit

Question 93. **A loan to finance the purchase of real estate (e.g., a house and/or other property) usually with a specified period within which to pay back the loan plus interest (e.g., 15 years at 5% interest):**

a. payday loan

b. title loan

c. mortgage

d. demand loan

e. easy-access credit loan

 Expenses, Bills and Budgets

Answer 91. **c – Rent:** money you pay to a landlord every month for the use of an apartment, office or house.

Answer 92. **b – Apartment lease.** Before you can rent an apartment, you usually must sign a lease. A lease is a written contract between you and the owner of the rental property (the landlord) that covers a specified time period and spells out what you will pay the owner for use of the property. (Leases also set limits on how you can use the property, e.g., no pets, no smoking.) Often you must pay an upfront "security deposit" equal to 1-2 months' worth of rent; the landlord can retain all or a portion of your deposit should you cause serious damage or fail to pay your rent prior to vacating the apartment.

Answer 93. **c – Mortgage:** a loan to finance the purchase of a house or other real estate. Most people do not have sufficient funds to purchase a house outright, so they make a down payment of 10-20% of the appraised value of a house and then take out a mortgage loan to cover the rest of the price. With a mortgage, a bank or similar lender typically agrees to loan the borrower a certain amount of money for a specified time period plus interest (e.g., 15 years at 5% interest). Should the borrower fail to keep up with regular payments, the lender retains the right to take possession of the house.

Mortgage

A mortgage is a means to acquire and keep a roof over your head. The word "mortgage" is said to come from two French words - mort meaning death and gage meaning pledge or agreement. In other words, a "death contract" in which the pledge ends (dies) when either the obligation (to repay a loan) is fulfilled or the property is taken back.

Expenses, Bills and Budgets $10

Question 94. **A bill can mean:**

a. paper money of a certain amount

b. an amount owed for services or products provided

c. a statement from your bank

d. a bank deposit

e. a shipper's packing slip

Question 95. **Ways to pay bills:**

a. Pay cash at a store location.

b. Pay by check in person at a store.

c. Mail a check to a merchant.

d. Pay with a credit or debit card in person or online.

e. Arrange an electronic payment from your bank.

Question 96. **Good bill-paying habits:**

a. Verify all charges are correct.

b. Pay bills before due date.

c. Pay down debt with the highest interest rate first.

d. Pay bills that will charge interest if left unpaid.

e. Pay the minimum amount for each bill.

$10 Expenses, Bills and Budgets

***Answer 94.* a,b – Bill:** Either paper money (e.g., a $5 bill) or a document that details an amount owed for a product or service that has been provided.

***Answer 95.* a,b,c,d,e – Payment methods.** Some ways of making a payment:

- Pay with cash in person.
- Pay by check in person.
- Pay with a check mailed to a merchant. (Note: It is not safe to mail cash.)
- Pay with a credit or debit card at a store.
- Pay online with a credit or debit card.
- Pay with funds electronically transferred from your bank account.

***Answer 96.* a,b,c,d – Good bill-paying habits.** Some good habit are:

- Never ignore bills. (If you ignore a bill, you risk having to pay late fees and interest charges.)
- Verify all charges are correct.
- Pay bills before their due date.
- Pay down debt with the highest interest rate first.
- Pay bills that will start to charge interest if left unpaid.
- Pay the full amount of every bill every month, if possible. If you can't pay the full amount, pay as much as you can. Always try to pay more than the minimum payment.
- Arrange for automatic payment of monthly bills using your bank account or credit card.

Expenses, Bills and Budgets $10

> ***Budgeting Using the 50/30/20 Rule of Thumb***
> *(coined by Harvard bankruptcy expert Elizabeth Warren and her daughter, Amelia Warren Tyagi, in their book, "All Your Worth: The Ultimate Lifetime Money Plan.")*
>
> 1. **Calculate Your After-Tax Income.** *Your after-tax (disposable) income is the amount of money you have left after you've paid your taxes (federal and state income taxes, local taxes, Medicare, Social Security, etc.)*
> 2. **Spend at least 20 percent on Savings** *(emergency fund and your retirement accounts)* **and Debt Repayments.**
> 3. **Limit Your Needs to 50 Percent.** *"Needs", such as groceries, housing, utilities, and insurance, should be no more than 50 percent of your total after-tax income.*
> 4. **Limit Your Wants to 30 Percent.** *Wants include cable or satellite TV, fancy tech toys, dining at restaurants, fast food/ casual eateries, beyond-the-basics clothing, subscriptions, club dues, hobbies, sports, lessons, trips, gifts, etc.*

 Expenses, Bills and Budgets

A CASH FLOWCHART

Cash Flow – *a pattern of money coming in and going out. Your cash flow history can be very helpful when preparing a budget.*

In the diagram on the facing page, imagine that money from various income sources converges into a river flowing downstream; portions of the money stream are diverted into various expense categories in order of priority.

Taxes - *income taxes are usually deducted from paychecks by employers. If you earn additional income from other sources, then you'll have to include that income on your income tax form and possibly pay more taxes later.*

Debt – *if you have a loan (e.g., car) with fixed payments, then you must make the payments on time or you will lose the property. To avoid paying high interest rates on a credit card, it's best to pay the full amount of your credit card bill every month, even if you have to cut back on amounts you're saving in "pay yourself first"categories.*

Savings - *it's fairly easy to save money if you are able to pay yourself first (the "golden rule" of personal finance), i.e., set aside money for "rainy day" emergencies and short and long-term goals before paying for needs and wants. Most people do the opposite, spending money on bills and fun first and then saving the rest. This approach usually results in having little or nothing left over for savings goals.*

Living Expenses - *these are needs you should pay for before spending any money on wants.*

Donations to Nonprofits – *this includes religious organizations, charities, favorite causes. For some people, this could be a higher priority than it appears in this diagram.*

Discretionary Spending – *after spending money on the higher priorities above, the money left over is available to spend on wants.*

Expenses, Bills and Budgets $10

A CASH FLOW FLOWCHART

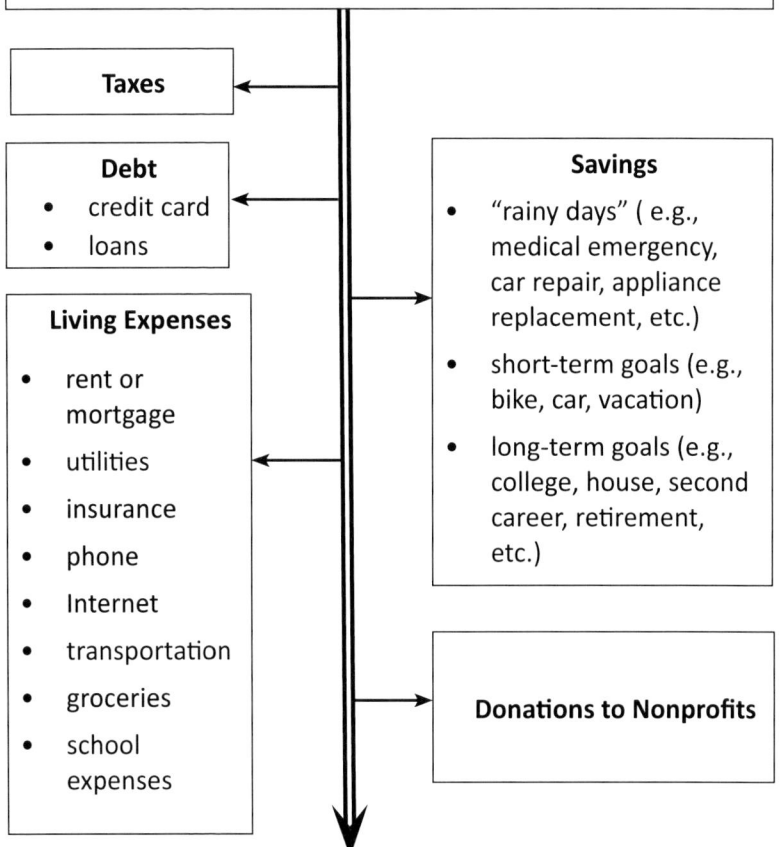

$10 Expenses, Bills and Budgets

Cash Flow Journal

You can use a computer spreadsheet to keep a cash flow journal of money as it flows in and out of your life. This can help you keep track of income and expenses and provide the basis for a budget.

Date	Description	Income	Expenses
6/1	Pay from part-time job	$85	
6/2	Bus fare		$2
6/3	School lunch		$5
6/4	Babysitting	$20	
6/5	Birthday gift money	$50	
6/9	Allowance	$25	

Income and Expense Statement

Referring to your cash flow journal, you can summarize your cash flow activity over a month in a cash flow or income and expense statement. This is a detailed picture of how money has passed in and out of your life over a period of time.

Income			
Part-time job	$250		
Allowance	$40		
Gift money	$35		
Total Income		$225	
Expenses			
Bus fare	$22		
School lunches	$50		
Entertainment	$100		
Total Expenses		$172	
Net Income			$53

Expenses, Bills and Budgets 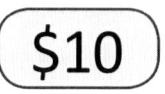 $10

Question 97. **A plan for spending and saving money during a given time period:**

a. a credit report
b. a savings account report
c. a credit card statement
d. a budget
e. a net worth statement

Question 98. **A budget must include dollar amounts for:**

a. anticipated income
b. projected expenses
c. savings targets
d. costly items you need to buy
e. taxable income

"Sir, I'm sorry about your job loss, but we don't cover financial emergencies. Do you have any 'rainy day' savings?"

$10 Expenses, Bills and Budgets

Answer 97. **d – Budget:** a plan for spending and saving money during a given time period in the future. Ideally, you should prepare a budget for a whole year and monitor it once a month. When you create a budget, you do your best to forecast the future based on how much money you expect to come in, pay out, and put aside in savings. Of course, it's impossible to completely foresee the future, so a budget is not a fixed picture. You may get a raise or financial windfall; you may lose your job or have a medical emergency. Such events will necessitate adjustments to your budget. Still, as you become more familiar with the process of maintaining a budget, the more accurate you are likely to become in projecting income and expenses and setting realistic savings goals.

Answer 98. **a,b,c,d – Key elements in a budget.** A budget must include dollar amounts for anticipated income and projected expenses (including an amount to be saved). You can't pull these amounts out of thin air, though. You need to assemble the most accurate information you possibly can.

Your history of earning money and spending is the basis for projecting your future income and spending in a budget. A cash flow journal and an income and expense statement (see page 170) are good sources of information to draw on when creating a budget. If you need or want to make a big purchase, you can also do research on the Internet or in stores to determine how much to include in your budget.

You will probably discover that it's not easy to find hard data to support proposed savings targets. But it's critical to build up your savings, so you need to pick an amount and include it as a fixed expense in your budget. Then, as you go along, you can adjust the amount to more accurately reflect reality.

Expenses, Bills and Budgets $10

***Question 99.* Budgets are good for:**

a. businesses
b. government
c. families
d. adults
e. kids

Question 100. A budget for one person is called a:

a. personal budget
b. family budget
c. household budget

***Question 101.* Items in a family or household budget might include:**

a. utility expenses – electricity, water, heat, phone
b. anticipated home improvements
c. donations to charities
d. miscellaneous small expenses
e. savings for education and other goals

Online Budget Worksheet

An online worksheet can be a useful aid when developing a budget. It takes you step by step through the process of inputting income and projecting expenses and can be adapted to suit your particular circumstances.

See: tinyurl.com/k4frsrj

$10 Expenses, Bills and Budgets

Answer 99. **a,b,c,d,e – Budgets are good for everyone** – kids, adults, families, businesses and governments.

Answer 100. **a – A personal budget.** This is a budget you create just for yourself. It should include: income from jobs and your allowance, expenses (e.g., for lunch and snacks, bus fare, school books, school uniforms and presents for friends and family) and savings goals.

Answer 101. **a,b,c,d,e – Family budget.** This is a budget created for an entire household. It identifies all sources of family income and lists expenditures such as rent or mortgage payments, other loan payments, utility expenses (e.g., electricity, water, heat, phone), groceries, tax allocations, anticipated home improvements, savings and donations to charities. Small expenditures are usually covered in a "miscellaneous" category; it's important to keep track of these expenses, because they can add up fast. A family budget also spells out an amount to be saved for various goals, including education, family entertainment and vacations.

Check Out This Cool Financial Website - mint.com

This free online servce has helped over 10 million users set up a budget and create a plan to reach their personal financial goals.

The Mint automatically pulls all your money information into one place, so you can get the big, financial picture (your net worth). You can see what's happening with all your accounts – checking, savings, investments, retirement – at any moment of the day. Free mobile apps mean you can track your money on-the-go. You can track your progress online or stay up-to-date with monthly emails. It can also help you achieve your goals faster with helpful free advice.

Expenses, Bills and Budgets — $10

Question 102. **To create a budget:**

a. Select a time period.

b. List amounts of income and total them.

c. List expenses and total them.

d. Subtract total expenses from total income.

e. Calculate your net worth.

$10 Expenses, Bills and Budgets

Answer 102. **a,b,c,d – To create a budget:**
1. Use paper and pencil or a computer program.
2. Select a time period, e.g., one month.
3. List the amounts of income and total them.
4. List the fixed and variable expenses and total them.
5. Subtract total expenses from total income to get discretionary income (money still available to save/spend).

BUDGET FOR JUNE			
Income	$250		
Part-time job	$25		
Babysitting	$40		
Yard work	$50		
Allowance	$35		
Total Income			$400
Expenses			
Fixed Expenses	$100		
Transportation (bus fare)	$22		
School lunches	$50		
Total fixed expenses		$172	
Variable Expenses			
School fees	$23		
Clothing	$60		
Entertainment	$40		
Miscellaneous	$35		
Total Variable Expenses	$25	$183	
Total Expenses			$355
Discretionary Income			$45

Question 103. When creating a spending plan or budget, which items should should take top priority?

a. things you would like to buy
b. things you need to buy

Question 104. A "smart" budget includes money set aside for financial emergencies.

a. true
b. false

Question 105. To prepare for a possible job loss, it's ideal to have enough saved to cover living expenses for:

a. 1 month
b. 2 months
c. 3 months
d. 4 months
e. 6 months or more

Question 106. In a balanced budget, the total income is:

a. greater than total expenses
b. equal to the total expenses
c. less than the total expenses

Question 107. A surplus occurs when:

a. expenses are greater than income
b. income is greater than expenses

Question 108. A deficit occurs when:

a. expenses are greater than income
b. income is greater than expenses

 Expenses, Bills and Budgets

Answer 103. **b – Needs come first.** When creating a spending plan or budget, first include items you need to spend money on, then add things you would simply like to spend money on.

Answer 104. **a – Prepare for financial emergencies.** It's smart to set aside money for various financial emergencies (e.g., unexpected car or appliance repairs) in a "rainy day" fund (e.g., a savings account).

Answer 105. **e – Prepare for a job loss.** Losing your job can be a very serious financial emergency. To take care of yourself in such a situation, it's ideal to have enough funds on hand to cover living expenses for 6 months or more. Obviously the more you have in your emergency fund, the better.

Answer 106. **b – A balanced budget** is a plan for balancing income and spending where total income is equal to total expenses.

Answer 107. **b – Surplus.** If your income is greater than your expenses, the result is a surplus.

Answer 108. **a – Deficit.** If your expenses are greater than your income, the result is a deficit.

"Money is better than poverty, if only for financial reasons."

— Woody Allen

Expenses, Bills and Budgets $10

Question 109. **The overall degree of comfort enjoyed by an individual, household or population, as measured by the amount of goods and services consumed:**

a. lifestyle
b. gross national product
c. income
d. assets
e. standard of living

Question 110. **Ways to balance your budget when it shows a deficit:**

a. obtain a loan
b. reduce spending on non-essentials
c. buy budget insurance
d. reduce your fixed expenses (e.g., rent, car payment)
e. increase your income

Question 111. **Common reasons for budgets failing:**

a. lack of commitment (self-discipline)
b. unrealistic wants and goals
c. unexpected financial emergencies
d. saving too much money
e. a financial windfall

$10 Expenses, Bills and Budgets

***Answer 109.* e – Standard of living** – the overall degree of comfort enjoyed by an individual, household, or population, as measured by the amount of goods and services consumed. The higher the standard of living, the more money is spent. Standard of living is not the same thing as quality of life. It's possible to lower your standard of living (and thus your expenses) and still have a good quality of life in which your basic needs are fulfilled and you find pleasure in having things and doing activities that don't cost a lot.

***Answer 110.* b,e – Balancing your budget.** If your budget shows a deficit (negative balance), you need to re-balance it by reducing your expenses (i.e., lowering your standard of living), increasing your income or both. You need to refrain from spending money on nonessential things and find ways to earn more money (e.g., doing odd jobs). For most people, reducing fixed expenses (e.g., rent, car payments) is not an option.

***Answer 111.* a,b,c – Reasons why people fail to stay within their budget.** Spending and expenses may exceed the amounts alotted in a budget due to:

- a lack of commitment (self-discipline)
- unrealistic wants and goals
- unexpected financial emergencies (e.g., health crisis, job loss, major car or appliance repairs)

Even when a budget fails, it serves a useful purpose. By studying this budget you can see where you've made miscalculations in projecting income and expenses. Equipped with this information, you can be more realistic when you revise your budget for the next time period.

Expenses, Bills and Budgets — $10

Question 112. **One of the biggest benefits of maintaining a budget is that it:**

a. makes you more aware of how you spend your money

b. makes it possible to buy all the things you want

c. allows you to spend more money

d. lets you borrow more money

e. keeps you from spending any money

Question 113. **A budget can help you to:**

a. pay bills

b. pay off debts

c. make wise purchases

d. reduce frivolous spending on nonessentials

e. save money for short and long-term spending goals

Simple Budgets for Kids

Parents: When teaching kids about budgeting, it's best to create a simple budget tailored to their age and skill level. Try not to overwhelm them with too much information at the beginning. As kids mature, add more details to income and expense categories. Eventually, you can use the family budget as a learning tool.

$10   Expenses, Bills and Budgets

Answer 112. **a - One of the best reasons for maintaining a budget** – increased awareness of where your money is going, which makes it easier to control your spending and maintain a balance between what comes in and what goes out.

Answer 113. a,b,c,d,e – Benefits of budgets. A budget can help you to:

- pay bills (A budget helps you keep track of all the bills you need to pay.)
- pay off debts and stay out of debt (A budget helps you to maintain a balance between your income and your expenses so you can stay out of debt. If you have accumulated some debt, a budget can also help you pay it down more quickly by allotting a regular amount toward that end.)
- make wise purchases (A budget helps limit your spending to what you can afford and avoid frivolous spending.)
- save money for short- and long-term goals, e.g., trips, a new laptop, college, etc. (A budget shows how well you're doing in setting aside money for your goals and gives you a sense of accomplishment as the amount increases.)

"Your ability to manage your money directly affects your ability to have the life you want."

— Colin Ryan, youth financial literacy speaker

Prepaid Cards

Prepaid Cards

HOW PREPAID CARDS WORK

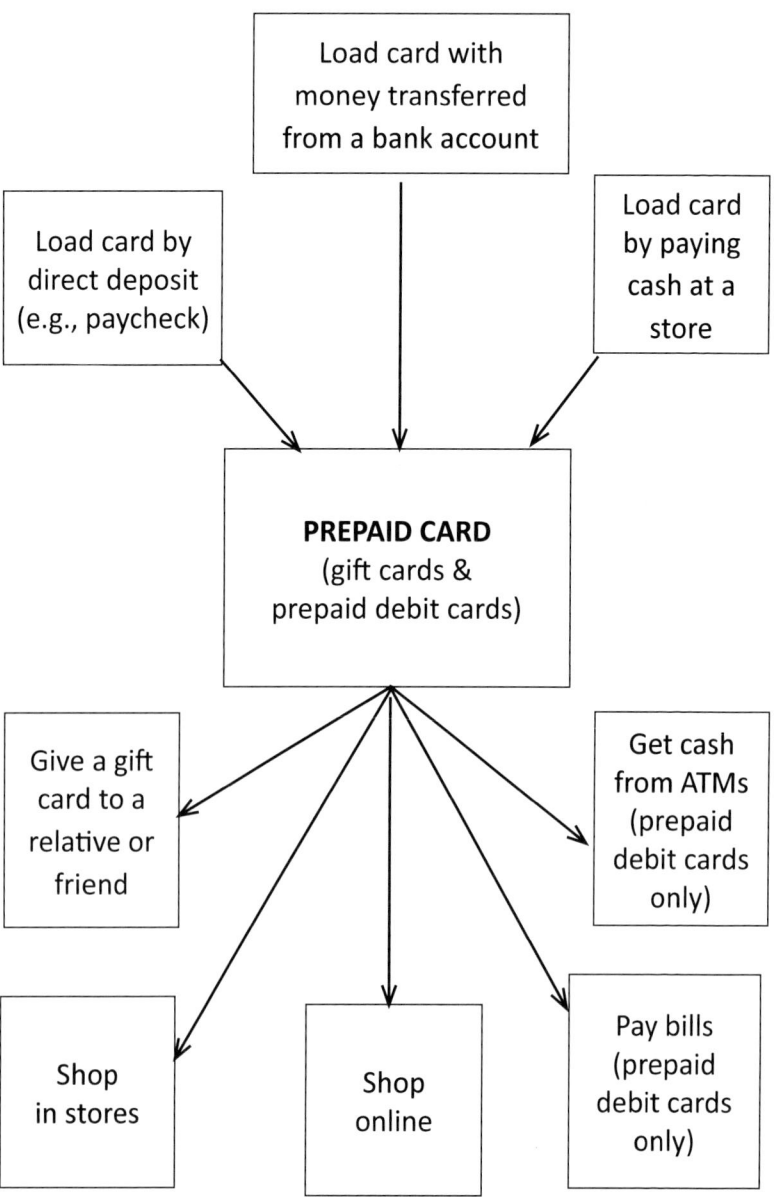

Question 1. **Prepaid cards can best be described as:**

a. "borrow money now" cards
b. "check" cards
c. "pay before" cards
d. "pay now" cards
e. "pay later" cards

Question 2. **To obtain a prepaid card, you need to:**

a. have a good credit score
b. have a bank account
c. shop around for one that best suits your needs
d. find a store/website where you can obtain the card you want
e. preload the card with a minimum amount of money

Question 3. **All prepaid cards are alike:**

a. true
b. false

Question 4. **Some places you may be able to use prepaid cards include:**

a. supermarkets
b. clothing stores
c. drugstores
d. gas stations
e. Internet

$20 Prepaid Cards

Answer 1. **c – "Pay Before" cards.** You must load a prepaid card with money before you can use it. *There are two main types of prepaid cards: gift cards and prepaid debit cards.*

Prepaid cards are becoming popular because of their convenience. They are easier to manage than coins and bills in your wallet. Some people use prepaid cards instead of cash, checks or credit cards. People often use prepaid cards as a convenient way to give a gift to family and friends. The cards can be used to buy restaurant meals, books, music, online games, and many other entertainments.

Answer 2. **c,d,e – Getting a prepaid card.** To obtain a prepaid card, you don't need a good credit score or a bank account. All you need is some cash to load onto the card. Companies sell many types of prepaid cards. As the terms of use vary, it's wise to shop around for a card that suits your needs and offers the best deals (on the web, in stores, at banks etc.). Some card providers charge upfront fees for purchasing a prepaid card.

Answer 3. b – **Not all prepaid cards are alike.** The world of prepaid cards is in flux, and the features associated with these cards differ from one card to the next.

Three ways prepaid cards may differ:

1. Some cards are reloadable, some are not.

2. Some cards are tied to a specific store (or group of stores), some are not.

3. Some cards are linked to a payment card network (Visa, Master Card, American Express or Discover), some are not.

Answer 4. **a,b,c,d,e – Where you can use prepaid cards:** clothing stores, supermarkets, drug stores, gas stations, on the Internet.

Prepaid Cards

$20

Question 5. **Prepaid gift cards:**

a. are popular because anyone can acquire one
b. carry no age restrictions
c. are an easy way to give a gift
d. are usually reloadable
e. are like cash

Question 6. **Closed-loop gift cards:**

a. can be used only at select retailers
b. do not carry a payment card network logo
c. can be used at any store
d. are always reloadable
e. require a signature when used

Payment Card Networks

A "payment card network" is an electronic payment system used to accept, transmit or process transactions made by payment cards (such as prepaid cards and credit cards) for money, goods or services. These networks are also used to transfer information and funds among issuers, acquirers, merchants and payment card users. Visa, Mastercard, American Express and Discover are payment card networks. An acquiring bank (or acquirer) is a bank or financial institution that processes credit or debit card payments on behalf of a merchant.

Prepaid Cards

Answer 5. **a,b,c,e – Prepaid gift cards.** This type of card can usually be loaded with money just once. When the balance reaches zero, the card becomes useless. Prepaid gift cards are popular because: anyone can buy a gift card; there are no age restrictions on buying a card; and it's an easy way to give a gift.

Save your receipt when you buy a card. Gift cards are like cash – anyone can spend the money on a gift card, since it carries no name and does not require a signature. Should a gift card be lost or stolen, it's important to act fast. You may be able to get what money remains on it if you still have your receipt.

Answer 6. **a,b – Closed-loop, prepaid gift cards** – a type of gift card that can only be used in one store or a set of related stores. There are no payment card network logos (e.g., Visa). Typically, these cards cannot be reloaded. However, some store-branded cards can be reloaded. If you often go to a particular store, e.g., a convenience store or coffee shop, it may make sense to obtain one of these no-fee, reloadable cards.

```
$50 - $500

My Favorite Store
Gift Card

5890 6739 0040 9858
```

A sample closed loop (store) gift card which can be used only in one store or a set of related stores. Note: there is no payment card network logo (e.g. Visa, Mastercard, American Express, Discover).

Prepaid Cards

Question 7. **When you see the logo of a credit card company (Visa, MasterCard etc.) on a prepaid card, this means:**

a. The cardholder can borrow money using the card.
b. The card is linked to a large payment card network.
c. The card can be used anywhere the logo is displayed.
d. The cardholder can use the card to withdraw money from his/her savings account.
e. The cardholder will be billed at a later date for the purchase made using the card.

Question 8. **Open-loop gift cards:**

a. include a payment card network logo (e.g., Visa)
b. can be used only at select retailers or malls
c. can be used at any store that displays the electronic payment network logo
d. can be used only by the person whose name is on the card
e. can be used on the Internet

Some Downsides to Gift Cards

- *Many can be used only in one store or a set of related stores.*
- *If a gift card is lost or stolen, it is often difficult to get your money back, as gift cards have less regulatory protection than bank debit cards or credit cards.*
- *Money put on a gift card may be wasted if the recipient only spends a portion of its value or never uses it at all.*
- *Some gift cards expire before recipients ever use them.*
- *Money put on a gift card may be wasted if the recipient only spends a portion of its value or never uses it at all. Some gift cards expire before recipients think to use them.*
- *Money on the gift card cannot be redeemed for cash or used for other purposes*

Answer 7. **b,c – Payment card network logos.** Some prepaid cards carry the logos of big, electronic payment card networks such as Visa, MasterCard, American Express and Discover. If you see such a logo on a prepaid card, it simply means that the card payment network associated with that logo will be used to process your transactions; it does not mean that you can use this card in the same way as a credit card (e.g., to borrow money). A prepaid card with a logo can be used anywhere that logo is displayed (including the Internet).

Answer 8. **a,c,e – Open-loop, prepaid gift cards** are different from closed-loop gift cards in that they carry a payment card network logo and are not restricted to select retailers. They can be used at any store that displays the logo. They can also on a store's website. These cards frequently require an activation fee.

```
$25
                Gift Card
             Provider Logo

                              Payment Card
                              Network Logo (e.g.,
5890 6739 0040 9858           Visa, Mastercard,
                              American Express,
Good Thru: 2/16               Discover)
```

A sample open loop prepaid gift card with a payment card network logo. The initial value of the card (e.g., $25 - $500) may appear on the front of the card.

Prepaid Cards

Question 9. **Prepaid debit cards:**

a. can be reloaded

b. can be purchased by people 18 years and older

c. can be used by anyone over 13 years old

d. are issued in the name of the cardholder

e. require a signature to complete a transaction

Question 10. **Prepaid debit cards are similar to credit cards in that both:**

a. have an payment card network logo on the front

b. can be used to borrow money

c. can be used to improve your credit score

d. have similar fees

e. provide the same protections against loss and theft

How to Avoid Prepaid Card Fees

You could be charged a fee for using an ATM to withdraw cash from your prepaid card. To avoid this, get "cash back" (add an extra amount to the purchase price and receive the added amount in cash) at a store register when making a purchase with your prepaid card. You can also avoid fees by using an ATM that is linked to your card's electronic payment network. You could be charged a fee for checking your balance at an ATM or speaking directly to a customer representative. Check to see if your provider offers free balance updates online or via an automated phone system or text messaging.

***Answer 9.* a,b,c,d,e – Prepaid debit cards.** This is the other main type of prepaid card. Unlike most gift cards, a prepaid debit card is reloadable and always carries a payment network logo. After spending down the balance on these cards, you simply add more money to them; they can be used indefinitely. To acquire this type of card, you must be 18 years of age or older. However, teens who are at least 13 years old may use prepaid debit cards, as long as an adult buys the card for them. Prepaid debit cards are issued in the name of the cardholder and usually require a signature in order to complete a transaction.

***Answer 10.* a – Prepaid debit cards and credit cards are different.** It's easy to mistake a prepaid debit card for a credit card. They look alike – both show the owner's name and a payment card network logo on the front. Both can be used for many of the same purposes and both are safer to carry around than large amounts of cash.

However, unlike a credit card, you can't borrow money with a prepaid debit card. You can only spend money you've already loaded onto a prepaid debit card. The word "debit" on the front of the card makes this clear. Because you are not borrowing and repaying money with a prepaid card, you can't build a credit history (see p. 208) or improve your credit score (see p. 210). Prepaid debit cards and credit cards also differ in terms of the fees charged for various services as well as the protections afforded against, loss, theft and disputed charges (prepaid cards have less protections).

Prepaid Cards

Question 11. **Prepaid debit cards are similar to debit cards issued by banks in that both:**

a. are linked to a checking account

b. are safer than carrying around large amounts of cash

c. charge overdraft fees for exceeding the balance

d. can be used to get cash from ATMs

e. have the same consumer protections

Question 12. **Prepaid debit cards can be used to:**

a. withdraw cash from ATMs

b. make purchases and pay bills online

c. make electronic transfers between accounts

d. receive direct deposits

e. borrow money to make purchases

General Purpose Prepaid Debit Card

5890 6739 0040 9858

Good Thru: 2/16

Cardholder Name

Payment Card Network Logo (e.g., Visa, Mastercard, American Express, Discover)

A sample prepaid debit card. The cardholder whose name appears on the front can use the card wherever the payment card network logo is displayed.

Answer 11. **b,d – Two types of debit cards.** It's easy to get confused about debit cards, because there are two types. A *bank account debit card* is linked to a checking account at a bank (see "Banking" chapter p. 122); a *prepaid debit card* is not. These two types of cards look the same; they both have the owner's name, a payment card network logo (e.g., Visa) and the word "debit" on the front. Both cards can be used for many of the same purposes and both are safer to carry around than cash.

The main differences between these two types of cards are:

1. With a prepaid debit card, you are charged a small fee when you attempt to spend more than the remaining balance on your card. With a bank account debit card, you are charged a substantial overdraft fee when you attempt to spend more than the balance in your checking account (unless you opt to pay for the bank's overdraft protection service).

2. Prepaid debit cards usually have fewer consumer protections than bank account debit cards in the event of loss or a disputed charge.

Answer 12. **a,b,c,d – Using prepaid debit cards.** These cards can be used to:

- withdraw cash from ATMs
- make purchases
- pay bills online
- transfer money electronically between accounts.
- distribute pay to employees who don't have bank accounts and are not able to enroll in direct-deposit programs.

Prepaid Cards

Question 13. **Ways to add money to a prepaid debit card:**

a. arrange for paychecks to be directly deposited onto the card
b. transfer money electronically from a bank account
c. do a "swipe reload" at a participating store
d. buy a "reload pack" at a participating store
e. charge an amount to your credit card

Question 14. **Prepaid debit card fees. Typically, fees are charged for:**

a. adding money to the card by direct deposit of paychecks
b. monthly service
c. adding money to the card using a "reload pack"
d. out-of-card-network ATM cash withdrawals
e. requesting a paper statement to check your balance

"Wow! Look at all these fees hidden in the fine print. There's a fee for literally everything I do with my card."

Prepaid Cards

***Answer 13.* a,b,c,d – Adding money to a prepaid debit card.** There are many ways to add money to a prepaid debit card. Be careful, sometimes a fee is charged. Ways to add money:

- Arrange for your paycheck or government benefits to be directly deposited onto the card (Typically there is no fee.) If your wages or benefits are deposited directly onto the card, make sure you know the amounts and deposit dates.
- Transfer money onto the card from a bank account.
- Transfer money from another prepaid card (no fee).
- "Swipe reload" with cash at a store register. You give cash to the clerk, who in turn swipes your card through the register to directly add the money to your card. You can also ask the store clerk to cash your payroll or government benefits check and add all or part of it to your prepaid debit card.

***Answer 14.* b,c,d,e – Prepaid debit cards fees.** Card fees vary widely, so be sure to carefully read the fee information in the cardholder agreement or on the website. Typically, there is no fee for having paychecks electronically deposited on your card. However, you may be charged a fee for:

- monthly service (maintenance fee)
- adding money to the card at a store by cashing a check, using the swipe method or buying a "reload pack"
- making cash withdrawals or balance inquiries at an out-of-network ATM
- making a purchase (transaction fee) or having a purchase declined because your purchase exceeds the balance remaining on the card
- calling customer service and talking to a live agent
- requesting a paper statement to check your balance
- not using the card during a 12-month period!

***Question 15.* How to check your prepaid debit card balance for free:**

a. do a balance inquiry at any ATM associated with your card's payment network

b. call customer service

c. log in to your account on the prepaid card website

d. send a text message to the card provider

e. send an email to the card company

***Question 16.* A "hold" on a prepaid card means:**

a. The card is no longer usable.

b. A merchant has temporarily charged you a greater amount of money than the actual cost of the goods or services they are providing to you.

c. You may have less money available on your card than you think.

d. Money cannot be loaded onto the card.

e. Security has put your card on "hold" after detecting a suspicious transaction.

Returning Purchases Made with Prepaid Cards

Store return policies vary and are becoming more stringent. Depending on the particular store and its restrictions, you may be able to receive a cash refund, a store credit, or a credit on your prepaid card. A credit to your card may take up to a week to process. In the meantime, you may have less money on the card than you think.

Prepaid Cards

***Answer 15.* a,c,d – Checking your prepaid card balance for free.** It's always advisable to know the balance on your prepaid debit card. Then you can avoid the distressing situation of having a transaction declined due to lack of money. Card providers allow you to check your balance in various ways, but it can cost you money (e.g., doing a balance inquiry on an out-of-network ATM, speaking to a live customer representative). So read the card agreement or go to the card company's website to determine, which methods are available for free. It's free to:

- do a balance inquiry at any of your provider's ATMs
- check your balance online by logging in to your account on the card provider's website
- send a balance inquiry text message (if this service is available)

Card companies will not reply to emails requesting a balance.

***Answer 16.* b,c – Temporary "holds" on prepaid debit cards.** A merchant may temporarily charge more money to your prepaid card than the actual cost of the goods or services they are providing. They do this to ensure that enough money will be available to complete the transaction. For example, holds may be placed on your card when you check into a hotel, rent a car, or buy gas. You can continue to use the card, provided you still have some money left on it. After at may take a few days for the hoild to be removed, so make sure there's enough money remaining on your card to cover additional purchases; otherwise your purchases could be declined.

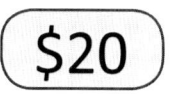

Question 17. **When you try to spend more money than your prepaid card balance:**

a. Your card will be cancelled.

b. Your card transaction will be declined.

c. You may be charged a fee for a declined transaction.

d. Your credit score will be lowered.

e. You will be charged an overdraft fee.

Question 18. **How to protect your prepaid debit card:**

a. Carry your card in a safe, secure place (e.g., snugly in your wallet or purse).

b. Keep your card number, PIN and customer service phone number in a safe place at home.

c. Only share your PIN with close friends.

d. Report a lost card right away.

e. If your wages or other benefits are deposited directly onto a card, verify the amount and date of the deposit.

Spending Rules for Prepaid Cards

Before giving a prepaid card to a teen, parents need to discuss their spending rules and how and where the card can be used. If their teen does not follow the rules, then the parents can suspend the card and reactivate it at a later time.

Answer 17. **b,c – Charging more than your prepaid debit card balance.** If you try to purchase an item of greater value than the balance on your prepaid debit card, your card will not be cancelled, but the purchase transaction will be declined and you may be charged a fee.

One solution, when making a purchase that could exceed the balance on your card, is to pay for part of the cost with your card and the rest with cash or a check. Just tell the cashier how you want to divide your payment before completing the transaction.

Answer 18. **a,b,d,e – Protecting your prepaid debit card.** Take the following precautions:

- Carry your card in a safe, secure place (e.g., snugly in your wallet or purse).
- Make sure you know your card issuer's policies for lost or stolen cards.
- Keep your card number and the customer service phone number in a safe place at home.
- Keep your PIN secret. Don't even share it with friends.
- If your card is lost or stolen, minimize your losses by letting the card issuer know right away. Most card issuers will freeze the funds so the card can't be used. They will then send you a new card with your remaining balance on it.

***Question 19.* Advantages of prepaid debit cards:**

a. less chance of spending more than you can afford

b. more widely accepted than checks

c. don't require a minimum balance

d. can help you track your spending

e. let you spend money you don't have right now

***Question 20.* Disadvantages of prepaid debit cards:**

a. There are lots of fees.

b. If a prepaid card is lost, stolen or used by unauthorized parties, there are fewer federal regulatory protections than for bank account debit cards or credit cards.

c. You can't use a prepaid card to improve your credit rating.

d. Merchants can place "holds" on a prepaid debit card for higher amounts than the actual service being provided

e. Overusing a prepaid card can increase your debt.

Special Prepaid Debit Cards for Teens and Students

Special prepaid debit cards for teens and students make it easy for parents to load money onto the card and monitor their kids' spending online or with text and email alerts. As with all prepaid cards, pay close attention to the fees listed in the fine print of card agreements.

Answer 19: a,b,c,d – **Advantages of prepaid debit cards.** If you have trouble managing your money, you may be better off with a prepaid debit card than with cash, a credit card or a bank account debit card. You can only spend the money that's been loaded onto a prepaid card. There's no danger of your spending more than you can afford on your credit card or overdrawing your checking account.

Other advantages of prepaid debit cards include:

- bank-like services for people who do not have bank accounts
- wide acceptance (checks and bank debit cards are less widely accepted)
- no required minimum balance
- no danger of overdraft fees or a bank account being drained by fraudsters
- an easy way to track spending
- some protection against loss or theft

Answer 20: a,b,c,d – **Disadvantages of prepaid debit cards.** Prepaid cards won't solve all your money management problems. There are a number of big disadvantages:

- fees, fees, fees! You can rack up a lot of charges just for the convenience of using a prepaid card (See Answer 14 above)
- fewer federal regulatory protections. Prepaid cards have less protection against loss or theft than credit or debit cards. In a worst case scenario, if the loss of a prepaid debit card is NOT reported to the card issuer within 60 business days, a thief could steal all the money on your card.
- no improvement to your credit score. (See Answer 10 above)
- holds (see Answer 16).

Credit

Credit

"He's on a revolving line of credit. He borrows money on his credit card for a month, repays it, then borrows money again next month, and so on..."

Credit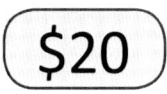

Question 21. **An agreement in which a borrower obtains something of value now and agrees to pay back the lender at some later date:**

a. credit
b. payoff
c. debit
d. ransom
e. tribute

Question 22. **The term "interest" refers to:**

a. a charge assessed when borrowing money
b. the original amount of money invested in a stock
c. the original amount of money borrowed for a loan
d. an outstanding loan balance
e. a reward for paying off a loan

Question 23. **A type of credit that allows a person to borrow money for an indefinite period of time is:**

a. revolving credit
b. unlimited credit
c. open-end credit
d. line of credit
e. closed-end credit

$20   Credit

Answer 21. **a – Credit** – a contractual agreement in which a borrower receives something of value (money, goods or services) now and agrees to pay back the lender at some later date.

Answer 22. **a – Interest.** Creditors/lenders charge you interest for the privilege of borrowing their money. Charging interest is the main way banks and credit card issuers make money. Interest continues to be charged until you repay all the money you owe.

Answer 23. **a,c,d – Revolving or "open-end credit"** – a type of credit in which a financial institution agrees to loan money to a borrower for an indefinite period of time, as long as the borrower repays what is owed (all or a portion of the balance due, along with finance charges) according to a certain schedule (usually every month). Credit cards are an example of revolving credit. Other terms used to describe this type of credit are "line of credit" and "revolving credit." In contrast to closed-end credit (e.g., car loans), open-end credit does not have a fixed number of payments.

Credit

Question 24. **Your credit history includes information on:**

a. how many credit accounts you carry

b. how long your credit accounts have been open

c. how many credit hours you have earned in college

d. how much you owe on your credit accounts

e. whether you pay your credit card bills on time

Question 25. A good credit history makes it easier to:

a. obtain loans or credit cards

b. be admitted into college

c. rent an apartment

d. open utility accounts without paying a large deposit

e. obtain lower car insurance rates

Review Your Credit Report Yearly

To reduce the risk of identity theft, it is advisable to review your credit report at least once a year. At the web site annualcreditreport.com, you can request a credit report once every 12 months from each of the three nationwide consumer credit reporting companies: Equifax, Experian and TransUnion. Do not provide personal information to any other companies purporting to provide credit reports.

Credit

Answer 24. **a,b,d,e – Your credit history** – a report that contains a lot of information about your finances and your ability to repay money you have borrowed. It consists of: your bank balances, the number and types of credit accounts carried (installment loans, credit card accounts, etc.), the period of time each account has been open, amounts owed and your bill-paying habits (whether or not you routinely pay your credit-related bills in full and on time). It also contains information about whether you have experienced any bankruptcies or other situations indicating an inability to repay loans.

Answer 25. **a,c,d,e – Advantages of a good credit history.**
It is important to develop and maintain a good credit history, because your credit history impacts so many aspects of your life. Potential creditors/lenders (e.g., banks, credit card companies) consult credit history reports when deciding whether or not to provide individuals with loans or credit cards. The interest rate that a lender charges a borrower is also largely determined by the individual's credit history; the better your credit history, the lower the interest rate you will have to pay.

A good history may also help when:

- renting an apartment
- opening utility accounts (electricity, phone)
- seeking to obtain a good rate on car insurance
- looking for a job (potential employers may review your history during the hiring process)

Beware !! A poor credit history can take years to improve.

Credit $20

Question 26. **Your credit score is:**

a. a numerical expression of your creditworthiness
b. established by the United States Government
c. based on a statistical analysis of your credit history
d. often called a FICO score
e. determined by a credit bureau

Question 27. **The percentage cost of credit on an annual basis which must be disclosed by law:**

a. Annual Percentage Yield (APY)
b. Annual Percentage Rate (APR)
c. Annual Yearly Percentage (AYP)
d. Annual Real Percentage (ARP)
e. Annual Percentage Cost (APC)

Creditworthiness

Creditworthiness is the likelihood that a specific borrower has sufficient assets, income and/or inclination to repay a loan. A credit score is a numerical expression of a person's creditworthiness.

 Credit

***Answer 26.* a,c,d,e – Your credit score.** A credit score is a numerical expression of creditworthiness. It is based on statistical analysis of a person's credit history. Credit scores are often referred to as FICO (Fair Isaac and Company) scores. Actually, there are three FICO scores, one for each of the three credit bureaus that operate in the United States. As the information in your credit history changes, your credit scores change as well. The maximum score is 850; lenders consider a score above 700 to be a good risk.

***Answer 27.* b – Annual percentage rate (APR)** – the annual cost of a loan (or credit) expressed as a percentage rate of the loan amount. This percentage is arrived at through complex, standardized calculations that factor in the basic interest being charged plus other costs associated with a certain loan. Lenders must by law disclose this number.

Loans can have fixed rates (e.g., car loans) or variable rates (e.g., credit card loans). Whether you're seeking a fixed or variable rate loan, the APR you obtain will depend in large part on your credit score -- the higher your score, the lower your rate. With car loans (fixed rate), APR's will not change once set. With credit card loans, however, the APR can go up and down all the time (despite the fact that it's called an annual percentage rate). So, when you start with a new credit card, you will be given an APR; but this rate will fluctuate depending on how well you do at paying off your bills. If you don't pay your bills in full, you will be charged the APR on your remaining balance and the APR could go up on subsequent bills.

Credit $20

Question 28. **Comparing APR's tells you, which loan or credit card:**

a. costs the least

b. offers you the most money

c. is the easiest to obtain

d. is the least complicated

e. performs the best

$20 Credit

Answer 28. **a – Comparing APR's.** When you're shopping for a loan or credit card, you need to compare annual percentage rates to determine what the various options will cost over the duration of an agreement. It's important to do this, as APR rates may vary considerably from one lender to another. This is because lenders set up interest rates and fees in many different ways.

Before the advent of the APR, borrowers had no way of comparing one loan/lender with another. Now, however, with the APR, they have a bottom-line number to use in comparing rates charged by various potential lenders. Usually the higher the APR on a loan, the more you'll have to pay. Don't be fooled by lenders who advertise low monthly interest rates. They are trying to create the impression that you can borrow money from them cheaply. To see a truer picture of how much a loan will cost, always refer to the APR.

> *"Nothing seems expensive on credit."*
> — Czech proverb

Credit Cards

Credit Cards

What's the main problem with credit cards?

The pain of payment is divorced from the pleasure of consumption.

Credit Cards $20

Question 29. **A credit card can be described as a:**

a. "pay before" card
b. "pay now" card
c. "pay later" card
d. "pay whenever" card
e. "pay on time" card

HOW CREDIT CARDS WORK

Ways To Use Your Credit Card

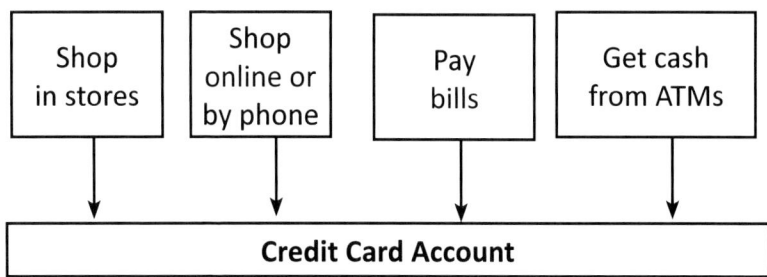

Ways To Pay Your Credit Card

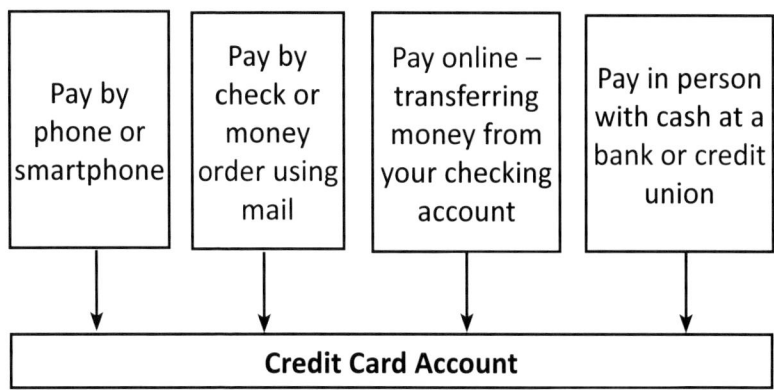

215

 Credit Cards

Answer 29. **c – A "pay later card."** A credit card is a plastic card that links to an electronic payment card network. A credit card can be described as a "pay later card", because it allows you to spend borrowed money now on condition that you pay back the lender (card provider) later. If you don't pay the full balance on your credit card once a month, you will be charged interest. This kind of credit is sometimes referred to as "short-term financing" (as opposed to long-term financing, such as a mortgage loan, which is paid off during a long and defined period of time).

```
                 Credit Card

             5890 6739 0040 9858

  Cardmember since: 2001      Payment Card
                              Network Logo (e.g.,
  Good Thru: 2/16              Visa, Mastercard,
  Cardholder Name              American Express,
                                   Discover)
```

Sample Credit Card - front

The front of the credit card includes an account number and the cardholder's name. It may or may not include an expiration date and a payment card network logo (e.g., Visa, Mastercard, American Express, Discover).

Store-branded (or private-label) credit cards, in particular, do not have a payment card network logo. They can only be used with specificic merchants who offer the cards.

Credit Cards $20

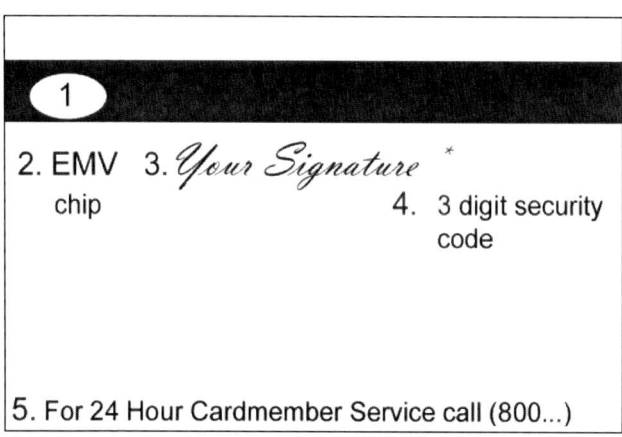

Sample Credit Card - back

The back of the card contains:

1. A magnetic strip that authenticates credit and debit card transactions.
2. Some cards in the U.S. may also have an EMV (Europay, MasterCard and Visa) chip. EMV chips make theft more difficult and are already common in European and other countries. Credit card companies plan to replace magnetic strips with EMV digital chips on all U.S. cards in 2015.
3. A place for the cardholder's signature
4. A 3 digit security code (often asked for by merchants) that helps prevent fraud by verifying the order is being placed by the actual cardholder
5. A service phone number to call if you have problems using the card or it is lost or stolen

Before using a new credit card, you need to sign the back of the card and follow the instructions to activate the card using a phone or the Internet.

 Credit Cards

Federal Protection from Unfair Credit Card Practices

Credit Card Accountability Responsibility and Disclosure Act of 2009 (Credit CARD Act of 2009) – *prohibits certain practices that are unfair or abusive such as hiking up the rate on an existing balance or allowing a consumer to go over-limit and then imposing an over-limit fee; makes the rates and fees on credit cards more transparent, so consumers can understand how much they are paying and can compare different cards.*

Equal Credit Opportunity Act – *a federal law that forbids lenders from discriminating against loan applicants on the basis of gender, race, marital status, religion, national origin, age, or receipt of public assistance.*

Fair and Accurate Credit Transactions Act (FACT Act) – *a federal law that gives consumers more ways to recover their credit reputations after they have been victims of identity theft and allows consumers to request one free copy of their credit report from each of the three major credit reporting agencies each year.*

Fair Credit and Charge Card Disclosure Act – *a part of the Truth in Lending Act (see page 242) that mandates that credit card companies provide a description on credit card applications of key features and costs such as APR, grace period, balance calculation, annual fees and penalty fees.*

Fair Credit Billing Act – *a federal law that addresses billing problems with open-end credit accounts. For example, it requires consumers to send a written error notice within 60 days of receiving the first bill containing the error. This prevents creditors from damaging a consumer's credit rating during a pending dispute.*

Fair Credit Reporting Act – *a federal law that covers the reporting of debt repayment information, requiring, for example, the removal of certain information after seven or ten years and giving consumers the right to: know what is in their credit reports, dispute inaccurate information and add a brief statement explaining accurate negative information.*

Credit Cards $20

Question 30: **To acquire a credit card of their own, a teen:**

a. just needs to fill out an application

b. needs a parent or legal guardian to cosign a credit card agreement (if the teen is under 18)

c. just needs to call a credit card company and request a card

d. must have a good income and be able to keep on top of their credit card bills (if they're over 18)

e. should be financially mature

"Oh my god! If I only make the minimum payment, it will cost me an extra $10,000 and 10 years to pay off this bill."

***Answer 30.* b,d,e – Acquiring a credit card.** Having a credit card is one of the best ways to build a credit history, but teenagers usually need some help getting their first card. In fact, before the age of 18, the main way for a teenager to get a credit card is for a parent or legal guardian to agree to be a cosigner. (See the next page for two other ways to obtain a credit card.)

After the age of 18, a young person can legally apply for their own for a credit card. But credit cards are tricky, so there are federal requirements that help protect young people from falling into serious credit card debt. Before providing a card to a young applicant, a credit card company must determine that the applicant has sufficient income and will be able to keep up with credit card payments. If not, the applicant will still need a trustworthy cosigner (a parent is again the best).

Parents should only agree to be a cosigner if they believe their teen is mature enough to use credit responsibly. This is because the parent, as a cosigner, has equal responsibility for paying the credit card bills. If a teen misuses the card, both the teen and parents will suffer the consequences, i.e., negative information in credit reports and lower credit scores.

Read the Fine Print First!

Before selecting a credit card, compare the terms and conditions for different credit cards. Often this important information is buried in the fine print on the back of the credit card statement. Credit providers charge a late payment fee if you fail to submit your payment on time. They will also charge you interest if you pay anything less than the full balance. It can become very costly not to pay the full balance when it's due.

Credit Cards $20

> ## Two Other Credit Card Options
>
> ***Be an authorized user.*** *Teens – you can ask your parents to put you forward as an authorized user on their credit card. This is similar to having a cosigner, but in this situation you are not responsible for paying the credit card bills. Even so, the payment history could help you obtain your own credit card later.*
>
> ***Acquire a secured credit card.*** *Another way of getting a regular credit card is to first obtain a secured credit card. This is an option if you have sufficient income to get a credit card but have been denied because you don't yet have a credit history. This type of card requires you to make a cash deposit up front to cover what you might owe should you default on your payments. After that, you're responsible for making regular payments toward the balance you accumulate. If you manage your card well for a certain period of time, the issuer may convert your card to a regular credit card.*

Question 31: **A credit card statement shows:**

a. the termination date of your credit card agreement

b. all purchases, payments and other debits and credits made to your credit card account within a billing cycle

c. the total balance due

d. the minimum payment due and the payment due date

e. the annual percentage rate that applies to your credit card

$20 Credit Cards

Answer 31. b,c,d,e – Credit card statement. Your credit card company sends you a billing statement periodically (usually monthly). It contains a lot of information including purchases, payments and other debits and credits made to your credit card account within the billing cycle (the time interval between the dates on which regular periodic statements are issued). Law requires that credit card billing statements be sent at least 21 days before the due date so you have time to make your payment on time and avoid finance charges.

ACCOUNT SUMMARY
Account Number: 1234 5678 0009 1000

Previous Balance	$1,719.40
Payment, Credits	-$1,760.38
Purchases	+$2,515.81
Cash Advances	$0.00
Balance Transfers	$0.00
Fees Charged	$0.00
Interest Charged	$0.00
New Balance	$2,474.83
Opening/Closing Date	03/27/13 - 04/26/13
Credit Access Line	$29,130
Available Credit	$26,655
Cash Access Line	$5,826
Available for Cash	$5,826

Sample Credit Card Statement - Account Summary

A Credit Card Account

- *tracks purchases, payments, interest, fees and balance*
- *creates a monthly statement with balance due and minimum payment (available on paper and online)*

Credit Cards

The statement must disclose:

- how long it would take you to pay off your current balance, plus the total amount you would end up paying, if you only make the minimum payment every month
- the monthly payment required to pay off your current balance in three years
- a late payment warning showing the consequences of sending your payment late, i.e., after 5 pm on the payment due date
- the late fee and the penalty APR that could be applied if you don't make the minimum payment by the due date

PAYMENT INFORMATION

New Balance	$2,474.83
Payment Due Date	05/23/13
Minimum Payment Due	$25.00

Late Payment Warning: If we do not receive your minimum payment by the date listed above, you may have to pay a late fee of up to $35.00 and your APR's will be subject to increase to a maximum Penalty APR of 29.99%.

Minimum Payment Warning: If you make only the minimum payment each period, you will pay more in interest and it will take you longer to pay off your balance. For example:

If you make no additional charges using this card and each month you pay...	You will pay off the balance shown on this statement in about...	And you will end up paying an estimated total of...
Only the minimum payment	13 years	$5,190
$89	3 years	$3,192 (Savings=$1,998)

If you would like information about credit counseling services, call 1-866-797-2885.

Sample Credit Card Statement - Payment Information

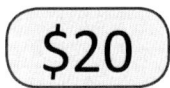 Credit Cards

Date of Transaction	Merchant Name or Transaction Description	$ Amount
ACCOUNT ACTIVITY		
	PAYMENTS AND OTHER CREDITS	
04/25	STAPLES 00104521 LATHAM NY	-46.99
05/20	Payment Thank You - Web	-2,474.83
	PURCHASES	
04/25	THE HOME DEPOT 1259 LATHAM NY	43.17
04/26	GULF OIL 91803816 TROY NY	50.59
04/25	STAPLES 00104521 LATHAM NY	75.59
04/26	RADIOSHACK 00113233 TROY NY	41.02
04/30	NETFLIX.COM NETFLIX.COM CA	18.78

Sample Credit Card Statement - Account Activity

INTEREST CHARGES

Your **Annual Percentage Rate (APR)** is the annual interest rate on your account.

Balance Type	Annual Percentage Rate (APR)
PURCHASES	
Purchases	17.24% (v)
CASH ADVANCES	
Cash Advances	19.24% (v)
BALANCE TRANSFERS	
Balance Transfer	17.24% (v)

(v) = Variable Rate

Sample Credit Card Statement - Interest Charges

Credit Cards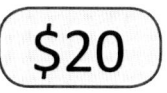

Question 32. **Verifying information on your monthly credit card statement will help you to:**

a. stay in control of your finances
b. detect and remove inaccurate or fraudulent charges
c. remove unfair or illegal finance charges
d. protect yourself from identity theft
e. prevent an unfair increase in your interest rate

Question 33. **The amount of money you currently owe your credit card company is referred to as your:**

a. debit
b. balance
c. credit
d. total
e. loan

Question 34. **Principal (for a credit card) is:**

a. the interest paid on a loan
b. a rule to follow when deciding how to spend your money
c. the amount of money borrowed on your credit card
d. an outstanding loan balance
e. the head of the personnel department in a company

Question 35. **The time during which a borrower can pay the full balance of credit due without incurring extra charges:**

a. time limit
b. deadline
c. grace period
d. pay period
e. loan period

***Answer 32.* a,b,c,d,e – Verifying information matters.** Do not assume that all the information on your credit card statement is correct. All those facts and figures can be intimidating, but it is critical that you check the information carefully. Reviewing your statement will help you:

- stay in control of your finances. (It's easy to keep adding charges to your credit card account without realizing how much money you're really spending.)
- detect and remove inaccurate or fraudulent charges
- avoid paying unfair finance charges
- protect yourself from identity theft
- prevent an unfair increase in your interest rate

***Answer 33.* b – Balance** – the amount of money you currently owe your credit card company. A *balance transfer* is the transfer of the balance in one credit card account to another credit card account, often held at another institution. Transfers are sometimes facilitated by companies trying to recruit new consumers. Sometimes transfers are accompanied by transaction costs paid by the consumer.

***Answer 34.* c – Principal** – the amount of money borrowed on your credit card (not including the interest).

***Answer 35.* c – Grace Period –** the span of time between the end of your credit card billing cycle and the due date of your payment. If you make your payment in full within the grace period, you will not be charged interest. By law, the grace period for credit cards should be at least 21 days. For example, if the end of the billing cycle is March 10 and your company has a 21-day grace period, your payment will be due on March 31. If you pay your bill in full on or before the 31st, there will be no interest charges.

Credit Cards $20

Question 36. **A "credit limit" is:**

a. the minimum amount a credit card company will allow you to charge on your credit card each month

b. the maximum amount a credit card company will allow you to borrow on a single card

c. a restriction placed on your credit card that prevents you from using it in certain stores

d. the maximum amount that a credit card company determines you will be able to repay, based on your credit score

e. a spending limit that can rise and fall depending on whether or not you consistently pay your monthly credit card bills on time and in full

Question 37. **A cash advance using your credit card:**

a. may make sense in a dire financial emergency

b. won't cost you a dime if you pay your credit card bill on time

c. usually comes with a transaction fee

d. has no grace period – interest charges start immediately

e. has a higher interest rate than a standard purchase

Alerts

Take advantage of automated alerts from your card issuer (by cell phone or email). Alerts include: payment reminders, balance notifications and warnings of possible fraudulent activity.

Answer 36. **b,d,e – Available credit limit** – refers to the maximum amount a credit card company will allow a cardholder to borrow on a single card. Credit card companies set an individual's credit limit based on their credit score and information in their credit card application. A borrower's credit limit can go up and down depending on their repayment patterns, i.e., whether or not they consistently pay their monthly credit card bills on time and in full.

Having a high credit limit on one or more cards might seem like a good thing; but if you want to apply for additional credit, potential creditors may be reluctant to take you on. They may be concerned that you are already carrying a lot of debt and might not be able to repay all that you owe in the future.

Answer 37. **a,c,d,e – Credit card cash advance.** You can obtain a "cash advance" using your credit card at an ATM or a "convenience check" supplied by your card provider. Doing this is a bad financial move except in a dire emergency, e.g., when your car breaks down and the mechanic demands payment in cash.

Getting cash with your credit card always costs more money than a regular credit card purchase. First, it usually comes with a $10-$20 transaction fee. There is no grace period for cash advances, which means that your credit card company immediately starts charging interest on the cash advance.

The interest rate on cash advances is often significantly higher than it is on purchases made using your credit card. And when you make a partial payment of your credit card bill, the payment applies first to your regular purchases. This means that you could still be paying for the cash advance at the higher interest rate in subsequent months. Note: you cannot generally take a cash advance for the full amount of your available credit.

Credit Cards $20

Question 38. **Finance charges are:**

a. a way for credit card companies and banks to make money

b. a bill received from a financial planner

c. fees added to the original amount of money you borrow

d. fees you pay for the privilege of borrowing money

e. fees that can be avoided by paying a credit card in full and on time

Question 39. **Not paying your credit card bill on time results in:**

a. cancellation of your card

b. no financial penalty

c. a late fee

d. possibly having to pay higher interest rates

e. an automatic withdrawal from your bank account

> *"All I know is God help me if I don't pay the full credit card bill every month. Then I'll have to dive into the fine print of the credit card agreement...which is really scary!"*
>
> — Anonymous

Credit Cards

***Answer 38.* a,c,d,e – Finance charges.** Credit card companies and banks make money by charging customers finance charges. Finance charges include: interest added to an outstanding balance, service fees for transactions and late fees. You can avoid finance charges by paying your credit card balance in full before the grace period ends.

***Answer 39.* c,d – Late fees/penalties.** If you fail to make a payment on time (at least the minimum amount due on your credit card balance), you will have to pay late fees. You may also find your interest rate increases after a certain number of late payments.

If you pay the full amount on time	*Credit Provider charges no late payment fees or interest*
If you pay the full amount but late	*Credit Provider charges a late payment fee and may raise your annual interest rate*
If you make only the minimum payment	*Credit Provider charges interest on the remaining balance due*
If you make only the minimum payment but late	*Credit Provider charges a late fee plus interest on your remaining balance and also raises your annual interest rate*
If you fail to make the minimum payment	*Credit Provider charges a late fee plus interest on the entire remaining balance and raises your annual interest rate significantly, e.g., from 17.25% to 29.9%.*

Credit Cards $20

Question 40. **Minimum payment on a credit card bill is:**

a. the lowest payment your credit card company will accept per month toward your balance without adding a penalty fee

b. the smallest purchase listed on your credit card statement

c. the minimum payment required to avoid an interest charge

d. a charge for not paying the bill on time

e. the minimum expense you can charge on your card

Question 41. **If you pay your credit card bill on time but make only the minimum payment due, in the next billing cycle you will have to pay:**

a. interest on the unpaid credit card balance

b. an overdraft fee

c. a transaction fee

d. a late payment fee

e. a recording fee

Question 42. **If you don't even make the minimum payment due on your credit card balance:**

a. an automatic withdrawal will be made from your bank account

b. you will incur a late payment fee

c. you will be charged interest on your outstanding balance

d. your interest rate could be increased

e. your card will be cancelled

Answer 40. **a – Minimum payment –** the minimum amount that a credit card company will accept from you as a payment (usually on a monthly basis) without adding a penalty fee. You can maintain a good credit score if you pay at least the minimum. A minimum payment is usually about 5% of the current balance due and includes a portion of the money you have borrowed (the principal) and of the interest charges you have accrued so far.

Answer 41. **a – Paying only the minimum.** If you only pay the minimum amount due on your monthly credit card balance, the credit card company will add interest to the remaining balance even if you pay on time. If you do this consistently, it could take a long time and a lot of money to completely repay your balance. Many people fall into this minimum payment trap. It's a very costly habit.

Answer 42. **b,c,d – Failing to pay the minimum.** If you don't pay even the minimum due on your credit card balance, there will be serious consequences. You will be charged interest on your outstanding balance along with a late payment fee, adding more money to your credit card debt. Your interest rate could be increased substantially, and obviously, you could be paying off what you owe for a long time. Also, your credit score could be lowered.

Question 43: **To keep your credit cards safe from fraudsters:**

a. Use as few credit cards as possible.

b. When turning over your card to a clerk or waiter, keep your eyes on the card.

c. Check your credit card statements often for unknown charges.

d. Report card losses ASAP.

e. Wait until you receive your next statement to report a lost card.

Question 44: **To avoid losing your credit cards:**

a. Remain aware of your card's whereabouts at all times.

b. Only carry the credit cards you'll need.

c. Carry your credit cards in a safe, secure place.

d. Make sure a sales clerk returns your card after you make a purchase.

e. Put your card back in its safe place immediately after you use it.

Question 45: **To be prepared in case your credit card is lost or stolen:**

a. Make a photocopy of all your cards and give it to a friend.

b. Make a photocopy of your cards and post it on a bulletin board near your desk.

c. Store your credit card contact list in a safe, accessible place.

d. Make a photocopy of all your cards and keep it in a safe deposit box or other secure location.

e. Have a second, backup credit card.

$20 Credit Cards

Answer 43. **a,b,c,d – Keep your credit cards safe.** To keep your cards safe from fraudsters:

- Use as few credit cards as possible. (It's hard to keep track of a lot of cards.)
- Check your credit card statements often for unknown charges.
- Report card losses ASAP.

Answer 44. **a,b,c,d,e – Avoid losing credit cards.** Take these steps to protect your cards:

- Remain aware of your card's whereabouts at all times.
- Carry only the credit cards you'll need on a shopping trip. (Leave the others at home.)
- Carry your credit cards in a safe, secure place. (Don't put credit cards loose in a pocket or the bottom of a purse. It's too easy for them to fall out.)
- Make sure your cards fit snugly in your wallet. (Buy a new wallet if your old one is worn out.)
- Make sure a sales clerk returns your card after you make a purchase.
- Always put your card back in its safe place after using it.

Answer 45. **c,d,e – Be prepared.** Despite all precautions, it's possible you will someday lose a credit card or have one stolen. To be able to respond promptly, it's important to:

- Create a list of your card providers' phone numbers and store it in a safe, accessible place.
- Make a photocopy of all your cards and keep this documentation in a safe deposit box or secure location.
- If you are able to manage your primary card without trouble, keep a second card just for emergencies.

Credit Cards

Question 46. Advantages of credit cards:

a. They can be used to obtain an "instant loan."
b. They can be used to make purchases in a store and online.
c. They offer better fraud protection than checks, debit and prepaid cards.
d. They have no credit limit.
e. They allow you to track your expenses.

Question 47. Disadvantages of credit cards:

a. Interest rates are usually high.
b. Low introductory interest rates frequently increase.
c. Many cards charge annual fees.
d. If you are late or miss a payment, you will be charged late fees and your interest rate could increase dramatically.
e. If you fall behind in your payments, your credit score may be lowered.

"When I pay with cash, I see money disappearing from my wallet and stop spending when it's gone. When I pay with a credit card, I risk buying too much and going into debt, because I don't check my balance as often as I should."

$20   Credit Cards

***Answer 46.* a,b,c,e – Advantages of credit cards.** Credit cards are used almost universally nowadays and for good reasons. They:

- are more widely accepted than checks
- allow you to obtain small, short-term loans that enable you to purchase things you need or want on the spot ("instant loan")
- allow you to make purchases in a store without having to carry cash or a checkbook
- allow you to make purchases online
- offer better fraud protection than checks, debit or prepaid cards
- provide an easy way to track your expenses
- offer rewards (including cash)

***Answer 47.* a,b,c,d,e – Disadvantages of credit cards.** Despite their convenience, credit cards do have some disadvantages:

- Interest rates are high and low introductory rates frequently increase (up to 30% or more).
- You often have to pay annual fees.
- You will be subject to late fees and your interest rate could increase dramatically if you are late or miss a payment.
- If you fall behind in your payments, your credit score may be lowered.
- You can easily spend more than you can afford.
- You will be less able to save money for your long-term goals when you are paying high interest on your credit card debt.

Loans

"Now that I know the down payment, the monthly payment, the length of the loan, the APR and the total cost of the car, I'm thinking maybe I should just rent one occasionally."

"I would really like to go to this college,
but their 18% student loan rate is excessive."

Loans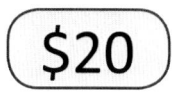

Question 48. **Loaning money to a friend or relative can be risky because:**

a. There could be misunderstandings about how the loan is to be repaid.

b. Problems with repayment could damage your credit score.

c. The borrower may fail to repay a loan.

d. Failure to pay back a loan could hurt your chances of landing a job.

e. Problems with repayment could damage your relationship.

Question 49. **When negotiating a personal loan for a significant amount of money with friends or relatives, specify in writing:**

a. the amount of the loan

b. the loan duration or payback date

c. the interest rate, if the borrower is expected to pay interest

d. what will happen if the borrower can't repay the loan

e. what the borrower may be putting up as collateral

Question 50. **Don't loan money if…**

a. you feel pressured to loan money

b. you don't know the person well

c. the person already owes you money

d. you don't have enough money to pay your own expenses

e. you are not prepared to forgive the loan

> "Acquaintance: a person whom we know well enough to borrow from, but not well enough to lend to."
> — Ambrose Bierce, a 19th century American writer

Loans

Answer 48. **a,c,e – Loan money, lose a friend.** If you loan money to a friend or relative to buy a cup of coffee, it's not really important whether or not they pay you back. However, if you loan them a significant sum, you could be setting yourself up for problems. If misunderstandings develop about how the loan is to be repaid or the borrower fails to repay the loan altogether, you risk damaging or even losing your relationship with them. When someone you know needs money, it's really preferable for them to go through a professional organization, such as a bank or credit union.

Answer 49. **a,b,c,d,e – Negotiating a personal loan.** If you do decide, despite the risks, to loan a significant amount of money to a friend or relative, it is very important that the parties agree on the loan conditions and put them in writing. The loan agreement should specify: the loan amount, the payback date, interest rate (if the borrower is expected to pay interest), and what happens if the borrower can't repay the loan. Perhaps, your agreement could specify what item of value – a tablet computer, for instance – the borrower would give you in place of the money owed. This alternate form of potential payment is called "collateral."

Answer 50. **a,b,c,d,e – Reasons not to loan money.** Don't loan money if you feel pressured to do so. Don't loan money to a person you don't know well – you can't be sure they will repay you. Don't make a loan if: a person already owes you money, you don't have enough money to pay your own expenses, or you're not prepared to forgive a loan (accept that you'll never be repaid) in order to keep a friend.

Loans $20

Question 51. When borrowing money to buy a car, you need to know:

a. how much money you can afford to put down
b. who the loan manager is
c. the annual percentage rate (APR) of interest
d. if you can afford the monthly payment
e. the payback period of the loan

> **An Upside-Down Car Loan**
>
> *If you start with a small down payment, and then the value of your car drops rapidly (depreciation), you could end up in a situation where the car is worth less than what you still owe on it ("upside-down").*

Question 52. A loan that helps you buy a house is:

a. a credit card loan
b. a consumer loan
c. a home equity loan
d. a mortgage loan
e. a demand loan

> *"A bank is a place that will lend you money if you can prove you don't need it."*
>
> — Bob Hope

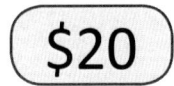 Loans

***Answer 51.* a,c,d,e – Borrowing money to buy a car.** If you borrow money to buy a car, you need to know:

- how much money you can afford for the down payment and monthly payments. If you put too much money down and/or the monthly payments are high, you may not have enough money for other necessities.
- the annual percentage rate (APR) of interest to be paid. To keep the cost down, you want to get the lowest APR possible.
- the time it will take you to repay the loan, plus interest (payback period).

Answer 52: **D - Mortgage Loans** – long-term loans used to buy so-called "real property", such as a house and the land on which it sits.

Loans: Closed-End vs. Open-End

A closed-end loan is for a fixed amount (principal) and must be repaid in full (plus any interest and finance charges) by a specified date. The loan may require periodic payments (a portion of the principal plus some of the interest) or may require the entire payment of the principal at maturity. Most real estate and auto loans are closed-end credit loans. Credit cards and home-equity lines of credit are examples of open-end loans that can go on indefinitely.

Truth in Lending Act

A federal law that requires financial institutions to disclose specific information about the terms and cost of credit, including the finance charge and the annual percentage rate (APR).

Loans

Question 53. "Easy access" credit loans include:
a. payday loans
b. car-title loans
c. mortgage loans
d. pawnshop loans
e. rent-to-own loans

"Sorry...we don't loan money for old, trashy, beat-up, broken-down stuff."

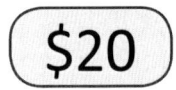 Loans

***Answer 53.* a,b,d,e – "Easy access" credit loans.** It's possible to obtain short-term "easy access" loans even if you have a poor credit history or none at all. The lenders who offer these loans usually charge high interest rates (as high as 500%!) which is why they are often called "loan sharks".

- **Payday loans/deposit advances** – a high-interest loan made with the understanding that it will be repaid when the borrower receives his/her next paycheck. It works as follows. The borrower writes a personal check in the amount they wish to borrow plus a fee, and in exchange receives the cash. The check is typically written with a date in the future. The lender holds the check and cashes it on the borrower's next payday. These loans are also called cash advance or check advance loans. "Deposit advance" loans offered by some banks are similar to payday loans except that the bank repays itself from the borrower's account.

- **Car title loans** – a high-cost loan that uses a borrower's automobile as collateral. Typically you will be able to borrow only a small portion of what your car is worth, and you could lose ownership of the car if you fail to repay the loan according to the agreed-upon terms.

- **Pawnshop loans** – a high-interest loan obtained from a pawnbroker. The deal is that you give the pawnbroker something of value as collateral and he loans you money in exchange. When you repay the loan plus the interest, you get your collateral back. If you don't repay the loan, the pawnbroker keeps the collateral.

- **Rent-to-own** – a plan to buy a product with little or no down payment by renting it (in a sense borrowing it) until the final payment is made, at which point the total paid will far exceed the product's original price. If you fail to keep up with your payments, the product will be seized and you will lose your investment in it.

Loans

***Question 54.* Student loan rules of thumb:**

a. Borrow as much as you can to pay for the degree you want.

b. Don't borrow any money to go to college; you'll just end up with a pile of debts you can't afford.

c. Go for federal student loans first; avoid private, bank, or credit card debt.

d. Don't borrow more money than your anticipated annual salary for the first year out of school.

e. Use your credit card as an alternative way to finance college costs

---

Types of Student Loans

Stafford loans – *the most common federal education loans. They may or may not be subsidized (provided at a reduced rate).*

Perkins loans – *low-interest federal loans, administered by a school, for students who demonstrate exceptional financial need.*

PLUS loans – *federal loans that cover expenses not met by other federal financial aid.*

Consolidation loans – *multiple federal student loans can be combined into one new loan with a single monthly payment and a fixed interest rate. The new loan will generally be for a longer term.*

Institutional loans – *non-federal aid that schools loan to their students.*

Private and state loans – *loans that do not come from the federal government but which can help students ineligible for federal aid or those who do not receive enough aid to cover the full cost of attendance.*

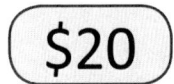 Loans

Answer 54. c,d – Student loan rules of thumb:

- As federal student loans have relatively low interest rates, try for them first. Avoid private, bank and credit card loans.
- Try to limit your total college debt to your anticipated annual salary for the first year out of school. (This may not be possible, but it's still a good rule of thumb.)
- Try not to spend more than 10 percent of your annual pretax income on student loan payments.

To estimate your entry-level or first-year earnings, go to Glassdoor.com and/or tinyurl.com/lhral66. These tools allow students to check out salaries by job title, location and in some cases, employer.

If you borrow too much money to get the degree you want, you may doom yourself to a life of struggling with college debt. On the other hand, if you don't invest in a college education, you may be crippling your chances of developing a satisfying career with a good salary.

Avoid Fine-Print Traps

Whenever you enter into a financial agreement (e.g., a car loan), make sure you read and understand the fine print. If you don't understand it, find someone who does (e.g., a lawyer). Not reading or understanding the fine print in a financial agreement can result in paying higher interest rates, fees and charges than you ever expected.

Debt

Debt

> "Annual income twenty pounds, annual expenditures nineteen nineteen and six, result happiness. Annual income twenty pounds, annual expenditures twenty pounds ought and six, result misery."
> — Charles Dickens

Debt $20

Question 55. **Debt is:**

a. money you have borrowed and have yet to pay back

b. money you own

c. money you loan

d. money you borrowed and have repaid

e. money you lost

Question 56. **Liability:**

a. an unfulfilled financial obligation

b. an unpaid credit card bill

c. a bank loan not paid back

d. payments still due on a car loan

e. money still owed to a family member or a friend

Question 57. When you are in debt:

a. You owe someone money.

b. It's OK if you forget to repay the debt.

c. You can pay the money back whenever you like.

d. You will likely have to pay interest.

e. You don't owe money if the lender forgets about it.

Question 58. **Which of the following are examples of debt?**

a. a bank loan not yet paid back

b. a 15- year mortgage loan not yet paid off

c. payments remaining on a student loan

d. an unpaid credit card balance

e. money borrowed from a relative you have not yet repaid

 Debt

Answer 55. **a – Debt** – money that you have borrowed and have yet to pay back.

Answer 56. **a,b,c,d,e – Liability** – an actual or potential financial obligation or responsibility. All debts are liabilities.

Answer 57. **a,d – Conditions that apply to debt.** When you are in debt, you are expected to pay back the loan within an agreed upon time frame and often with interest.

Answer 58. **a,b,c,d,e – Examples of debt** – money owed to a bank (e.g., for a personal loan or mortgage), government agency (e.g., for a student loan), credit card company or relative.

"For better, for worse, for richer, for poorer, in sickness and in health, to love and to cherish, till *debt* do us part."

Debt $20

Question 59: **Dumb habits that can lead to debt:**

a. writing checks without knowing the account balance

b. using your credit card to get cash

c. paying only the minimum due on your credit card

d. borrowing more money than you can afford to repay

e. taking out a new loan to make a payment on an existing loan

Question 60. **Not all debt is bad.**

a. true

b. false

> "Creditors have better memories than debtors."
> — Benjamin Franklin

 Debt

Answer 59. **a,b,c,d,e – Dumb habits that can lead to debt. Things to avoid include:**

- buying things on impulse that you want but don't need
- writing checks without knowing your checking account balance
- using your credit card to get cash
- paying only the minimum due on your credit card
- paying bills with your credit card when you can't pay the full balance every month (In effect, you may not have paid your bills.)
- taking out a loan for more money than you can afford to repay
- taking out a new loan to make a payment on an existing loan (This is not the same as consolidating several loans into one, which could be a good thing to do.)
- failing to pay attention to "gotchas" (hidden tricks and traps) buried in the fine print of loan agreements
- ignoring mail, email and phone calls from lenders
- gambling

Answer 60. **a – Good debt vs. bad debt.** Not all debt is bad. Sometimes a loan is a good investment that will pay off later.

Good debt – debt you take on that has a good chance of increasing your earning power and enhancing your lifestyle. Of course, it's essential that you manage the debt well by paying back the loan according to the agreed-upon terms.

Bad debt – debt you've accumulated for things you don't need and can't afford (that trip to Disney World, for instance). One of the most expensive forms of debt is credit card debt, since it usually carries a high interest rate.

Debt $20

***Question 61.* It makes sense to borrow money to:**

a. buy something you really need to earn a living

b. buy something you really want, but don't need

c. invest in education that prepares you for a future job or career

d. buy something that's on sale

e. finance certain big purchases (e.g., a car or house)

***Question 62.* Does paying off debt really matter?**

a. No. There are much more important things in life.

b. No. You can pay later when you have more money.

c. Yes. Debt will grow if you don't make payments.

d. Yes. You could damage your credit score.

e. Yes. Debt can make your life more difficult and stressful.

***Question 63.* The failure to meet a financial obligation:**

a. default

b. deficit

c. loss

d. defect

e. summons

> *"Default is not in our stars, but in ourselves."*
> — Paul Krugman, New York Times columnist

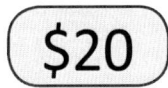 Debt

Answer 61. a,c,e – When borrowing makes sense.

In life, you may need to borrow money for a few really important things that cost way more than you can afford at a particular moment in time. But it costs money to borrow money, and you should borrow only when you can afford to make the monthly payments. It makes sense to borrow money to:
- buy something you need to earn a living (e.g., tools, a car to drive to work)
- invest in education that prepares you for a future career or job
- purchase a house (Note: Everyone needs a roof over their head. Owning a house can be a wise, long-term investment, but only if you are able to keep up with loan payments and maintenance. If not, it is better to rent.)

Answer 62. **c,d,e – Yes! Paying off debt matters.** When you borrow money, you make a promise (usually in writing) to pay it back. Some people try to ignore this obligation. They want to believe that other things in life are more important than repaying the money they owe. But debts are a big problem, because they keep growing; the longer you stay in debt, the more problems you will have. Until you start managing your debt, it'll feel like there's a big black cloud parked over your head, making your life more and more difficult and stressful.

Answer 63. **a – Default.** A borrower is in default when they fail to make a scheduled payment of money owed to a lender. Existing and potential lenders will see a default as a sign that a borrower may not be able to make future payments and is not a good risk.

Debt $20

Question 64. **Consequences of default:**

a. You will likely have to pay more interest on the remaining balance still owed on the loan.

b. Your default may trigger certain penalties and fees.

c. You will be asked to pay off other debts as well.

d. Your credit score will drop.

e. Inflation will cause your loan to grow larger.

Question 65. **Debt and default could threaten your:**

a. happiness

b. ability to earn a living (livelihood)

c. personal safety

d. everyday comfort

e. health

Question 66. **If you default, a lender could:**

a. send you a letter asking you to pay up

b. send you to jail

c. hire a debt collector to confront you

d. put out a press release announcing that you have defaulted

e. call your friends in an effort to force them to pay your debt

---

National Foundation for Credit Counseling

The NFCC, the nation's largest financial counseling organization, provides financial counseling and education to millions of consumers each year in person, over the phone, or online (nfcc.org). To locate an NFCC Member Agency in your area, call 800-388-2227.

   Debt

***Answer 64.* a,b,d – Consequences of default.** If you default on a loan, the amount you owe will increase, because the lender will see you as a bad bet and will likely raise the interest rate on the remaining balance owed. The lender will also tack on various penalty fees. Your credit score will drop and you will probably have to pay higher interest rates to obtain new loans or credit cards. In fact, you may find it difficult to borrow any more money at all.

Some of your wages could be withheld to repay your debts (garnishment). You could lose certain possessions (e.g., your car). And, as you attempt to catch up with overdue payments, you could find yourself short of money for basic necessities, such as food, electricity, phone and Internet service. In the worst case, you could run out of money altogether and tumble into bankruptcy.

***Answer 65.* a,b,c,d,e – More consequences of debt and default.** Debt can result in severe personal problems and unhappiness. Your livelihood and safety could be jeopardized (e.g., no car to travel to work, no phone to call 911). Lacking everyday comforts (e.g., electricity and heat) and weighed down by worry, you could fall ill. This could lead to a whole new set of troubles.

***Answer 66.* a,c – Lender pressure tactics.** Lenders may first send a polite letter asking you to fulfill your repayment obligations. If that doesn't work, they may phone you, urging you to pay up. If that still doesn't work, they may turn your debt over to a collection agency.

> ### *Fair Debt Collection Practices Act*
> *A federal law that prohibits debt collectors from engaging in unfair, deceptive, or abusive practices such as calling people at work after being told not to do so.*

Debt $20

***Question 67.* Collection agency:**

a. a business that collects and recycles clothes

b. a business that buys and sells collectibles

c. a group that collects money for the poor

d. a company hired by a lender to collect unpaid, past-due debts from a borrower

e. a business that collects bottles and cans

***Question 68.* A court-ordered procedure that sets aside a portion of an employee's wages for repayment of debt:**

a. tax penalty

b. fine

c. bankruptcy

d. garnishment

e. impound

***Question 69.* A lender can take away your car if you fail to make a payment on your car loan:**

a. true

b. false

 Debt

Answer 67. **d – Collection agency** – a company hired by lenders to collect unpaid, past due debts. A collection agency usually earns a percentage of the funds or assets it recovers for the lender, so the agency has a strong incentive to make you pay up. Debt collection agencies use aggressive methods to force you to pay your unpaid debt. They may send strongly worded letters to your home, phone you multiple times, list the debt on your credit report and sometimes even take you to court.

Answer 68. **d – Garnishment.** This is a procedure whereby a collection agency obtains a court order compelling your employer to set aside a portion of your wages to pay your debt. You are the "garnishee." The collection agency may also be able to gain access to your bank account without your permission and keep withdrawing money until the debt is paid.

Answer 69. **a – Repossession.** This term is most often used in connection with vehicles. When you take out a loan to buy a car, the lender holds important rights to the vehicle until you've paid off their loan, plus interest. If you fail to keep up with your loan payments, the lender may have the right to repossess (take back) your car. If your car is repossessed, this fact will appear on your credit report for years and you will owe any expenses associated with the repossession (e.g., attorney's fees), as well as the difference between what the lender can sell the car for and what was still owed on the loan.

"Gee, I never thought I'd lose my car because of a missed payment."

Debt $20

Question 70. **When a person is in bankruptcy, they:**

a. are unable to pay back their debts

b. are sometimes referred to as a vagrant

c. have broken into a bank

d. are sometimes said to be insolvent

e. have filed papers in court to gain legal protection from creditors

Question 71. **Assets protected by federal bankruptcy laws:**

a. a car (under a certain value - approximately $2500)

b. some money paid toward the purchase of a home

c. individual retirement accounts

d. clothing

e. lottery winnings

Question 72. **Good advice about debt:**

a. Stay out of debt as much as possible.

b. Don't borrow money to buy things you don't need.

c. Shop around for the lowest interest rate when borrowing.

d. Pay off high-interest debts first.

e. Pay off smallest debts first.

> "Don't spend your money till you have it."
> — Thomas Jefferson

Debt

Answer 70. **a,d,e – Bankruptcy.** A person who feels like they are drowning in debt may seek relief from their debts by declaring bankruptcy. Often the debtor goes to court and files papers in order to be declared bankrupt. This releases the debtor from the obligation to repay some or all of their debts in exchange for giving up some of their assets. Declaring bankruptcy may allow a debtor to breathe a little easier but it comes at a high cost: it will taint his/her credit record for ten years. The *Bankruptcy Abuse Prevention and Consumer Protection Act* is intended to make the system fairer for creditors and debtors and make affordable credit available to more people.

Answer 71. **a,b,c,d – Protected assets.** United States federal bankruptcy laws exempt (protect) certain assets from creditors, as do laws in all 50 states. This means a debtor cannot be forced to let go of certain possessions in order to free up money to repay creditors. Exemptions may include: a car (under a certain value – approximately $2500), some money paid toward purchase of a home (equity), individual retirement accounts, clothing, or other personal property.

Answer 72. **a,b,c,d – Good advice about debt:**
- Stay out of debt as much as possible.
- Don't borrow money to buy things you don't need.
- Look for the lowest interest rate when shopping for a loan.
- Pay off high-interest debts first.
- Read the fine print of loan agreements.
- If you are having trouble making your loan payments, contact lenders to try to arrange new terms for your loan.
- If you think you have a problem with debt, seek help as soon as possible from a reputable credit counseling service.

Risk

Risk

Risk — $50

Question 1. **The chance that something bad may happen:**

a. probability
b. likelihood
c. actuality
d. risk
e. certainty

Question 2. **Activities that could put you in serious danger:**

a. talking to a friend on the phone
b. gambling
c. investing in the stock market
d. reading a book
e. starting a new business

Question 3. **The process of calculating risk and devising methods to minimize or manage loss:**

a. formulation
b. hedging your bets
c. risk management
d. statistical analysis
e. equivocation

> *Risks are the spice of everyday life. Some risks are potentially rewarding and some are not. The trick is to distinguish between foolhardy gambles and reasonable risks.*

 Risk

Answer 1. **d – Risk** – the chance that something bad may happen. We are all vulnerable to physical, financial and other misfortunes. That's just the way it is – to be alive means having to contend with risk.

Answer 2. **b,c,e – The range of risk.** The potential for something bad to happen ranges from minimal to extreme. Some activities, like talking to a friend on the phone or reading a book, are not at all risky. Others, like jogging or riding a bicycle, can be moderately risky. Still others could put you in serious danger. Examples include: smoking, driving a car, starting a new business, investing in the stock market, gambling and posting personal information on the Internet.

Answer 3. **c – Risk management** – the process of calculating risk and devising methods to minimize or manage loss. The term "risk management" usually refers to financial matters, but in fact, can be applied to all aspects of life. We can't prevent all negative events – accidents, fires and damaging storms are beyond our control – but often we have a choice about what risks are worth taking, how to reduce or handle potential negative occurrences, or how to take advantage of certain opportunities that may arise in the midst of a crisis. We are engaged in risk management when we decide to buy a car, for instance. We know that driving can be dangerous, but because we need the car to travel to work, we are willing to take the risk. To minimize the potential financial drain that an accident could trigger, we buy car insurance.

Risk

Question 4. **When your physical health is at risk, your financial health is also at risk.**

a. true
b. false

Question 5. **Dangerous physical activities can result in:**

a. pain
b. permanent injury
c. inability to work
d. huge medical expenses
e. death

Question 6: **You can stay healthy by:**

a. eating healthful foods
b. maintaining a healthy weight
c. getting regular exercise
d. not smoking
e. wearing safety gear when engaged in harmful or dangerous activities

---

Rewards of a Healthy Lifestyle

Good health is a great physical asset, like money in the bank.

You need to be healthy to feel positive about life. Every day that you feel good is a day that you're getting a dividend from your good health bank.

If you have an unhealthy lifestyle (not getting enough sleep or exercise, using drugs, smoking, overeating, eating unhealthy foods, etc.), you increase the risk of developing health problems that could deplete your financial resources and, worse still, diminish your energy and enjoyment of life.

 Risk

Answer 4. **a – Physical health and financial health.** When your physical health is at risk so is your financial health. Health problems can lead to expensive health care costs, job loss and even bankruptcy. In a sense, your body is your most valuable asset, so it's vital that you take good care of it.

Answer 5. **a,b,c,d,e – Avoid dangerous activities.** The thrill of dangerous activities attracts many young people. What makes this attraction especially perilous is that young people are also prone to believing that they are invincible. But no one is completely safe, so it is always sensible to refrain from unnecessarily risky activities, like texting while driving or speeding on a motorcycle. Such activities could result in pain, permanent injury, inability to work, huge medical expenses and even death. Some potentially hazardous activities, like skiing or scuba diving, can be done safely, but only if you are properly trained and equipped.

Answer 6. **a,b,c,d,e – Take steps to stay healthy.** There is much you can do every day to prevent or reduce potential harm to your body. Here's a sampling:

- Eat healthful foods.
- Avoid excessive eating or drinking and maintain a healthy weight.
- Avoid sitting for long periods of time.
- Exercise on a regular basis.
- Refrain from smoking or doing drugs.
- Wear safety gear when engaged in harmful or dangerous activities. This may include work gloves, seat-belts, bike helmets and/or life jackets.

Risk  $50

Question 7. **Ways to reduce financial risks include:**

a. setting financial goals
b. saving money
c. avoiding habits that lead to long term debt
d. buying insurance
e. refraining from gambling

Question 8. **Lack of health insurance poses a big financial risk.**

a. true

b. false

Question 9. **To be prepared for the unexpected, it's important to have:**

a. pocket money
b. a credit card
c. a "rainy day" fund
d. loot
e. spare change

"If you don't stick your neck out once in a while, you'll never go anywhere in life."

Risk

Answer 7. **a,b,c,d,e – Reduce financial risks.** You can't escape all financial troubles, but there are certain wise practices that will help keep you safe. They include: setting financial goals, saving your money, avoiding habits that lead to long term debt (not paying off credit card bills), refraining from gambling activities that could lead to big financial losses, staying healthy and buying insurance (health, car, home, personal property).

Answer 8. **a – Lack of health insurance.** This is one of the biggest financial risks you can take. Even though you strive to stay healthy, you cannot always control what happens to your body. It is essential that you have health insurance to protect yourself from expensive health care costs.

Answer 9. **c – Prepare for the unexpected.** When you get up in the morning, you never know for sure what's going to happen. Sometimes it's a day full of good events, but sometimes you run into trouble and need extra money to cover the cost of dealing with an emergency. To be prepared for the unexpected, it's important to have money set aside in a "rainy day" fund.

Having a credit card in your wallet when you are hit with a large, unexpected expense (e.g. a car breakdown) can be helpful. But if you don't have enough money in your "rainy day" fund to pay your credit card bill when it's due, you'll end up paying a high interest rate on your credit card balance.

> *"What we anticipate seldom occurs;*
> *what we least expect generally happens."*
> — Benjamin Disraeli

Insurance

Auto Insurance Reduces Financial Risk

In the United States, 16- to 19-year-old drivers have the highest average accident and traffic violation rates of any age group and traffic crashes are the leading cause of death among this group.

Teenagers tend to take more risks while driving because they can be overconfident about their driving abilities. Young drivers are more likely to engage in risky behaviors such as texting, using a cellphone, speeding, tailgating, running red lights, violating traffic signs and signals, making illegal turns, passing dangerously and failing to yield to pedestrians.

Refraining from risky behaviors is the best way to reduce the chance of having a traffic accident. But accidents still happen. For one thing, even if you are a "safe" driver, you have no control over the risky behavior of other drivers.

Accidents not only result in physical injuries and property damage, they can also lead to substantial financial losses. You can reduce the risk of such consequences, however, by making sure you have adequate auto insurance.

Insurance

Question 10. **Taking out an insurance contract is a way to protect yourself from the costs associated with:**

a. unexpected property losses
b. gambling losses
c. bad loans
d. spending too much
e. serious medical problems

Question 11. **The maximum amount of money an insurance company is willing to pay you for a loss:**

a. is flexible
b. decreases if you win the lottery
c. increases if you lose your job
d. varies depending on the inflation rate
e. is stipulated by the company

Question 12. **An insurance premium is:**

a. high-quality, expensive insurance
b. the amount you pay if you make a claim
c. the amount an insurer requires a client to pay in order to continue insurance coverage
d. an extra amount you pay if you miss a scheduled payment
e. the amount you overspent on insurance

Question 13. **A deductible on an insurance policy is:**

a. the extra cost to cover valuable things
b. a measure of how reasonable your claim is
c. the amount you overspent on insurance
d. a deduction on your tax return
e. an amount you must pay for a loss before the insurance company starts paying you

Answer 10. a,e – Insurance – a way to protect yourself from the potentially overwhelming costs of living in a complex and sometimes dangerous world. When you buy an insurance policy, you enter into a contract with an insurance company/insurer who agrees to pay you a specified amount of money to cover certain costs – routine or unexpected – that you will incur. Your insurance coverage helps you pay for such things as routine health maintenance, which has become very costly. It can also help you cover costs associated with unexpected events, such as property damage from fires or storms, auto accidents and serious medical problems. The insurance company is able to help you pay your costs, because it collects money from a large group of other policyholders who are not likely to submit claims all at once.

Answer 11. e – Limits to insurance. An insurance company typically sets maximum liability limits, that is, it stipulates the maximum amount of money it is willing to pay you for a loss. For example, you could buy an auto insurance policy that covers losses up to but not exceeding $1 million.

Answer 12. c – Premium – the amount that an insurer requires a client (the insured individual) to pay routinely in order to maintain coverage under a given insurance plan.

Answer 13. e – Deductible – the amount you have to pay up front for a loss before the insurance company will start paying you. Your policy may specify a dollar amount or a percentage of the loss that you could incur. The higher the deductible, the lower the cost of the premium.

Insurance

Question 14. **In an insurance policy, exclusions are:**

a. people not covered by the policy

b. objects you asked to be included in the policy

c. objects you asked not to be included in the policy

d. objects or circumstances an insurance company will not cover in its policy

e. belongings you don't want insured

Question 15. **When you file a claim, you are asking an insurance company to:**

a. write you a letter

b. define the terms of your insurance

c. pay you money for a loss based on the terms of your policy

d. pay you a refund

e. start a legal action

Question 16. **It makes sense to pay a relatively small amount of money to an insurance company every year to prevent losing a large amount of money should you experience a disastrous event.**

a. true

b. false

Question 17. Insurance can help you cover the costs of:

a. car accidents

b. health problems

c. lost income

d. house fires

e. gambling losses

Answer 14. **d – Exclusions** – objects or circumstances an insurance company will not cover in its policy.

Answer 15. **c – Claim** – a request you make to your insurance company to pay you money for a loss covered in your insurance policy

Answer 16. **a – The benefits of insurance.** It makes sense to pay a relatively small amount of money to an insurance company every year so you can be protected from losing huge amounts of money should you experience a disastrous event. For example, paying a yearly premium of $150 in renter's insurance could protect property up to $75,000 in total value.

Answer 17. a,b,c,d – Insurance Coverage. Having insurance can help to cover the costs of such things as:

- car accidents
- health care
- lost income if you get sick, injured or die
- damages to your home or other property (e.g., fire or flood)
- theft of your property
- damages you cause to someone else – physical or property

> *"Most people don't expect anything bad to happen to them until it already has."*
>
> — Larry Winget, speaker, author and TV personality

Insurance

$50

***Question 18.* Auto insurance:**

a. is not required to legally drive a car

b. provides financial protection against damages resulting from auto accidents

c. is required by law in all 50 states

d. varies from one insurer to another in terms of cost and coverage, so it pays to shop around

e. costs less for drivers with a good driving record

"See what happens when you text and drive...
Wait till you see your next insurance bill!!"

Insurance

Answer 18. **b,c,d,e – Auto Insurance** – provides you with financial protection against a variety of damages resulting from auto accidents. Laws in all 50 states in the U.S. require that you carry some form of insurance to cover bodily injuries as well as damage to cars. Typically you are required to have some liability coverage in the event that someone other than yourself is injured. However, minimum requirements for car insurance vary from state to state. Because many auto accident losses routinely surpass the minimum limits, it is advisable to get more than the minimum coverage.

When buying insurance, it pays to shop around, because the costs and coverage vary from one insurer to another. Drivers with good driving records can expect to pay less for insurance.

Types of Car Insurance Coverage	
Collision	Covers damage to your auto, even if you're responsible.
Property Liability	Covers damage you do to another's car.
Bodily Injury Liability	Covers medical bills and lost wages for the other persons you injure.
Uninsured/ Underinsured Motorist	Covers your medical expenses if an uninsured or underinsured motorist injures you. Consider increasing your Supplemental Underinsured Motorist (SUM) coverage to equal your liability coverage limit.
Comprehensive	Covers damage caused by something other than an accident, such as fire or vandalism.
Medical	Covers medical expenses for you and your passengers, regardless of fault.

Insurance

Question 19. **A type of auto insurance that covers such things as vandalism:**

a. property liability

b. bodily injury liability

c. uninsured/underinsured motorist coverage

d. collision coverage

e. comprehensive

Question 20. **Insurance that replaces a portion of income lost when a person cannot work because of illness or injury.**

a. injury insurance

b. disability insurance

c. Medicaid

d. Medicare

e. long-term care insurance

Question 21. **Insurance that covers specific medical costs associated with wellness, illness and injury:**

a. health insurance

b. disability insurance

c. long-term care insurance

d. life insurance

e. malady insurance

$50   Insurance

Answer 19. **e – Comprehensive auto insurance** – covers damage caused by something other than an accident, such as fire, theft or vandalism.

Answer 20. **b – Disability insurance** – replaces a portion of income lost when a person cannot work because of illness or injury.

Answer 21. **a – Health insurance** – covers specific medical costs associated with wellness, illness and injury. Except for Medicare and Medicaid, which are government-run health insurance programs, health insurance in the United States is provided by private for profit and nonprofit companies. Typically, health insurance providers require that in addition to a monthly premium, the people they insure pay a small, fixed fee, called a "copay", whenever they visit a doctor or fill a drug prescription.

"Oh dear! He's suffered a relapse.
He was doing so well until he saw his hospital bill."

Insurance

Question 22. **A federal government program financed by deductions from wages that pays for certain health care expenses for citizens 65 or older, disabled and retired workers:**

a. Medicaid

b. Health Care for All

c. Social Security

d. Senior Health Care

e. Medicare

Question 23. **A program financed by state and federal government tax revenues that pays specified health care costs for those who cannot afford them:**

a. Medicare

b. Medicaid

c. health insurance

d. disability insurance

e. long-term care insurance

Question 24. **Insurance that covers custodial care costs in a nursing facility or at home:**

a. custodial care insurance

b. nursing insurance

c. disability insurance

d. health insurance

e. long-term care insurance

Insurance

Answer 22. **e – Medicare health insurance** – a program administered by the federal government (the Social Security Administration) since 1965 that guarantees access to health insurance for Americans aged 65 and older, as well as other people who may be younger but have certain disabilities. It is financed by deductions from wages. The intent of the Medicare program is to spread the financial risk associated with illness across society so as to protect everyone.

Answer 23. **b – Medicaid health insurance** – a program financed by state and federal government tax revenues that pays specified health care costs for those who cannot afford insurance.

Answer 24. **e – Long-term care insurance** – covers specific costs of custodial care in a nursing facility or at home. ("Custodial care" means helping people with basic needs, such as eating and dressing.)

Living Will

This is a document that specifies a person's desires for specific medical treatment in the event that they are unable to make their own medical decisions due to illness or incapacity; also known as a **health care directive.**

Another document often used when a person becomes incapacitated is a **power of attorney** *or* **health care proxy.** *This empowers a spouse, friend or family member to make health care decisions in the event that the primary individual is incapable of executing such decisions.*

It's important to complete these documents ahead of time, while you are still healthy and of sound mind. People are often encouraged to complete both documents to provide comprehensive guidance regarding their care.

Question 25. Insurance that provides property damage and liability coverage for your house under specific circumstances:

a. house insurance

b. homeowners insurance

c. property insurance

d. liability insurance

e. storm damage insurance

Question 26. Insurance that provides protection from losses due to damage to the contents of a rental dwelling:

a. dwelling insurance

b. property insurance

c. contents insurance

d. renters insurance

e. home insurance

"May you live all the days of your life."
— Jonathon Swift

Insurance

Answer 25. **b – Homeowners insurance.** If you own your home, this type of insurance provides property damage and liability coverage under specific circumstances (e.g., fire, flood).

Answer 26. **d – Renters insurance** – covers damage to your personal property when you rent an apartment. The landlord's insurance won't cover loss of your belongings if something is stolen or if there's a flood or fire. Renters insurance covers these losses as well as items lost in transit or damaged in storage.

Insurance

Question 27. **Insurance that protects you from others' claims of loss due to the your alleged or actual negligence or improper actions:**

a. no-fault insurance
b. negligence insurance
c. liability insurance
d. health insurance
e. life insurance

Question 28. **Umbrella insurance:**

a. provides coverage against storm damage to your house

b. provides extra insurance that goes beyond the limits of your homeowners and auto policies

c. provides health care coverage for weather-related illness

d. provides an additional layer of security for those at risk of being sued

e. protects against libel, vandalism, slander and invasion of privacy

Insurance

Answer 27. **c – Liability insurance** – gives you financial protection from others' claims of loss due to your alleged or actual negligence or improper actions. If you own a small business, you may need liability insurance to protect yourself from customer or client lawsuits claiming you are responsible for a loss or injury.

Answer 28. **b,d,e – Umbrella insurance.** This is extra liability insurance coverage that goes beyond the limits of insurance you are carrying on your home or auto. It provides an additional layer of security for those who are at significant risk of being sued for damages to other people's property or for injuries caused to other people in an accident. An umbrella insurance policy is very helpful when the insurancd person is sued and the dollar limit of the original policy (home or auto) has been exhausted. The added coverage provided by this type of liability insurance is most useful to individuals who own a lot of assets and/or very expensive assets. Umbrella policies also protect you against being sued for libel, vandalism, slander or invasion of privacy.

Trust

A legal relationship in which one party, known as a trustor, gives another party, the trustee, the right to hold title to property or assets for the benefit of a third party, the beneficiary.

For example, if the beneficiary of an estate is underage or has a mental disability, a trust can be set up to manage the estate for the benefit of the beneficiary.

Insurance

Question 29. **A type of insurance that provides financial security to a family should the primary breadwinner die:**

a. auto accident insurance
b. death insurance
c. health insurance
d. family assistance insurance
e. life insurance

Question 30. **A person or organization named to receive assets after an individual's death.**

a. winner
b. policy holder
c. beneficiary
d. will
e. survivor

Estate

An estate is the total of all the assets and debts that a person leaves at death. Assets include everything of value an individual owns, such as real estate, art collections, collectibles, antiques, jewelry, investments and life insurance. Accurately establishing the value of a personal estate usually becomes very important upon the death of the person, because those in line for inheritance often have to pay an inheritance tax on their share of the estate.

Will

A legal declaration of a person's wishes for disposing of his or her estate after death. If you do not have a will, the distribution of your property is left up to the government; the property may even end up becoming state property. A will makes it easier for your heirs to carry out your wishes.

 Insurance

Answer 29. **e – Life insurance** – a type of insurance that provides financial security to a family should the primary breadwinner die.

Such a policy gives the policy holder (the breadwinner) peace of mind in knowing that his/her family or dependents would not suffer financial hardship if he or she were to die. (A dependent is a person who relies on another individual for support.)

You may receive solicitations that strongly encourage you to buy life insurance, but it is not essential unless others are depending on your income for food, shelter and other basic support.

Answer 30. **c – Beneficiary** – a person or organization named to receive assets after an individual's death. Wills and life insurance policies specify the person(s) who will be the beneficiaries in the event of a death.

"As none of you have shown an ability to manage money wisely, I have decided to donate all my wealth to my favorite charities."

Gambling

> "I get dozens of letters, almost daily from people who have financial difficulties for one reason or another. And they overwhelmingly come from three sources: One is health problems, people run into unexpected medical bills and it gets them into a tough situation. Second, they get into trouble on credit cards, frequently a credit card is a temptation to many people. But the third thing I hear about is people who have an addiction to gambling. And they've used thousands and thousands or tens of thousands of dollars that the family needs and they just can't get off the hook and they find themselves in enormous financial trouble, sometimes that interacts with the credit card situation."
>
> — Warren Buffett

> "By gaming we lose both our time and treasure – two things most precious to the life of man."
>
> — Owen Feltham (1602-1668), English author

> "Gambling promises the poor what property performs for the rich – something for nothing."
>
> — George Bernard Shaw

> "Playing the lottery is practically a religion among poor people in the United States. It is yet another corrosive addiction that preys upon the greed and hopeless dreams of those trapped in poverty."
>
> — Palash R. Ghosh, journalist, International Business Times

Gambling

Question 31. **Risking the loss of something valuable in the hopes of gaining something else of greater value when the chances of winning are extremely low:**

a. investing in a money market account
b. hoarding
c. gambling
d. saving
e. hedging

Question 32. **Examples of gambling:**

a. buying a raffle ticket
b. betting on a sporting event
c. playing bridge
d. playing poker for money
e. buying a lottery ticket

Question 33. **Investing money in any high-risk venture (certain high-risk stock offerings, real estate projects and/or business startups) can also be considered a form of gambling.**

a. true
b. false

Question 34. **A bet with odds of 100/1 means:**

a. a win is likely to happen once in a hundred times
b. if you placed a $1 bet you could win $100
c. there is a good chance of winning
d. the chance of winning is very small
e. the risk of losing money is high

"*Lottery: a tax on people who are bad at math.*" — Unknown

$50 — Gambling

***Answer 31.* c – Gambling.** In the usual sense, to gamble is to risk losing something of value, like money, in the hopes of gaining something of greater value. Often, gambling refers to playing a game of chance for money or other rewards. The lure of a big win can make gambling very exciting, even though the chances of winning are extremely low.

***Answer 32.* a,b,d,e – Examples of gambling –** buying a raffle or lottery ticket, betting on a sports event, playing poker for money, playing roulette at a casino. Playing a game of bridge is not gambling as it does not involve risking money.

***Answer 33.* a – High-risk investments are a form of gambling.** Investing money in any high-risk venture (certain high-risk stock offerings, real estate projects, or startup businesses) can also be considered a form of gambling. Some individuals are fooled into thinking they are making wise investments in such ventures when, in fact, they are taking big risks with their money, i.e., they are gambling.

***Answer 34.* a,b,d,e – A bet with odds of 100/1 means:**

- a win is only likely to happen once in a hundred times
- if you placed a $1 bet you could win $100
- the chance of winning is very small
- the risk of losing money is high

> "Shockingly, a University of Pennsylvania study says the number of young people addicted to gambling - largely due to increased exposure to the Internet and Internet gambling - grew by an alarming 20 percent between 2004 and 2005 alone."
> — Spencer Bachus, member of the United States Congress

Question 35. **When people gamble with money, the odds are high (there's a high probability) they will win money and the odds are low (there's a low probability) they will lose money.**

a. true

b. false

"You can be lucky for a little while, but if you play long enough, you will surely lose. The odds always favor the house."

Gambling

Answer 35. **b – Gambling odds/probabilities.** When people gamble, the odds are high (there's a high probability) they will lose money. Many people have irrational ideas about gambling. They believe that they're luckier than others or that some oddball belief orpractice (e.g., keeping a rabbit's foot in their pocket) will make them a winner. But the reality is that when you gamble, the odds are always against you. There's a small chance (low probability) you will be a winner and a big chance (high probability) you will be a loser. Of course, some games give you a better chance of winning than others, but the odds of winning are still not great.

- **Playing at the casino.** If you play a casino game long enough, you will certainly lose. This fact has nothing to do with luck and everything to do with probability theory, statistics and casino business practices. The real math behind casino games makes sure the "house" (casino owner) always wins in the long run. You may be gambling with your money but you can be sure the casino is not.

- **The house edge** is a casino's profit expressed as a percentage of the player's original bet. Casinos offer games with a variety of house edges ranging anywhere from less than 1% to more than 25%.

- **Playing the lottery.** If you think casino games are a bad bet, consider government-run lotteries. The odds in favor of the government for a typical lottery are 50% or more. With state-run lotteries this means that for every $10 million dollar lottery, the state always walks away with $5 million or more, whereas your chances of winning a million are only one in many millions.

Why do people (especially the poor who can least afford to gamble) keep falling for these bad bets? Maybe it's because the lottery is selling the next-to-impossible dream of living the life of a millionaire.

Gambling

Question 36. **Your chances of winning a lottery jackpot are less than your chances of:**

a. winning an Academy Award
b. getting hit by lightning
c. dying in an auto accident
d. dying of cancer
e. being killed by an asteroid

Question 37. **You improve your chances of winning at gambling by:**

a. wearing a lucky charm
b. developing a fool-proof system/strategy for winning
c. refraining from singing or whistling while gambling
d. gambling more often
e. none of the above

Question 38. **When you gamble, you risk:**

a. losing money you can't afford to lose and having trouble paying for everyday expenses
b. gambling away valued possessions
c. losing lots of money and going into debt
d. neglecting other important aspects of your life
e. developing a gambling addiction

Question 39. **If you think you have a gambling problem, you should:**

a. Hide it - don't let anyone know about your problem.
b. Try a different form of gambling.
c. Call a gambling helpline.
d. Try to become better at gambling.
e. First, win big, then quit for good.

$50   Gambling

***Answer 36.* a,b,c,d,e – The odds are against you.** The chances of winning a lottery jackpot are infinitesimal (e.g., typically, Powerball players have a 1 in 175 million chance of winning). You have a much greater chance of dying of cancer, being killed in a car accident, winning an Academy Award, getting hit by lightning on your birthday, or even being killed by a falling asteroid than of winning the lottery.

***Answer 37.* e – Tricks won't help.** People may offer you tips that they say will help you win at gambling, such as wearing a lucky charm or refraining from singing or whistling while gambling. Don't fall for it. Tricks don't improve your odds, and neither will developing a system or strategy. And gambling longer and more often doesn't work either – it just increases your risk of serious loss.

***Answer 38.* a,b,c,d,e – Risks of gambling.** These include: being short of money to pay for everyday needs; squandering money that should be reserved for long term goals; gambling away valued possessions; having to borrow money to keep on gambling; going into serious debt and perhaps bankruptcy; wasting time and neglecting family, friends, school, work, or real fun; and developing a gambling addiction that could ruin your life.

***Answer 39.* c – Where to look for help.** Young people are gambling a lot these days. Poker is very popular and online gaming opportunities abound. For some, gambling is just fun, but for others, it can become a serious problem. If you feel compelled to gamble even when you're finances are in a shambles, you may be addicted. There is no shame in admitting this. You are not alone. Many people have struggled with gambling, but then overcome their problem with the help of others. If you think you are on a slippery slope, don't wait. Seek the help of people who understand your problem. Call a gambling helpline or visit gamblersanonymous.org

Fraud

Fraud

The Vocabulary of Frauds

Judging from the number of colorful words that are widely used to describe the act of fraud, it is something that happens a lot. To defraud is to: bluff, burn, cheat, chisel, con, deceive, delude, double-cross, dupe, entice, exploit, finesse, flimflam, gyp, have, hoodwink, impose on, jockey, juggle, lure, manipulate, mislead, play, play for a sucker, rook, rope in, scam, seduce, shave, snow, stick, string along, suck in, take, take in, trick.

The Most Common Form of Online Fraud

This scheme usually goes like this - you order an item online and make an online payment, but you receive nothing. Or you receive an item that is a poor example of the item advertised (e.g., a toy camera instead of a high-quality camera). Sometimes items are defective or have been obtained illegally (stolen). Scam artists are particularly likely to offer tempting big-ticket equipment such as computer hardware.

Fraud

Question 40. **An intentional deception or trick perpetrated by one person in order to gain a benefit, usually money, at the expense of another:**

a. prank
b. fraud
c. slander
d. libel
e. affront

Question 41. **Examples of fraud:**

a. identity theft
b. counterfeiting checks or money orders
c. selling bogus goods
d. making fun of someone
e. bait and switch tactics

An Example of Fraud

Someone claiming to be a tourist or military person sends you an email or makes contact in an Internet chat room. He/she asks you for help cashing a check or money order. Being sympathetic, you agree; so the correspondent sends you a check, which you deposit in your bank account. You keep a small portion of the money as payment for your assistance and wire the rest of the money to the person, usually overseas.

But the check is fake! Eventually the bank discovers this and demands that you pay back the money.

$50 — Fraud

Answer 40. **b – Fraud or Scam** – a deception or trick perpetrated by one person in order to gain a benefit at the expense of another. Often a victim is persuaded to give up money or something else of value, thus leaving him or her in a worse position than before the fraud occurred. Fraud is most common in the buying or selling of property, including real estate, personal property and intangible property, such as stocks, bonds and copyrights.

Answer 41. **a,b,c,e – Examples of fraud.** This is just a sampling!

- identity theft (acquiring your personal information without your consent)
- counterfeiting checks or money orders
- selling bogus goods, including health care products, which are not what they claim to be
- selling goods or services with no intention of delivering them
- bait and switch tactics - Merchants lure customers to their stores by advertising products or services at a low price ("baiting"). When customers arrive, however, they discover that the advertised goods are not available. Salespeople then pressure the customers to consider items that are similar but higher priced ("switching").
- rigged gambling games

Fraud

Question 42. As long as you are not involved in criminal activity, you have every right to keep your personal information private or confidential.

a. true
b. false

Question 43. When someone acquires your personal information without your consent and uses that information to steal your money, they are engaging in:

a. defamation
b. restitution
c. identity theft
d. counterfeiting
e. trafficking

Question 44. Documents that help prove your identity:

a. birth certificate
b. store gift card
c. driver's license
d. passport
e. student or employee identification card

Question 45. Thieves are looking for personal information, such as your:

a. name
b. email address
c. blood type
d. bank and credit card account details
e. Social Security number

 Fraud

Answer 42. **a – Your personal information belongs to you!** As long as you are not involved in criminal activity, you have every right to privacy – to keep your personal information private or confidential. It is up to you, and only you, to decide who can obtain or use this information.

Answer 43. **c – Identity theft.** You have become a victim of identity theft when someone acquires your personal information without your consent and uses that information to steal money from you or obtain credit and other benefits.

Answer 44. **a,c,d,e – Documents that prove your identity.** The most common identity documents are: your birth certificate, driver's license, state-issued non-driver ID card and passport (United States or foreign). Other possible identity documents include: a military ID card, a certificate of naturalization, a student or employee ID card or a health insurance card.

Answer 45. **a,b,d,e – What thieves want to know about you.** Thieves are looking for personal information such as: your street address, email address, bank and credit card account details and Social Security number.

> *To keep up with the latest frauds,*
> *visit www.fbi.gov/scams-safety/*

Fraud

Question 46. **Why is identity theft a problem?**

a Someone could incur debts in your name.

b. Your name could be attached to a criminal character n a novel.

c. Your bank account could be drained.

d. Your credit rating could be downgraded.

e. Your name could be linked to a crime.

Question 47. **Why banks ask you to prove your identity:**

a. Banks share identity information with other banks.

b. Banks are overly cautious.

c. Banks try hard to protect you and your money.

d. Banks want to hassle you a bit so you'll think twice before making withdrawals for frivolous purposes.

e. Banks want to prevent dishonest people from using your personal information to withdraw money from your account.

Question 48. **Some ways to manage important papers to foil thieves:**

a. Put bill-payment envelopes directly in a United States postal box; don't leave them in your mailbox for the mail carrier to pick up.

b. Shred important documents containing personal information as soon as possible.

c. Store important papers in a safe deposit box.

d. Don't carry photo ID.

e. Leave your passport at home when traveling to a foreign country.

Fraud

***Answer 46.* a,c,d,e – Why identity theft is a problem.** It's very serious problem, because:

- Someone could rack up big debts in your name and even drain your bank account.
- Your credit rating could be downgraded.
- Your name could be linked to a crime you did not commit, which could ruin your reputation.

***Answer 47.* c,e – Why banks ask for ID.** Banks try hard to protect you and your money, so don't be annoyed when they ask you for ID. They want to prevent dishonest people from using your personal information to withdraw money from your account.

***Answer 48.* a,b,c – Managing important papers to foil thieves.** Several things you can do:

- Put bill payment envelopes directly in a United States postal box rather than leaving them out in your mailbox for the mail carrier to pick up. This is just an invitation to a thief to snatch some personal information.
- As soon as possible, shred important documents that link your name with information, such as your address, credit card and bank account numbers and Social Security number. This includes credit card and ATM receipts.

Of course, you must keep some information forever (birth certificate, Social Security card) or at least, for a number of years (tax returns). For these documents, store them in the safest place you can find (in safe deposit box at a bank or in a fireproof safe or locked file cabinet at home).

Fraud $50

Question 49. **Ways to avoid being a victim of fraud in connection with your credit, debit or prepaid money cards:**

a. Review your credit card statement frequently.

b. Look for charges or withdrawals that look suspicious.

c. Watch for small, recurring charges or withdrawals that you have not authorized.

d. Report suspicious or unauthorized activity to your card provider.

e. Use the same PIN for all your money cards

Question 50. **Stealing a victim's credit or debit card number using a small, handheld electronic device is called:**

a. hacking

b. skimming

c. scoring

d. pinching

e. pillaging

Question 51. **Common locations where credit and debit card skimming occurs:**

a. restaurants

b. banks

c. bars

d. gas stations

e. airports

303

Fraud

***Answer 49.* a,b,c,d – Avoid being a money card victim.** Even though your money cards are tucked safely in your wallet, thieves can still find ways to acquire your card numbers and use them to gain access to your accounts. Review your card and bank statements frequently to spot charges or withdrawals that look suspicious, especially small, recurring charges or withdrawals that you have not authorized. Report suspicious or unauthorized activity to your card provider and/or bank as soon as you discover such activity.

Credit card companies also try to protect you from fraud. If they notice unusual charges to your account or charges made in locations far from your home, they will notify you of such activity. If your account has been compromised, they will issue you a new card with a new number.

***Answer 50.* b – Skimming.** This is an electronic means of gaining access to your credit or debit card account. With a quick swipe, thieves can procure your credit or debit card number using a small, handheld electronic device called a skimmer that records the data contained in the magnetic strip on your credit card. With skimmers, thieves can store information on hundreds of victims and may either use the captured information themselves or sell it to other criminals.

***Answer 51.* a,c,d,e – Where skimming happens.** Skimming can occur right under your nose during ordinary business transactions. Restaurants and bars are easy places for thieves to practice skimming, because a server takes your card away briefly in the process of settling your bill. In just a second, an unscrupulous server can scan your card before returning it to you. Other common skimming locations include gas stations and airports.

Fraud

Question 52. **If any of your money cards are lost or stolen:**

a. Report the loss to your card provider ASAP.

b. Wait until you receive your next statement to report the loss.

c. Promptly report the loss on the provider's website (if you have online access to your account).

d. Forget about it, because the card provider will automatically spot the fraudulent use.

e. Check your card agreement for your provider's specific rules pertaining to loss or theft of your cards.

Question 53. Information you should have available when you call to report a lost or stolen money card:

a. your account number
b. the date you noticed your card was missing
c. the date and amount of your last purchase or withdrawal
d. your Social Security number
e. your birth date

"Oh my god! I don't recognize a lot of these credit card charges...They could be fraudulent...I'm calling the credit card company right now."

Fraud

Answer 52. a,c,e – Report loss or theft of cards ASAP. If any of your money cards (ATM, credit, debit, or prepaid cards) are lost or stolen, report the loss to your card provider as soon as possible. Phone them, or if you have online access to your account, report the loss on the provider's website. The card provider will issue you a new card with a new number.

Different types of cards have different levels of protection against fraudulent use. Credit cards have the most protection. Check your card agreements for the provider's specific rules pertaining to loss or theft of your cards.

Answer 53. a,b,c,d,e – Be ready to report. It's important to prepare in advance in case your card is lost or stolen. This is the information you need to have available when you call in a report:

- your card issuer's phone number and/or website
- your account number
- the date you noticed your card was missing
- the date and amount of your last purchase or withdrawal
- your Social Security number
- your birth date

Avoid Credit Card Shutoffs

When you travel far from home, notify your credit card company ahead of time; otherwise, they may suspect your card has been stolen and shut off your card. You can call them on the phone or complete an online travel notification form. You'll need to provide your departure and return dates, as well as your away destination(s).

Fraud

Question 54. **How to fight telemarketing fraud:**

a. Don't give out personal information over the phone to unknown persons.

b. Don't be pressured into accepting an offer from a telemarketer.

c. Don't pay with a debit card for goods or services ordered over the phone.

d. Change your phone number often.

e. Don't accept free trial offers over the phone.

"Hey...I don't care if the prize is a gold Cadillac... I don't give out personal information over the phone."

Fraud

Answer 54. a,b,c,e – **Telemarketing fraud.** For years telemarketers have sold bogus products and services over the telephone. Scams often involve offers of free prizes, low-cost products, inexpensive vacations and other "deals" like no-interest loans, low-interest credit cards and debt relief.

There are warning signs. If a salesperson says something like "You can't afford to miss this high-profit, no-risk offer," just say "no thank you," and hang up. It's very difficult to recover your money if you've been cheated over the telephone, so:

- **Never give out personal information,** such as your credit card number and expiration date, bank account numbers, date of birth, or Social Security number, to unknown persons over the phone.
- **Don't respond to pressure.** Always take time making a decision and never accept an offer you don't understand.
- **Don't buy from an unfamiliar company.** Request written material on the company and check them out with the Better Business Bureau or similar watchdog group. Always obtain a salesperson's name and contact information before transacting business.
- **Don't pay with a debit card for goods or services ordered over the phone or Internet.** Use your credit card instead. If you pay with a debit card, you have paid in advance for the goods or services you ordered and have little or no recourse if you never receive your order.
- **Don't pay for "free" prizes or accept free trial offers.** If you accept a free trial offer over the phone for magazines, CDs or other products, you may find yourself inadvertently billed for additional products even though you didn't explicitly order them.

Fraud — $50

***Question 55.* The real purpose of many work-at-home schemes is:**

a. to give people with little education the opportunity to make a lot of money doing a simple task

b. to assist legitimate nonprofit organizations with completing simple work, like stuffing envelopes for fundraising appeals

c. to give people a chance to make a lot of money quickly

d. to extort money from victims by charging a fee to join the scheme

e. to give people the opportunity to make money while staying at home

***Question 56.* A type of electronic fraud where a seemingly legitimate person or business sends you an email asking you to supply financial or other confidential information in order to steal money from your accounts:**

a. scanning

b. fishing

c. forgery

d. phishing

e. conspiracy

> "I'm acutely aware that the possibility of fraud is even more prevalent in today's world because of the Internet and cell phones and the opportunity for instant communication with strangers."
> — Armistead Maupin, novelist

Fraud

Answer 55. **d – Fraudulent work-at-home schemes** – a get-rich-quick scam in which a victim is lured into performing some simple, short-term task – usually done at home – with the promise of substantial payment upon completion of the task. Such offers may appear on websites, radio, TV, posters around your neighborhood, or in the newspaper. The perpetrator's real purpose in making such offers is to extort money from the victim, either by charging a fee to join the scheme, or requiring the victim to invest in products whose resale value is exaggerated.

There are more work-at-home scams than there are real work-at-home job listings, so you need to be really careful when searching for and evaluating these types of "opportunities." Presume that the position is a scam, unless there is compelling evidence to the contrary. If it sounds too good to be true, it is.

Legitimate work-at-home opportunities do exist but these jobs usually require some relevant form of post–high school education and some prior experience in an office or other supervised setting. Take the time to research the position and the company. Talk to other people who work there. This way, you won't be scammed and may be able to find a legitimate work-from-home job.

Answer 56. **d – Phishing.** A type of electronic fraud where a seemingly legitimate person or business, usually posing as a financial institution, sends you an email or instant message. They ask you to supply financial or other confidential information, such as credit card numbers and passwords, often via a link to a fake website that mimics the real one. Your information is then used to steal money from your accounts.

Fraud

Question 57. **Precautions to take to avoid online fraud:**

a. Buy things only on secure websites.

b. Use the same, easy-to-remember password in all your transactions with online businesses.

c. Keep your anti-virus, anti-spyware, firewall and other security software updated.

d. Avoid using public computers to do online banking.

e. Never provide personal information in an email or on social media sites.

Keep Your Social Security Number (SSN) Safe

- *Do not use your SSN as a username, password or PIN.*
- *Make sure your SSN does not appear on your printed checks, driver's license or ID cards.*
- *Don't carry your SSN card; keep it at home in a safe place.*
- *Don't give out your SSN to any organization unless absolutely necessary and only to reputable, known groups.*
- *Ask organizations to use other types of identifiers instead of your SSN.*

Fraud

***Answer 57.* a,c,d,e – Avoiding Online Fraud.** Take these precautions:

- Visit and use legitimate online businesses only (e.g., eBay). These businesses work hard to prevent fraud.
- Don't buy anything online unless you are sure the website is secure. (A secure website is identified by "https.")
- When setting up accounts with online businesses, create unique passwords for each business that would be difficult for fraudsters to decipher.
- Protect your computer by installing security software (antispyware, antivirus, firewall).
- Keep your computer software up-to-date (operating system, web browser, security software).
- Block spam emails.
- Do not use computers at public places (such as libraries or Internet cafes) to do online banking.
- Never provide credit card numbers or other personal information in an email or on social media sites.

How Online Credit Card Fraud Can Happen

Scammers may use the Internet to install spyware on your computer in order to obtain your credit card details. These fraudsters employ all kinds of tricks to get their spyware loaded onto your computer, like sending you an email that entices you to click on a link to a website that they have set up solely to infect your computer. They may also sneak into your computer via free games or music that you have downloaded from the Internet.

Fraud

Beware of Fraud on Social Networks (e.g., Facebook)

Social networking sites have become an easy way to stay in touch with family and friends and to share information and pictures. But whatever you post online is potentially accessible to anyone, including thieves seeking to steal your identity and money.

Fraudsters try to collect any information about you they can. You may not think that revealing a few personal details about yourself on the web is taking a risk. However, fraudsters are good at combining all these bits of information to steal your identity.

Fraudsters go after the easiest victims first. They target social networking accounts that are not using the security features available on the site, in the Internet browser or in security software on your computer.

One of the easiest ways for fraudsters to get access to your information is to send you a "friend request" or something similar. Many people assume that only people who know you or have contacts in common would send you a request, but this is not the case.

Once fraudsters have access to or control of your profile, they can use this information for identity theft. They can also try to use your account to commit other types of fraud, like sending a message to your friends and family telling them you are in trouble and asking them to send money to help you.

 Fraud

How to Reduce Risks When Using Social Networks

- *Do not post personal information such as your home address or telephone number, names of your children and their schools, your employer, or specific details about when you will be away from home. (If you wouldn't post something on a bulletin board in a grocery store, don't post it online.)*
- *If you don't want the world to know something about you or see a raunchy photo of you, don't post it or share it with "friends."*
- *If you have to post your date of birth, do not include your year of birth.*
- *Only allow approved people to access your profile.*
- *Ignore "friend requests" from people you do not know.*
- *Pick a non-obvious, strong password that uses a mix of numbers, symbols and letters. Use different passwords for different applications such as social networking sites, email, online banking, etc. Change your passwords often.*
- *Choose a social network's enhanced privacy settings when creating a profile or setting up an account. It is important to know how they protect your data and what they are allowed to do with it. Check whether the site is allowed to sell your information to other companies.*
- *Do not use public Wi-Fi hotspots to access social networking sites. Use secure Internet access only.*
- *Learn in advance what you should do if your account or profile is hacked or taken over. That way, if your account is compromised at some point, you will be able to take action quickly to have your account returned to you.*

Business

Business

Preparing to Start Your Own Small Business

- *Build skills and knowledge related to your talents and interests; keep them up-to-date.*
- *Find an unserved new market for products and services related to your skills, knowledge and expertise.*
- *Develop a business plan with clearly defined goals and objectives.*
- *Find a mentor.*
- *Dedicate your life to fulfilling your small business dream.*
- *Have faith in your idea and your ability to succeed.*
- *Persevere through setbacks and adversity.*

Resources For Starting a Small Business

- *10 Businesses Your Teens Could Start This Summer*
  tinyurl.com/lzlvf5t
- *Junior Achievement - JA Be Entrepreneurial*
  tinyurl.com/lfuanx9
- *PBS Biz Kids TV Program*
  bizkids.com
- *US Small Business Administration*
  archive.sba.gov/teens/
- *Wall Street Journal Classroom Edition*
  guides.wsj.com/small-business
- *Wikipedia - How to Start a Business As a Teenager*
  wikihow.com/Start-a-Business-As-a-Teenager

Business

Question 58. A continuous and regular activity that has income or profit as its primary purpose:

a. nonprofit
b. stock market
c. shopping
d. government
e. business

Question 59. A set of moral principles or beliefs that govern business behaviors:

a. invisible hand
b. business acumen
c. business ethics
d. monopoly
e. corporation bylaws

Question 60. A formal statement of business goals:

a. business mission
b. business plan
c. prospectus
d. business financial plan
e. budget

Question 61. A legally binding agreement between two or more parties with mutual obligations:

a. verbal agreement
b. business plan
c. contract
d. FICA
e. mutual fund

Business

Answer 58. e – **Business** – a continuous and regular activity that has income or profit as its primary purpose. Businesses range in size from one person operations to giant international companies. But, regardless of size, all businesses share certain common features.

Answer 59. c – **Business ethics** – a set of moral principles or beliefs that govern business behaviors. Example: environmental sustainability has become a goal for many well-meaning businesses. Good corporate citizenship is now studied, advocated and sometimes practiced.

Answer 60. b - **Business plan** – a formal statement of business goals along with an explanation of why these goals are attainable and how they will be achieved.

Answer 61. c – **Contract** – a legally binding agreement between two or more parties with mutual obligations.

"This rain is really watering down our profits."

Business

***Question 62.* An entrepreneur is:**

a. a French chef
b. a risk-averse person
c. an investor
d. a person who starts a new business
e. a bon vivant

***Question 63.* The positive difference between total revenue and total expenses of a business or investment:**

a. loss
b. profit
c. yield
d. cash flow
e. dividend

"Whoopee! Our first business venture made a profit. That is, if we don't count all the money wasted buying that junk in the first place."

Answer 62. **d – Entrepreneur** – a person who invests personal time and money in starting a new business. Entrepreneurs hope to earn a good income from a successful business; however, they also accept the possibility that a business may fail and that they may lose some or all of the money invested in it.

Answer 63. **b – Profit** – the positive difference between total revenue and total expenses of a business or investment.

Inventions Created by Kids

Television *– Philo Farnsworth first conceived of the "electronic television" in 1920 when he was 14 years old. By the age of 21, he had developed a working model that served as the basis for all later televisions. In 1929, he televised an image of a dollar sign.*

Braille *– In 1821, Louis Braille, at the age of 14, created a finger touch system as a way for blind people to read books. Blind people around the world still use the Braille system to read.*

Earmuffs *– On a very cold day in 1873, Chester Greenwood, a 15-year-old kid in Maine, was trying to keep his ears warm while skating. All his attempts seemed awkward, so he conceived of the idea of covering two wire loops with tufts of fur.*

The Popsicle *– Frank Epperson of San Francisco invented the popsicle one cold night in 1905 when he was just 11 years old. In 1923, 18 years later, Frank applied for a patent for what he called the "frozen ice on a stick" and started selling it.*

Glo-Sheets *– Rebecca Shroeder created these sheets in 1974 when she was 14 years old. The sheets allow a person to read information in the dark. They are widely used by doctors in hospitals and by astronauts in space when they power down the space shuttle.*

Economics

"As you can see, economic history is a series of booms and busts. Eventually the recession will end, then we can graduate and start looking for a job."

Economics

Why Learn About Economics?

Learning about economics will help you function more effectively as an investor, consumer, citizen and individual.

As an investor, you will have a greater understanding of the how the marketplace works and how you can invest your money to greatest advantage. You will learn about various economic factors and indicators that can lead to wise investment strategies.

As a consumer, you will have a better sense of when to sit tight and save your money and when to take advantage of certain market situations, like low interest rates, to spend money and make your dreams come true.

As a citizen, you will be better able to interpret the daily news. You will understand how national economies and markets operate, how the U. S. economy interacts with the global economy and how global competition in the modern day impacts all the citizens of the world, including yourself. And you will be better informed when you enter the voting booth to express your opinion on government actions.

As an individual, by observing the day-to-day actions of business and government, you will improve your own ability to analyze complex situations and develop better problem-solving skills. This will be a benefit to you in your chosen work and in your personal life.

Human Capital

This term refers to the skills, knowledge and experience possessed by an individual or population, viewed in terms of their value or cost to an organization or country, is often referred to as human capital.

Economics

Question 64. **The study of how people, governments, firms and nations use limited resources to try to satisfy unlimited needs:**

a. informatics
b. accounting
c. statistics
d. resource management
e. economics

Question 65. **The total system of economic activity in a particular country or area, comprising all the production, labor, trade and consumption that takes place:**

a. fiscal scheme
b. economy
c. monetary regime
d. market
e. financial system

Question 66. **A place or sphere where buyers and sellers come together to exchange goods or services:**

a. commons
b. domain
c. market
d. precinct
e. arena

Capitalism

Capitalism is an economic and political system in which a country's trade and industry are mostly controlled by a few owners for their own profit (and their stockholders). The resources and means of production are privately owned and prices, production and the distribution of goods are determined mainly by competition in a free market.

Answer 64. **e – Economics** can be defined as the study of resource allocation, production, trade and consumption of goods and services. It can also be described as the study of how various agents (individuals, businesses, governments, nations) interact to use limited resources in an attempt to satisfy unlimited needs.

The subject is broadly divided into two main branches: microeconomics and macroeconomics. *Microeconomics* looks more closely at the economic choices of individual agents (consumers, households, businesses) and the factors that influence their choices, as well as how each choice affects another choice. *Macroeconomics* looks at the bigger picture and analyzes entire economies and how national trends, such as unemployment, inflation, economic growth, and government monetary and fiscal policy, affect these economies.

Answer 65. **b – Economy** – the total system of economic activity in a particular country or area, comprising all the production, labor, trade and consumption that takes place.

Answer 66. **c – Market (marketplace)** – a place or sphere where buyers and sellers come together to exchange goods or services after agreeing on prices and conditions of sale (payment methods, warranties, delivery, etc.). Early on, human beings met face to face in a market to conduct business and we still do. But with ever-improving methods of communication (e.g., the Internet) and transportation, markets are now global, with goods being exchanged over vast distances.

A *free market economy* is an economy in which the allocation of resources is determined only by the supply of resources and the demand for them. This is mainly a theoretical concept, because all countries, even capitalist ones, regulate or restrict some market operations.

Economics

Question 67. **In economics, the term used to describe how many people are interested in buying a particular product or service and how much they are willing to pay for it:**

a. inclination
b. interest
c. incentive
d. demand
e. motivation

Question 68. **In economics, the term used to describe the amount of products or services available for purchase at a given price:**

a. stockpile
b. stash
c. reserve
d. surplus
e. supply

Question 69. **The term used to describe a situation in which two or more producers attempt to win the business of a buyer by offering the best terms:**

a. cooperation
b. price-fixing
c. competition
d. collaboration
e. collusion

Question 70. **A market in which there is only one seller or supplier of a product or service:**

a. duopoly
b. monopoly
c. competitive market
d. oligopoly
e. bull market

Answer 67. **d – Demand** – a consumer's desire to possess products or services and their willingness to pay the asking price. Looking at the larger marketplace, the term "demand" refers to a group of people, how many of them are interested in buying a certain thing, and how much they are willing to pay for it. Businesses often spend lots of money trying to figure this out.

Answer 67. **e – Supply** – the total amount of a product or service that is available to consumers. The interaction of supply and demand forms the basis of our modern economy. If people want a product and are willing to pay more for it, producers will add to the supply in order to increase their profits. Then as the supply increases, the price will fall provided the demand remains the same.

Answer 69. **c – Competition.** Competition arises when two or more producers, working against each other, attempt to win the business of a buyer by offering the best terms (price, warranties, loan arrangements, delivery time, etc.).

Answer 70. **b – Monopoly** – the domination of a market by a single entity who has become the only supplier of a product or service. In the absence of competition from others, the supplier usually restricts supply and increases prices in order to maximize profits. The United States has laws in place to restrict the formation of monopolies. The highly popular board game "Monopoly" is based on the economic concept of monopoly. Players move around a game board buying or trading properties, developing their properties with houses and hotels and collecting rent from their opponents. The ultimate goal is to drive opponents into bankruptcy.

A *cartel* is a group monopoly. This happens when a group of businesses agree to cooperate so as to restrict the output of a particular product and thereby drive up prices. Many countries around the globe strive to identify and break up cartels.

Economics

Question 71. **The difference between a country's imports and exports over a given time period:**

a. deficit
b. national debt
c. surplus
d. net profit
e. balance of trade

Question 72. **A tax on imported goods that is meant to protect domestic producers from foreign competition:**

a. tariff
b. sales tax
c. income tax
d. value-added tax
e. foreign-competition tax

Question 73. **The import and export of goods and services without tariffs or quotas being imposed:**

a. wholesale commerce
b. mercantilism
c. duty-free shopping
d. bartering
e. free trade

Question 74. **The term used to describe the free flow of money, goods and people across international borders:**

a. globalization
b. internationalism
c. protectionism
d. transnationalism
e. liberalization

Answer 71. **e – Balance of trade (trade surplus or deficit).** The balance of trade is the difference between a country's exports and imports. Picture a teeter-totter tipping toward the United States when we have a trade deficit, i.e., more imports than exports, or away when we have a trade surplus, i.e., more exports than imports.

This is a dynamic, global condition that can have a real impact on you as an individual, because it affects our domestic economy and can determine whether or not you have a job and how much you pay for basic needs.

Answer 72. **a – Tariff** – a tax on imported goods as they cross national boundaries, usually imposed by the government of the importing country to protect domestic producers from foreign competition. The words tax, tariff and duty are generally used interchangeably.

Cross-border trade wars may start between countries when one country decides that another is engaging in unfair trading practices. For example, Country A may raise tariffs on goods imported from Country B, so Country B retaliates with tariffs of its own and so forth.

Answer 73. **e – Free trade** – the sale and purchase of goods and services between countries without any governmental constraints, such as import tariffs, import quotas, or export subsidies (incentive payments to exporters). Since the mid-20th century, nations have increasingly reduced barriers to international trade.

Answer 74. **a – Globalization** – the free flow of money, goods and people across international borders. Today, the economies of nations around the world have become highly interdependent.

An example of this trend toward integration of national economies is the Eurozone which is an economic and monetary union of 17 European Union (EU) member states that have adopted the euro (€) as their common currency.

Economics

Question 75. **A severe, long-term decline in the economic activity of a nation during which output slumps, unemployment soars, consumer and business spending plummets, stock prices plunge and credit is scarce:**

a. recession
b. bear market
c. depression
d. bull market
e. depreciation

Question 76. **A relatively mild and short-lived decline in the economic activity of a nation:**

a. recession
b. bear market
c. depression
d. bull market
e. depreciation

"Don't worry, Mom. If it's only a recession and not a depression, I'll be out on my own again in six months."

329

Economics

Answer 75. **c – Depression** – a severe, long-term decline in the economic activity of a nation during which output slumps, unemployment soars, consumer and business spending plummets, stock prices plunge and credit is scarce. A devastating breakdown of an economy (essentially, a severe depression) is referred to as an economic collapse.

The Great Depression was a worldwide economic slump that lasted from 1929 to the mid-1930s. It started in the United States with the Wall Street Crash and spread around the world. Since the Great Depression, the governments and central banks of industrialized countries have monitored their economies, and when required, adjusted their economic policies in an effort to prevent another financial crisis of this magnitude.

Answer 76. **a – Recession** – a decline in the economic activity of a nation during which output slows, unemployment rises, consumer and business spending decreases and stock prices fall. The main difference between a recession and a depression is the severity of the decline in economic activity and the duration of the slowdown. Recessions are milder than depressions. They also occur more frequently and last for shorter periods of time. A recession is said to be underway after two calendar quarters of negative economic growth. The most recent recession, dubbed the "Great Recession", came to a head in 2008 in the wake of the housing finance crisis.

> *"It's a recession when your neighbor loses his job; it's a depression when you lose yours."*
>
> — an old joke told by Harry S. Truman as well as many economists

Economics

Question 77. The amount by which a government's expenses exceed its income in a single year:

a. surplus
b. debt
c. deficit
d. credit
e. loss

Question 78. The accumulation of yearly deficits amassed over a period of years by a central government:

a. government debt
b. public debt
c. national liability
d. national debt
e. biennial bill

Question 79. The central banking system of the United States:

a. the World Bank
b. the International Monetary Fund (IMF)
c. the United States Treasury
d. the Federal Reserve
e. the Federal Deposit Insurance Corporation (FDIC)

Question 80. The interest rate that banks pay to borrow money from a country's central bank:

a. base interest rate
b. bank interest rate
c. United States Treasury interest rate
d. national interest rate
e. World Bank interest rate

Economics

Answer 77. **c – Deficit** – the amount by which a government's expenses exceed its income in a single year. When there is a deficit, a government must borrow money to pay its bills.

Answer 78. **a,b,d – Government debt** – the accumulation of yearly deficits amassed over a period of years by a central government (also referred to as public debt or national debt). To finance its debt, the United States government sells Treasury notes and government bonds to investors. You can buy Treasury notes directly from the United States government or through a bank.

Answer 79. **d – The Federal Reserve.** The Federal Reserve System (also known as the Federal Reserve and, informally, as the Fed) is the central banking system of the United States. In the Federal Reserve Act, the United States Congress established three key objectives for United States monetary policy : (1) achieve maximum employment, (2) sustain stable prices and (3) keep long-term interest rates moderate. The Fed's duties have expanded over the years to include: overseeing the nation's monetary policy, supervising and regulating banking institutions, maintaining the stability of the nation's financial system and providing financial services to depository institutions (banks, credit unions), the United States government and official foreign institutions.

Answer 80. **a,b,d – Base interest rate** – the interest rate that banks pay to borrow money from a country's central bank (also referred to as the bank or national interest rate). In the United States, the Federal Reserve uses this rate to manage the ups and downs of the economy. When the Fed wants to stimulate the economy, it lowers the base interest rate. Banks then pass on this reduction to their customers; in essence, money becomes cheaper and easier to borrow. This helps to boost economic activity and increase the number of jobs available.

Economics

Question 81. A measure of the average change over time in the prices paid for consumer goods and services:

a. Goods and Services Average
b. Market Basket Average
c. Consumer Price Index
d. Shopper Outlay Index
e. Consumer Products Average

Question 82. In economics, the term used to describe an overall rise in the price of goods and services over a period of time:

a. deflation
b. recession
c. inflation
d. depression
e. expansion

Question 83. In economics, the term used to describe a general decrease in the price of goods and services over a period of time:

a. contraction
b. recession
c. inflation
d. deflation
e. depression

Exchange Rate

An exchange rate is the price of a currency in terms of other currencies expressed as a ratio. On July 11, 2013, one United States dollar was equal to 0.76 Euros. One Euro was equal to 1.31 United States dollars. The exchange rate changes daily.

333

$50   Economics

Answer 81. **c – Consumer Price Index** – a measure of the average change over time in the prices paid by urban consumers for a "market basket" of goods and services.

Answer 82. **c – Inflation** – an overall rise in the price of goods and services over a period of time. When this occurs, your dollar loses value and you can't buy as much as before. In most cases, inflation is reflected in the Consumer Price Index.

Answer 83. **d – Deflation** – a general decrease in the price of goods and services over a set period of time, meaning a dollar can buy more goods.

> ### *Gross Domestic Product (GDP)*
>
> *Gross Domestic Product is a measure of a nation's annual economic output - the market value of all officially recognized goods and services produced in a given period of time. Average GDP per capita tells us how big each person's share of GDP would be if it were divided into equal portions. GDP and GDP per capita are often considered by economists and policymakers to be measures of a country's standard of living and economic well-being. Countries are often ranked in terms of their GDP ratings.*
>
> *The problem with using average GDP per capita as a measure of the average citizen's standard of living is that a nation's income and wealth are not distributed evenly. Since the mid 1970s, increases in productivity and the GDP in the United States have mainly benefited the rich and failed to raise the living standards of average Americans.*
>
> *Other measures of national well-being include:*
> - *Better Life Index (oecdbetterlifeindex.org)*
> - *Gross National Happiness Index (grossnationalhappiness.com)*
> - *Happy Planet Index (happyplanetindex.org)*
> - *Social Progress Index (socialprogressimperative.org)*

Economics

Question 84. **Invisible hand:**

a. a term applied to government regulation

b. a term economists use to describe the theory that a marketplace will regulate itself to the benefit of all members of a society

c. a term first coined by the economist Adam Smith

d. a term referring to the claim that individuals, in striving to maximize their own gains in a free market, will benefit society as a whole

e. a term regulators use to describe insider trading on the stock market

Question 85. **Tragedy of the commons:**

a. when a human tragedy occurs in a public park

b. when a common market falls apart

c. when the common people lose a lot of money

d. when commoners are out of work due to no fault of their own

e. when multiple individuals, acting in their own self-interest, damage or deplete a shared and limited resource

> *"Practical men, who believe themselves to be quite exempt from any intellectual influence, are usually the slaves of some defunct economist."*
>
> — John Maynard Keynes

 Economics

Answer 84. b,c,d – **Invisible hand** – the term economists use to describe the self-regulating nature of the marketplace. This is a metaphor first coined by the economist Adam Smith to capture his important claim that individuals, in striving to maximize their own gains in a free market, will benefit society as a whole.

Answer 85. e – **Tragedy of the commons** – a term economists use to describe the depletion of a shared and limited resource (e.g., a fresh water aquifer) due to multiple individuals acting according to their own self-interests, even when it is clear that this will not be to anyone's long-term benefit. This concept is often cited in connection with the debate about global warming and with efforts toachieve sustainable growth by balancing economic success and environmental protection.

"I heard a bottling company upstream started capturing most of the water. Now there's none left for us."

Investing

Investing *is almost always for the long term;* ***spending*** *is for the present. Investing is putting money into things that will make life better tomorrow. Spending may help us feel good today, but won't necessarily improve our life in the long run. (In fact, spending today may deplete funds that could otherwise be available to improve our life later.)*

Most Americans have more money parked in their driveway than they do in their retirement account.

Now that most pension plans require participants to make their own investment decisions, most people are going to need some knowledge of investing.

The Gambler and the Investor

A gambler takes foolhardy risks that have little chance of success. An intelligent investor takes reasonable risks that have a good chance of success.

A gambler often risks money he/she can't afford to lose. An intelligent investor only risks money he/she can afford to lose without a significant decline in lifestyle.

Investing

Question 1. **Risking money in the present with a reasonable expectation that it grow in value over time:**

a. scamming
b. gambling
c. investing
d. hoarding
e. saving

Question 2. **Types of investments:**

a. stocks and mutual funds
b. a car
c. real estate
d. high-value collectibles
e. bonds

Question 3. **A car is:**

a. a savings vehicle
b. an investment
c. a depreciating asset
d. a potential liability
e. a capital loss

 Investing

Answer 1. **c – Investing** – risking some money in the present with a reasonable expectation that it will earn more money and/or grow in value (appreciate) over time. When you invest, you put your money to work for you.

Answer 2. **a,c,d,e – Types of investments.** When people hear the word "investment," they usually think of such things as stocks, mutual funds and bonds. But you can also invest in real estate (buildings and land) and high-value collectibles (e.g., fine art, antiques).

Answer 3. **c – A car is not an investment.** Even though you may spend a lot of money buying a car, it cannot be considered an investment (unless it's antique car that appreciates in value). Cars, like most of our possessions, are depreciating assets, i.e., they lose value over time.

"Dad, instead of buying a car, I'm saving money for college. I can always buy a car later, but my priority now is to get a good education."

Investing

Question 4. **Which of the following statements about investing and saving are true?**

a. When you buy investments, you can earn money or lose money.

b. When you put your money in a savings account, you know you will always earn some interest.

c. With investments, no one will insure you against potential losses.

d. If your bank fails, you will lose all the money in your savings account.

e. Investing in the stock market is safer than putting your money in a savings account.

Question 5. **Which of the following statements about investing and gambling are true?**

a. Your odds of earning money are much greater with gambling than with investing.

b. Investors tend to be more careful with their money than gamblers.

c. Investors are just as willing as gamblers to take big, spur-of-the moment risks.

d. Investors understand that it can take time for their investments to bring rewards, but gamblers are looking for instant gratification.

e. Investing is serious business, so you must be 18 years old to own stock; but gambling is just entertainment, so you are allowed to start at the age of 12.

$100 Investing

Answer 4. **a,b,c – Investing is different from saving.** The first difference has to do with earnings. When you invest your money, the outcome is uncertain. You could earn a little money or a lot; you could also lose all the money you invested. On the other hand, when you put your money in a savings account, the outcome is certain – you will always earn some money (interest), but never a lot. The other difference has to do with security. You're on your own when it comes to investments. No one will insure you against potential losses. However, money in your bank account is protected, because the FDIC (Federal Deposit Insurance Corporation) insures most bank accounts (including savings accounts) up to $250,000.

Answer 5. **b,d – Investing is different from gambling.** In general, investing is "smart" risk-taking whereas gambling is foolhardy risk-taking. Your odds of earning money with investments are usually much greater than with gambling. Investors are willing to take some chances, but they are much more careful with their money than gamblers. They approach investing seriously and often do a lot of research and carefully weigh the risks before handing over their money. Generally, they are patient, understanding that it can take time (sometimes years) for their investment to bring rewards.

Gamblers enjoy taking risks, no matter what the odds are. They gamble for the pure fun and excitement of the game, even when the odds of winning are low. Gamblers are impatient; they are hoping for the instant gratification of winning right now.

Interestingly, to legally gamble, you need to be 18 or older, whereas there is no minimum age to own stocks and similar investments. Theoretically, one can purchase a stock at any age, although a minor will usually require a parent or guardian to cosign a purchase agreement. A minor can also receive a stock as a gift or inheritance.

Investing

Question 6. **A term that refers to a variety of financing or investment instruments, including stocks, bonds and mutual funds:**

a. securities
b. guarantees
c. underwritings
d. leases
e. liabilities

Question 7. **The word "principal" means:**

a. the amount of money originally invested in a stock
b. a stockbroker's pledge of integrity
c. the original purchase price of a bond (face value)
d. the amount owing on a loan, separate from interest
e. the owner of a private company

Question 8. **When you buy stocks in a company:**

a. you have an ownership stake in the company
b. you own shares or equities of the company
c. you are called a stockholder or shareholder
d. you have the right to vote for the company's board of directors
e. you will find the value of your stocks going go up and down

Question 9. **The Dow Jones Industrial Average is:**

a. the most widely used index of United States stocks

b. an indicator of the overall condition of the United States stock market

c. published by the same company as the *Wall Street Journal*

d. a formula invented in 1790 by Alexander Hamilton, the first Secretary of the United States Treasury

e. an average of 30 significant stocks traded on the New York

$100 Investing

Answer 6. **a – Securities** – a general term that refers to a variety of financing or investment instruments. Companies issue securities to raise capital for various enterprises. Investors buy securities to obtain a return (make money). Stocks and bonds are two types of securities.

Answer 7. **a,c,d,e – Principal.** This term has several meanings. In the context of investing, it refers to the amount of money originally invested in a stock or bond, excluding any interest or dividends earned later. With regard to loans, principal is an amount borrowed or still owed on a loan, separate from interest. The owner of a private company is also referred to as the principal.

Answer 8. **a,b,c,d,e – Stocks.** When you buy stocks (also referred to as shares or equities), you gain an ownership stake in a company. As a stockholder/shareholder you have certain rights, including the right to vote for a company's board of directors and to benefit from a company's growth. But you're also taking a risk. The value of your stock may go up or down.

Answer 9. **a,b,c,e – Dow Jones Industrial Average (DJIA).** The DJIA is the most widely used index or indicator of the overall condition of the United States stock market. It is computed daily by the Dow Jones publishing and financial information company, which also produces the *Wall Street Journal* newspaper. The "Dow" is the average value of 30 significant stocks traded on the New York Stock Exchange. Charles Dow invented the index in 1896. Another index of the United States stock market is the Standard and Poors 500 (S & P 500). There are separate indexes for bonds.

Investing

Question 10. **A bond is a type of investment that:**

a. is issued by a company or government in order to obtain money for various projects and activities

b. is issued for a defined period of time

c. provides a bondholder with regular interest payments in return for loaning money

d. is referred to as a fixed-income security

e. is more risky than a stock

Question 11. **A document representing a loan to the federal government to be repaid with interest on a specified date.**

a. stock

b. mutual fund

c. United States Savings Bond

d. federal debt

e. Treasury bill

345

$100 Investing

Answer 10. a,b,c,d – Bonds. A bond is a loan of money for which you are the lender. This is how it works. A company or government entity issues bonds in order to raise money for various projects and activities. You buy one or more of the bonds in exchange for the issuer's promise to repay your loan at the end of a defined period of time and at a fixed interest rate. Interest is usually paid to bondholders every six months. The interest is your perk for having loaned the money. Individuals, mutual fund companies, government retirement programs and the like all buy bonds.

Bonds are issued for periods ranging from 90 days to 30 years and the date on which the loan must be repaid is called the maturity date. Bonds are referred to as "fixed-income securities," because you know the exact amount of cash you will receive if you hold the bond until maturity. For this reason bonds are considered safer than stocks. Still, there is always some risk involved, because certain borrowers may not be able to repay bond holders.

Answer 11. c – United States Savings Bonds. This is a familiar type of bond – you may already have received one as a gift from a relative. They are to be repaid with interest on a specified date. These bonds have significant tax benefits in that they are exempt from state and local taxes, and the federal government will not tax you until the bond comes due. Also, if you use your bond earnings on college tuition in the same year as the bond comes due, the interest earned may be exempt from federal taxes. Many people find these bonds attractive because, even though they don't earn a lot of interest, they are issued and backed by the federal government. United States Savings Bonds are issued in amounts ranging from $50 to $10,000.

Investing

Question 12. A type of investment that consists of a diverse set of securities purchased with a pool of money received from many small investors:

a. security reserve
b. multiple trust fund
c. mutual fund
d. joint stock reserve
e. cooperative fund

"Picking mutual funds and stocks online is not like gambling. I do extensive research before trading. The odds of profiting are much better."

$100 Investing

Answer 12. **c – Mutual fund** – a grouping of stocks and other securities assembled by a mutual fund company. The company uses money pooled from many small investors to purchase a diverse set of securities. When you invest in a mutual fund, you essentially become a shareholder in a group of investments. Traditional mutual funds have a manager or team of managers who do extensive research and analysis. Fund managers make frequent and conscious decisions about what stocks to buy and sell in an attempt to make money on stocks they think will go up in value. This approach is referred to as *active investing*.

Another type of mutual fund called an *index fund* does *passive investing*. With this type of fund, a decision is made up front about what securities to hold, often those found in a particular bond or stock index such as the Standard and Poors 500 Index of stocks. Then the fund simply tracks the ups and downs of that index. Management fees are low because, unlike traditional mutual funds, there are no managers actively buying and selling stocks. Index funds often outperform more actively managed stocks and mutual funds in the long run.

Mutual funds, including index funds, are a great way for young people to begin investing for several reasons:

- You don't need to know a lot about stocks to start investing.
- You don't need a lot of money to get started.
- You pay low management fees (especially for index funds).
- Your investments are less risky, because they're spread out (diversified) among numerous securities. One company in your mutual fund may fail, but many others will continue to thrive. If you were to put the same amount of money in the stock of a single company, you could lose everything should the company go belly up.

Investing

Question 13. **A place where stocks, bonds and other similar securities are bought and sold:**

a. chamber of commerce
b. capital market
c. stock market or exchange
d. money mart
e. securities store

Question 14. **The fluctuations in the price of a stock or other type of security:**

a. liquidity
b. excitability
c. buoyancy
d. volatility
e. unpredictability

Question 15. **When a stock market moves through wide price changes, it is said to be:**

a. a flat market
b. a bear market
c. a volatile market
d. a bull market
e. a recession

Question 16. **A legal document that provides detailed information about mutual funds, stocks, bonds and other investments offered for sale, as required by the United States Securities and Exchange Commission:**

a. an executive summary
b. a business plan
c. a budget
d. a prospectus
e. a securities summary

Investing

Answer 13. **c – Stock market or exchange** – a place, whether physical or electronic, where stocks, bonds and other securities are bought and sold. Stock markets or exchanges are crucial to: (1) companies seeking money to grow their businesses and (2) investors looking to make money as companies prosper. A stock market or exchange provides a regulated place where companies and stockbrokers/traders (acting on behalf of investors) can meet to transact business.

Most countries have a main exchange; many also have additional smaller, regional exchanges. There are quite a few exchanges in the United States. The New York Stock Exchange, located on Wall Street in New York City, is the largest. The NASDAQ (National Association of Securities Dealers Automated Quotations) was the world's first electronic stock exchange. It is a computerized system that facilitates trading on 5,000 of the more actively traded stocks in the United States. It is traditionally home to many high-tech stocks.

Answer 14. **d – Volatility.** This word refers to the fluctuations in the price of a stock or other type of security. If the price of a stock is prone to large swings in value, it is said to have high volatility.

Answer 15. **c – Volatile market.** When the whole stock market moves through wide price changes (sometimes on a daily basis), the market is said to be highly volatile. If the stock market is volatile, the value of your investments can go up and down very quickly.

Answer 16. **d – Prospectus** – a legal document that provides detailed information about stocks, bonds, mutual funds and other investments offered for sale, as required by the United States Securities and Exchange Commission (SEC).

Investing  $100

Question 17. **As a company becomes more and more successful, the price of its stock is likely to:**

a. remain constant
b. decrease
c. increase

Question 18. **Ways of making money with stocks:**

a. selling stocks for more than you paid for them
b. receiving company dividends
c. cashing in your stocks at a bank

Question 19. **An investment portfolio might include:**

a. stocks
b. bonds
c. mutual funds
d. lottery tickets
e. pawn slips

"Come on up to my apartment. I'll show you my stock portfolio."

$100 Investing

Answer 17. **c - Company success and stock value.** As a company becomes more and more successful, the price of its stock is likely to increase.

Answer 18. **a,b – Dividends and sales.** There are two ways to make money with stocks:

(1) sell a stock at a higher price than what you paid for it. (Put another way, you need to buy low and sell high.)

(2) receive dividends from the company in which you own stock

As a stockholder, you may receive regular dividends (payments) from a company. These payments constitute your portion of the company's earnings. Not all companies pay dividends, however. A rapidly expanding company often pays little or nothing, because most of its earnings are reinvested in the company. On the other hand, a well-established company with solid profits is likely to pay relatively high dividends.

You cannot cash in stocks at a bank.

Answer 19. **a,b,c – Portfolio** – the complete collection of securities (stocks, bonds, mutual funds, etc.) owned by an investor.

The Meaning of Wealth

Today we associate the word "wealth" with an individual's personal riches, namely an abundance of money and worldly goods. However, the original meaning of the word wealth came from the old English word "weal", which equated wealth with the well-being of an entire community.

Investing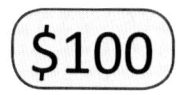

Question 20. **When you sell an investment for more money than you paid for it:**

a. You lose money.
b. You make money.
c. It's a potential tax deduction.
d. You may need to list it as a capital gain on your tax return.
e. You may need to list it as a capital loss on your tax return.

Question 21. **When you sell an investment for less money than you paid for it:**

a. You make money.
b. You lose money.
c. It's a potential tax deduction.
d. You may need to list it as a capital gain on your tax return.
e. You may need to list it as a capital loss on your tax return.

Question 22. **Measure(s) of investment performance:**

a. return
b. yield
c. interest
d. dividend
e. interest income

> ### *Winning the Game of Life*
>
> *You win the game of life by spending most of your days doing what you love to do. In the world of work, it's good if you can find a job you really enjoy. If that's not possible, do what you have to do every day to earn a living, but focus as much as you can on the longer term. This means saving and investing for the future, so you can develop a new career or retire sooner and get on with doing the things you really enjoy.*

Answer 20. **b,d – Capital gains.** If you hold stocks/shares in a successful company, the value of your holdings is likely to increase. If you sell your stocks for more than you paid for them, you make money. These earnings are referred to as capital gains and are taxable.

Answer 21. **b,c,e – Capital losses.** If you hold stocks/shares in a company that is not successful, the value of your holdings will likely decrease. If you sell your stocks for less than you paid for them, you lose money. These losses are referred to as capital losses and may be subtracted from earnings on income taxes.

Answer 22. **a,b – Measures of investment performance.** When you invest your money, you need to know how well your investments have performed or are expected to perform. There are two measures of investment performance that appear frequently – return and yield. Although these terms are often used interchangeably, they are not the same thing.

Return or total return is the full amount that an investment earns during a given evaluation period, including income (dividends on stocks, interest on bonds etc.) as well as capital appreciation (increase in the market price of certain securities). Example: this security earned $300 in the first half of this year.

Yield or annual percentage yield (APY), sometimes called *rate of return,* is the income generated by a security on an annual basis expressed as a percentage of the asset's purchase or market price. By law, the annual rate of return on an investment must be disclosed. The rate depends on the frequency of compounding.

Example 1: A $1,000 investment that earns 6% (compounded yearly) pays $60 at year-end and has an APY of 6%.

Example 2: A $1,000 investment that earns 6% (compounded monthly) pays $61.68 in one year and has an APY of 6.17%.

(See page 157 for an explanation of compund interest.)

Investing — $100

Question 23. **The chance that an investment will lose value:**

a. inconsistency
b. instability
c. variation
d. risk
e. liability

Question 24. **The degree of uncertainty that an investor is willing to accept with regard to a drop in the value of his or her investments:**

a. investor timidity
b. investor risk ratio
c. uncertainty principle
d. risk-aversion index
e. risk tolerance

Question 25. **With low-risk investments:**

a. chances are small that you will lose money.
b. chances are good that you will make a lot of money.
c. chances are, you will make some money but not a lot.
d. chance are, the value of your investment will remain stable.
e. chances are, you will make no money at all.

Question 26. **With high-risk investments:**

a. there's a lot of uncertainty
b. you could make a lot of money
c. you could lose a lot of money
d. their value tends to go up and down
e. you can be confident that your investment will be safe

Investing

Answer 23. **d – Investment risk** – the chance that an investment will lose value. When you buy an investment you are taking a risk. There is a business risk – the potential for the company (and it's stock) to lose value through competition, mismanagement, and financial insolvency (inability to pay debts). There is a valuation risk – although the company may be a great company, if the stock is over-valued at its current sky-high price, there may be little chance of a making a good return on your investment. There is also a liquidity risk – the chance that you might need some cash quickly and be forced to sell your investment at a loss when the stock price is low.

Answer 24. **e – Risk tolerance** – the degree of uncertainty that an investor is willing to accept with regard to a drop in the value of their investments. An investor needs to assess his/her risk tolerance before buying an investment. Risk tolerance varies according to age, personality, income requirements, financial goals, etc. For example, a 70-year-old will generally have a lower risk tolerance than a single 30-year-old who has more time to make up for any losses in the value of his or her stocks.

Answer 25. **a,c,d – Low-risk investments.** With low-risk investments, the chances are small that you will lose what you've invested. On the flip side, you are not likely to make a big return on such investments. It's important to note, however, that with all investments there is some degree of risk. Nothing is ever 100% safe. Low-risk investments tend to maintain a stable value, i.e., they're not volatile.

Answer 26. **a,b,c,d – High-risk investments.** The situation is more complicated and uncertain with high-risk investments. You could make a lot of money, but you could lose a lot, too. High-risk investments are volatile, i.e., they tend to go up and and down in value frequently.

Investing

Question 27. The principle that potential return from investments varies with the degree of risk involved:

a. risk ruler

b. risk ratio

c. risk-return trade-off

d. risk scale

e. risk measure

Question 28. The idea that money available at the present time is typically worth more than the same amount in the future because it has more purchasing power today than it will tomorrow.

a. compound interest

b. simple interest

c. exponential interest

d. time value of money

e. money multiplier

> "You don't need to be an expert in order to achieve satisfactory investment returns... Keep things simple and don't swing for the fences. When promised quick profits, respond with a quick "no."...In aggregate, American business has done wonderfully over time and will continue to do so (though, most assuredly, in unpredictable fits and starts). The goal of the nonprofessional should not be to pick winners – neither he nor his "helpers" can do that – but should rather be to own a cross section of businesses that in aggregate are bound to do well. A low-cost S&P 500 index fund will achieve this goal."
>
> — Warren Buffet

Answer 27. **c – Risk-return trade-off.** "Return" is the money you make from an investment. When you invest money, you need to balance how much risk you're willing to accept with how much return you want to make. Low-risk investments are relatively safe but usually yield low returns. With high-risk investments there's a slim chance of high returns but a greater chance of losing money.

Answer 28. **d – Time value of money.** The value, or purchasing power, of money changes from one moment to the next. It goes up, it goes down.

On the "up" side, money has the capacity to earn more money (grow in value) over time through the magic of interest. If you put $100 in your savings account today at 3% interest/year, you will earn $3 and have a total of $103 in your account by this time next year. If, instead, you wait out a year and don't put any of your paycheck in your savings account, that money will not be "at work" earning more for you. In other words, you will not have taken maximum advantage of your money's earning power and will have missed the opportunity to increase the value of your money over time.

On the "down" side, an opposing force – inflation – usually diminishes the value or purchasing power of your money as time goes by. The way things typically go, a dollar has more purchasing power today than it will next year – $1 will buy five apples this year, but only three apples next year.

So, given how the value of money changes over time, it is wise to save and invest every dollar you can as soon as you can. In this way, you can take advantage of your money's earning power to counteract the inflationary drag on your resources and thereby maintain financial equilibrium (provided, of course, the economy stays relatively steady and doesn't go into hyperinflation). If all goes well, you may be able to continue buying those 5 apples year after year without risking your financial well-being.

Investing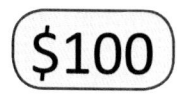

Question 29. **A rough calculation of the time or interest rate needed to double the value of an investment:**

a. double rule
b. rule of 72
c. investment double
d. double value
e. multiplier

Question 30. **How long will it take a sum invested at 8% to double in value?**

a. 5 years
b. 8 years
c. 9 years
d. 10 years
e. more than 10 years

Question 31. What percentage return do you need for an investment to double in value in 12 years?

a. 3%
b. 6%
c. 9%
d. 12%
e. more than 12%

High Returns, Low Risk – A False Promise

In 2009, Spanish bank officials talked 300,000 Spaniards into moving their money from safe savings accounts into a new investment "product". They promised a 7% return at no risk. Then, in the midst of a brutal recession, these people had their life savings virtually wiped out by what critics now call a deceptive and possibly fraudulent sales campaign conducted by the banks.

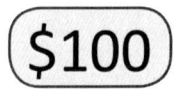

Investing

Answer 29. **b - Rule of 72** – a rough calculation of the time or interest rate needed to double the value of an investment. This is an important concept to understand when you are deciding how to spend and invest your money. Obviously, the sooner you can start investing your money, the more you will accumulate.

Answer 30. **c – Rule of 72: Calculation #1.** To calculate how many years it will take for a sum of money to double, divide 72 by the interest rate.

Example: If you want to know how long it will take to double your money at 8% interest, divide 72 by 8 (answer = 9 years).

Answer 31. **b – Rule of 72: Calculation #2.** To calculate the interest rate required for a sum of money to double in a fixed number of years, divide 72 by the number of years the money is invested.

Example: If you want to know what interest rate is required for a sum of money to double in 12 years, divide 72 by 12 (answer = 6%).

"A few years ago I changed my focus. I decided I wanted to retire at 40, so I started saving and investing 50% of my income."

Investing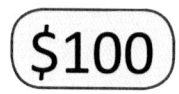

Question 32. **Generally, you should put money in investments only if you can afford to go without the money for several years.**

a. true
b. false

Question 33. **Investing a fixed amount in the same type of investment at regular intervals, regardless of price:**

a. dollar-cost averaging
b. diversification
c. phishing
d. rule of 72
e. day trading

Question 34. **Reducing risk by investing in a variety of investments:**

a. fencing
b. shorting
c. diversification
d. multi-risk investing
e. diffusion

Equity

Equity is the portion of any asset (e.g., a car or house) that you actually own. For example, if you own a car that's worth $5,000 and you still owe $1,000 on it, you have $4,000 of equity in your car. If you own a house that's worth $200,000, but still owe $50,000 on the mortgage, you have $150,000 of home equity. Stocks are equity because they represent ownership in a company.

$100 Investing

Answer 32. **a – Invest for the long term.** You can approach investing in a variety of ways; but because investments tend to gain value over the long term, you will do better if you can keep them working for you for several years. Advisors will tell you to buy investments only if you can afford to do without the money for several years. Investments rise and fall in value in the short term; so if you suddenly need the money, you risk selling at a loss.

Answer 33. **a – Dollar-cost averaging** – investing a fixed amount of money in the same type of investment (e.g., an index fund) at regular intervals, regardless of the share price. This means you will buy more shares when prices are low and fewer shares when prices are high. In the end, the cost per share averages out. This strategy reduces your risk of losing big and often yields greater returns over the long term than trying to predict the ups and downs of the stock market.

Answer 34. **c – Diversification** – putting your money in a variety of investments, thereby reducing your risk of losing big on a single investment. The idea is that when some investments are slipping, others will be doing well.

Social Security

A federal government program that provides retirement income, disability income, Medicare, Medicaid, death and survivorship benefits. It is funded by a tax on income, which appears on workers' pay stubs as a deduction labeled FICA (for Federal Insurance Contributions Act, the enabling legislation). The original program was part of President Franklin D. Roosevelt's New Deal plan to lift the United States out of the Great Depression.

Investing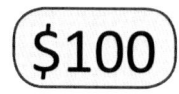

Question 35. **Investment tools that allow individuals to save for retirement on their own without involving an employer:**

a. government pension

b. a traditional IRA

c. defined-benefit company pension

d. a Roth IRA

e. a universal retirement instrument

> ***Retirement: Enough Time to Do Whatever You Want***
>
> *Imagine an endless summer holiday where you don't have to work anymore. Imagine being able to spend as much time as you want doing activities you find enjoyable and meaningful.*
>
> *To achieve this happy status, you will need to build up a substantial retirement "nest egg" that will provide the income you'll need in retirement.*
>
> *As soon as possible, set up an IRA (individual retirement account) and try to contribute as much money as you can every year. This money will be invested and grow in value as the years go by. When it comes time to retire, you'll have all the money you contributed directly to the account over the years plus the enhanced value of the investments in your account.*

***Answer 35.* b,d – Individual Retirement Accounts (IRAs).**
An IRA (Individual Retirement Account) is one of the best ways to accumulate retirement savings. With an IRA, you are investing part of your earnings in a variety of securities that will grow in value over the years. Plus, IRAs offer you various tax advantages. Two common types of IRAs are: a traditional IRA and a Roth IRA.

With a *traditional IRA,* while you work you are allowed to contribute 100% of your income – up to a maximum dollar amount. These contributions, under certain circumstances, are tax-deductible. However, when you retire, any funds you withdraw from your IRA will be treated as taxable income. But because your income in retirement is likely to be lower, your tax rate may also be lower – another tax advantage.

With a *Roth IRA,* you are still setting aside money for retirement, but the taxing conditions are different than with a traditional IRA. In fact, they are just the opposite. With a Roth IRA, you pay taxes up front on your contributions. Later on, your Roth IRA withdrawals will be tax-free. To make a tax-free withdrawal, you must typically wait at least five years after you establish your Roth IRA and be 59.5 years of age. Since distributions from a Roth IRA are always tax free (unless you withdraw early), a Roth IRA may be more to your advantage than a traditional IRA.

Employer-Sponsored Retirement Savings Plans

If you work for a corporation or a government, they may offer tax-deferred retirement savings plans. Maximize your benefits by enrolling in these plans as soon as possible. There are 401(k) plans for corporate employees and Section 457 plans for government employees. Some employers provide matching funds.

Investing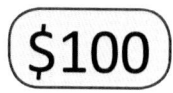

Question 36. **A federal law that attempts to strengthen employees' retirement security by, among other things, allowing employers to automatically enroll employees in retirement savings plans:**

a. Fair Pension Act

b. Pension Protection Act

c. Retirement Benefits Act

d. Pension Security Act

e. Retirement Protection Act

"How'd I make my first million? When I was just a little older than you, I started my own business and regularly invested 20% of my income in a Roth IRA."

 Investing

Answer 36. **b – Pension Protection Act** – a law that attempts to strengthen employees' retirement security by giving employers the right to automatically enroll their employees in a retirement savings plan. Not all employers opt to do this, however, so in such cases, employees should enroll themselves in their employer's pension plan or set up an IRA. Maximizing your contributions to a pension plan is one of the smartest financial moves you can make.

"Yeah, he's my financial advisor. Every time I'm about to do something stupid with my money, he hoots and I forget about it."

Investing — $100

Question 37. **Professionals who provide financial information and advice:**

a. financial planner
b. employee-benefits advisor
c. bank and credit union employee
d. credit counselor
e. accountant

Question 38. **Examples of financial goals:**

a. getting out of debt
b. saving enough money for a college education
c. saving enough money to buy something you really want
d. having money to spend on entertainment
e. having enough savings and investments to retire at a certain age

Question 39. **A measure of a person's financial condition at a given point in time:**

a. net worth
b. balance
c. income statement
d. portfolio
e. net wealth

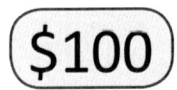

Investing

***Answer 37:* a,b,c,d,e – Financial advisers.** The world of investing is complicated. It's often wise to seek out professionals who can advise you on what steps to take in securing your financial future. People who can help you include: bank and credit union employees, financial planners, accountants, employee-benefit advisors, credit counselors, stockbrokers, insurance agents and attorneys.

***Answer 38.* a,b,c,d,e – Financial goal** – an objective expressed in or based on money. Examples include: getting out of debt; saving enough money for a college education; saving enough money to buy something you really want; having money to spend on entertainment; having enough savings and investments to retire at a certain age.

***Answer 39.* a – Net worth** – a measure of your financial condition or wealth at a given point in time. It is equal to what you own (assets) minus what you owe (liabilities).

"She may not be the next prom queen, but she's way ahead of us in net worth."

Investing

Negative Net Worth

ASSETS		
Home		
Car	3,000	
Jewelry	500	
Furniture	400	
Electronics (e.g., cell phone, TV)	1000	
Stuff you can sell for cash	300	
Cash	200	
Checking account	400	
Savings account	200	
Certificates of deposit		
Retirement account		
Investments (stocks, bonds, funds)		
Total Assets		**$9,000**
LIABILITIES		
Mortgage loan		
Home equity loan		
Car loan	2,000	
Student loan	20,000	
Credit card debt	3,000	
Unpaid bills/debts	1,000	
Taxes owing	250	
Total Liabilities		**$26,250**
Net Worth (total assets minus total liabilities)		**-$17,250**

 Investing

Positive Net Worth

Assets		
Home	200,000	
Car	10,000	
Jewelry	1000	
Furniture	4,000	
Electronics (e.g., cell phone, TV)	2,000	
Stuff you can sell for cash	800	
Cash	500	
Checking account	2,600	
Savings account	200	
Certificates of deposit	6,000	
Retirement account	50,000	
Investments (stocks, bonds, funds)	10,500	
Total Assets		**$287,600**
Liabilities		
Mortgage loan	100,000	
Home equity loan	5,000	
Car loan	6,000	
Student loan	10,000	
Credit card debt	1,000	
Unpaid bills/debts	1,500	
Taxes owing	500	
Total Liabilities		**$124,000**
Net Worth (total assets minus total liabilities)		**$163,600**

Investing

***Question 40.* A personal financial plan should account for:**

a. your needs and wants

b. your current financial health

c. net worth

d. your goals for the future

e. strategies for reaching your goals

Net Worth

Your net worth is calculated by subtracting all of your liabilities (what you owe) from your total assets (what you own). If your assets exceed your liabilities, you have a positive net worth. If your liabilities are greater than your assets, then you have a negative net worth.

Your net worth is a time-specific measure of how your financial "ship" is faring. It could be sinking fast, barely staying afloat, or sailing along with ease. You can improve your net worth by increasing your assets, reducing your liabilities, or a combination of the two.

Your net worth will vary a lot over your lifetime, responding to changes in your income, spending habits, personal circumstances and the state of the economy. It is a good idea to calculate your net worth on a regular basis. This not only gives you a picture of where you stand financially at a given point in time, but also allows you to see trends in your financial situation over the longer term.

To be financially secure when you retire, your net worth should continue to grow throughout your working life.

Investing

Answer 40. **a,b,c,d,e – Personal Financial Plan.** It's almost impossible to achieve big goals without a plan. This is particularly true when it comes to your finances. Your personal financial plan is a document that accounts for all critical areas of your financial life. It requires you to:

- think through what you really need and want in your life
- evaluate your current financial health, including your net worth
- set specific, achievable goals for where you want to be in the future
- develop strategies for reaching your goals, including how you will earn, save and invest your money and how you will manage debt and protect yourself financially with insurance
- implement and revise your plan as needed

Simple Money Management Rules

1. *Save, invest.*
2. *Pay for your needs.*
3. *Share some.*
4. *Have fun with the rest!*

Taxes

Taxes

"Mom says that our economic future depends on the taxes that she and Dad pay for schools."

> Nobody likes to pay taxes. But taxes are how we pay for public education, police, roads, clean water, national defense, Medicare for the elderly and Medicaid for the poor.

Taxes

Question 41. **Income taxes are collected by:**

a. the federal government
b. colleges and universities
c. state governments
d. some local governments
e. corporations

Question 42. **The official body of United States tax laws and regulations:**

a. United States Tax Law
b. United States Tax Regulations
c. United States Taxidermy Law
d. United States Tax Code
e. United States Tax Book

Question 43. **The agency that collects income taxes in the United States:**

a. Treasury
b. National Bank
c. Federal Reserve
d. Taxonomy Agency
e. Internal Revenue Service (IRS)

Question 44. **A tax that takes a larger percentage of income from high-income earners than from low-income earners:**

a. proportional tax
b. adequate means tax
c. proportional tax
d. progressive tax
e. regressive tax

Taxes

***Answer 41. a,c,d* – Income taxes.** Every year, if you earn more than a given amount of money (set by the federal government), you are required to pay income taxes to the United States government. Most states and some local governments collect income taxes as well. As everyone knows, the Boston Tea Party – a protest against Britain's unfair taxation of American colonists – was one of the first acts of rebellion that led to the formation of the United States. To this day, we all feel a bit like protesting at tax time; but without tax revenues, our government couldn't do the many things it does to help sustain our quality of life.

***Answer 42. d* – Tax code** – the official body of United States tax laws and regulations.

***Answer 43. e* – Internal Revenue Service (IRS)** – the agency that collects income taxes in the United States. The United States Social Security Administration also collects taxes on people's incomes.

***Answer 44. d* – Progressive income tax** – a tax that takes a larger percentage of income from high-income earners than from low-income earners.

"I believe in a progressive tax system. It seems only fair that those who have more should pay more. But I'm biased. I'm one of those who has less."

Taxes $100

Question 45. **Earned income consists of:**

a. royalty payments
b. salaries
c. lottery winnings
d. sales commissions
e. tips

Question 46. **Cash income is not taxable.**

a. true
b. false

Question 47. **Tip income is not taxable.**

a. true
b. false

Question 48. **Unearned income consists of:**

a. stock dividends
b. interest from investments and bank accounts
c. birthday presents
d. rental income
e. gambling winnings

Question 49. **All the taxable income you have received in a given year is referred to as:**

a. gross pay
b. gross income
c. total compensation
d. sum of benefits received
e. total earnings

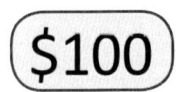

Taxes

Answer 45. b,d,e – **Earned income** – salaries, wages, sales commissions, tips. This is money you actually worked to acquire.

Answer 46. **b – Cash income is taxable.** In most cases, cash income (actual "greenbacks" and coins) is taxable under the requirements of the United States Tax Code. Failing to report cash income on your tax return is considered a crime. Those who do so run the risk of being audited, charged civil penalties or even subjected to criminal prosecution.

Answer 47. **b – Tips are taxable.** Tips include money and goods received for services performed by food servers, baggage handlers, hairdressers and others. Tips go beyond the stated amount of a bill and are given voluntarily. Tips are taxable and must be declared on your income tax return.

Answer 48. **a,b,d,e – Unearned income.** So-called "unearned" income is money you didn't work for, instead your money worked for you. It includes stock dividends and interest received on various types of securities (e.g., bonds) as well as interest received from certain bank accounts. It also includes rental income and royalty payments that the owner of intellectual property (such as patents and copyrighted books) receives from someone who uses this property. Gambling and lottery winnings are considered to be unearned income as well.

Answer 49. **b,e – Gross Income** – the total of all the income you received in a given year. It is the starting point for calculating your annual taxes. Income may be in the form of money, goods, property or services received. Social Security payments, unemployment compensation and certain scholarship funds are considered to be income. Welfare benefits are not. Amazingly, proceeds from criminal activities are considered to be income and are taxable. Failure to report this ill-gotten income on a tax return is a crime in itself!

Taxes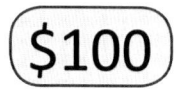

Question 50. **Expense(s) that a taxpayer can deduct from gross income to determine taxable income:**

a. home mortgage interest
b. charitable gifts
c. gambling losses
d. repair or replacement costs resulting from disaster damage
e. car expenses (when a car is used for business purposes)

Question 51. **Earnings, such as interest from municipal bonds, that are not considered part of your income:**

a. tax suspensions
b. tax credits
c. tax exemptions
d. tax deferrals
e. tax deductions

Question 52. **An amount that a taxpayer can subtract from what they would otherwise owe in tax payments to the government:**

a. tax deferral
b. tax credit
c. tax exemption
d. tax deduction
e. tax refund

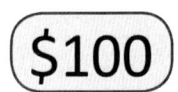 Taxes

Answer 50. **a,b,d,e – Taxable income and deductions.** Taxable income is determined by subtracting certain expenses (referred to as "deductions") from your gross income. Examples of deductions: home mortgage interest, contributions to charities, car expenses when you drive your vehicle for business, charitable or medical purposes and repair or replacement costs resulting from disaster damage.

Example: $50,000 (Gross Income) - $2,000 (Deductions, e.g., mortgage interest) = $48,000 (Taxable Income).

Answer 51. **c – Tax exemptions** – earnings, such as interest from municipal bonds, that are tax exempt and therefore not counted as part of one's gross income. Certain entities, such as schools and religious organizations, are also classified as tax exempt, which means they are not required to pay taxes to the government.

Example: $50,000 (Gross Income) - $2,000 (Exemptions, e.g., municipal bond interest) = $48,000 (Taxable Income).

Answer 52. **b – Tax credit** – an amount that a taxpayer is able to subtract from what they would otherwise owe the government. Unlike deductions and exemptions, which reduce the amount of your taxable income, tax credits reduce the actual amount of tax owed. Governments grant tax credits for a variety of things: fuel-efficient cars, new energy-efficient appliances, housing costs (low income taxpayers) and certain postsecondary school expenses.

To illustrate, suppose your taxable income is $50,000 and you have $10,000 in deductions. This reduces your taxable income to $40,000. on which you owe $8,000 in taxes. If you have a $7,500 credit for buying a fuel-efficient car, you can subtract that amount directly from the tax you owe ($8000), thus reducing your tax bill to $500.

Taxes 

Question 53. **An investment plan designed to encourage saving for the future higher education expenses of a designated beneficiary (typically one's child or grandchild):**

a. 401K Plan
b. 529 Plan
c. IRA Plan
d. Roth IRA Plan
e. education security plan

Question 54. **A feature of certain investments in which taxes due on proceeds (principal and/or earnings) are postponed until a later date when funds are withdrawn, often at retirement:**

a. tax deferral
b. tax abatement
c. tax relief
d. tax postponement
e. tax holiday

"Gee, if I'd only known I could use all those tax deductions, exemptions and credits to get a big cash refund, I'd have started filing returns years ago."

 Taxes

***Answer 53.* b – Tax-advantaged 529 college savings plan.** A "529" college savings plan is an investment plan designed to encourage saving for the future higher education expenses of a designated beneficiary (typically one's child or grandchild). The plans are named after Section 529 of the United States Tax Code and are administered by state agencies and organizations. Money contributed to such plans is invested and grows as the years go by. The main advantage of a 529 plan is that when money is withdrawn for the beneficiary's education expenses it is tax exempt. You cannot deduct contributions to 529 plans from your federal income taxes, but depending on where you live, you may be able to deduct them from your state taxes.

***Answer 54.* a – Tax deferral** – a feature of certain investments (e.g., IRAs) in which taxes due on proceeds (principal and/or earnings) are postponed until a later date when funds are withdrawn, often at retirement.

"Many thanks to my parents and their 529 college savings plan. It made this amazing day possible – graduating debt-free!"

Taxes

Question 55. The term "withholding" refers to:

a. tax refunds withheld by government
b. money taxpayers withold from the government
c. money employers withold from the government
d. money employers withhold from employee paychecks to be passed on directly to the government
e. money employers withhold from vendors

Question 56. Employers may deduct money from an employee's paycheck for reasons other than annual tax payments, including:

a. garnishment of wages by court order to pay for debts
b. automatic loan payments
c. political party dues
d. automatic charitable contributions
e. direct deposits into various types of bank accounts and savings programs

Question 57. Income retained after taxes have been subtracted:

a. total income
b. reduced income
c. free-and-clear income
d. net income
e. take-home pay

> "Taxes, after all, are dues that we pay for the privileges of membership in an organized society."
> — Franklin D. Roosevelt

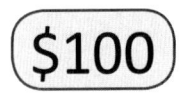

Taxes

Answer 55. **d – Withholding and other tax withdrawals.**
Throughout the year, employers withhold a portion of an employee's tax liability from his/her paychecks and pass on these funds directly to governments (federal, state, local). Such withdrawals are credited against (will reduce) an employee's income tax liability when he/she files a tax return.

Employers also collect money from employees that goes towards financing specific government programs, such as Medicare and Social Security (retirement, survivor and disability benefits). These are referred to as compulsory payroll taxes and are shown on an employee's pay stub as FICA withdrawals (Federal Insurance Contributions Act).

Answer 56. **a,b,d,e – Other types of payroll deductions.**
Employers may deduct additional money from an employee's paycheck for reasons other than annual tax payments.

Some deductions are mandatory. For instance, when an employee has fallen into debt, a court may order that a portion of his or her wages be withdrawn to pay back creditors (garnishment).

Some deductions are voluntary. Employees can ask their employer to automatically remove money for loan payments, charitable contributions and direct deposits into various types of bank accounts and savings programs.

Answer 57. **d,e – Net income** – income retained after taxes have been subtracted; sometimes referred to as take-home pay.

Taxes

Question 58. **Your income tax forms can be filed:**

a. electronically
b. whenever you want
c. on paper
d. with an IOU enclosed
e. after the deadline without penalty

Question 59. **Failing to pay or deliberately underpaying taxes due will result in:**

a. going to court
b. loss of bank accounts and property
c. financial penalties for tax evasion
d. bankruptcy
e. going to debtor's prison

Question 60. **Money the government returns to taxpayers when they have paid more taxes than they owe:**

a. profit
b. refund
c. return
d. yield
e. bonus

Transfer Payment

These are governments payments to certain citizens for which nothing is expected in return. Money is given out under various social welfare programs in the form of veterans' benefits, disability pensions, unemployment compensation, Medicaid benefits, food stamps, housing and child care assistance and more.

$100 Taxes

***Answer 58.* a,c – Filing a return.** The IRS and your state tax agency provide income tax forms that ask in step-by-step fashion for information on your income and guide you in calculating what you will owe. These forms must be completed and returned along with your payment (if your calculations reveal that you owe money) by the tax deadline. Late payment will result in penalties being charged (unless you formally request an extension of time). Nowadays, you can file your tax returns electronically or the old-fashioned way by mailing them to the IRS and your state tax agency.

***Answer 59.* c – Tax evasion** – failing to pay or deliberately underpaying taxes due. This can result in serious financial penalties.

***Answer 60.* b – Refund** – money the government returns to taxpayers when they have paid more taxes than they owe.

Taxes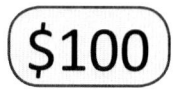

Question 61. **Taxes on real estate, as well as on boats, automobiles, recreational vehicles and business inventories:**

a. asset taxes

b. luxury taxes

c. property taxes

d. possession taxes

e. ownership taxes

Question 62. **A tax on retail products based on a set percentage of retail cost:**

a. consumption tax

b. goods and services tax

c. materials tax

d. corporation tax

e. sales tax

Question 63. **It is important to keep basic financial information, including:**

a. paycheck stubs

b. statements of interest or dividends earned on investments

c. rental income receipts

d. copies of tax returns

e. credit card statements

> "Our new Constitution is now established, and has an appearance that promises permanency; but in this world nothing can be said to be certain, except death and taxes."
> — Benjamin Franklin, 1789

Taxes

Answer 61. c – **Property taxes** – taxes you pay on property, especially real estate, but also on boats, automobiles (often paid along with license fees), recreational vehicles and business inventories.

Answer 62. e – **Sales tax** – taxes you pay on retail products based on a set percentage of retail cost.

Answer 63. a,b,c,d,e – **Recordkeeping.** It is very important to keep an orderly account of your financial affairs. Otherwise you could miss paying important bills, incur tax penalties and suffer a variety of other financial misfortunes. For tax purposes, you need to keep information pertaining to your income, such as paycheck stubs and tax returns. Also retain records of your expenditures, including your check register. Legal documents – loan agreements, house deeds and the like – should be kept safely stored, as well.

Except for certain legal documents, you don't have to keep all this paper forever. As far as taxes are concerned, the general advice is to keep your information 3 to 5 years from the date of submission in case the government wants to review it in connection with one of your tax returns.

> ### Records to Keep
>
> **Income Information for Tax Purposes:** *paycheck stubs, records of sales commissions and tips, statements of interest or dividends earned on investments, rental-income receipts, tax returns (3-5 years)*
>
> **Expenditures:** *check register, purchase receipts (especially for large items), receipts from service providers (doctors, accountants…), credit card statements*
>
> **Legal Documents:** *loan agreements, insurance policies, house deeds, wills, and power-of-attorney documents*

Money Tips For Teens

It pays in so many ways to start learning about money as a young person. When you know how to avoid common financial pitfalls and how to make your money work for you, you'll have more control over your life as it unfolds. And along the way, you'll be happier and better able to do what you really enjoy.

Reading this book is only the beginning of learning how to steer your financial ship. Throughout your life, you will need to seek out new ideas on how best to manage your money. The financial world we live in keeps evolving, so it's very important that you stay informed about the latest developments.

LEARN ABOUT MONEY

Take advantage of various ways to learn about money. You can: take classes your school may offer; read books, magazines, newspapers, web sites and blogs; watch YouTube videos, TV programs; listen to podcasts and radio programs; engage in money discussions with family and friends; and maybe even find a money mentor.

START EARNING MONEY

(Review Employment and Income and Business chapters.)

Earn your own money – don't rely on handouts. When you work for your money, you learn how many hours and how much effort goes into earning a certain amount. Then when you make a purchase with your hard-earned money, you value the purchase more. Plus, when you earn your own money, you have more freedom to do and buy what you want.

Earn money doing household and neighborhood chores. There's always something that needs to be done - washing windows, mowing lawns, taking care of pets, babysitting…

Use free time to develop job skills and experience. This can improve your chances of landing a job. For example, if you like sports, you could take a lifeguard course that might enable you to land a summer job as a lifeguard at a neighborhood swimming pool. This is a very responsible job that would enhance your resume.

Get a part-time or summer job at a local business. Having a job is a good way to earn and learn about managing money. (Just don't let your job interfere with your school work.) Be aware that your salary and tips may be subject to state and federal taxes if you earn more than a certain limit.

Try to avoid getting stuck in a boring, dead-end job. Some jobs offer no learning opportunities or other rewards. If you find yourself in this situation, start looking for another job that will give you more chances to learn new skills, earn more pay and perhaps have more fun, as well.

Start your own small business. Look for a need in your community, develop a product or service to meet the need and start marketing it. Earmuffs and popsicles were invented by kids. Check the Internet for more examples of practical kid inventions.

Maintain a work-play balance. Always take some time out from work to have fun.

KEEP YOUR MONEY SAFE
(Review Banking chapter.)

Open a bank account. Look for a bank (or credit union) that is FDIC-insured and offers the services you want for reasonable fees. Many banks offer accounts geared to teens and students that require less money to open and charge lower fees. Get a checkbook and a debit card for your account.

Prepaid cards are not a good alternative to having a bank account. They have many fees and don't provide the range of services that bank accounts do. (See Prepaid Cards chapter.)

Put money in a savings account. Your money will be safe and earn a bit of interest as well.

SAVE MONEY FOR "RAINY DAYS"
(Review Saving and Risk chapters.)

Save for emergencies. Put some money in a savings account for "rainy days" when you'll need extra money to pay for financial emergencies, such as a computer replacement or car repairs.

Save in case of job loss. If you're working and living on your own, it's wise to put some money in a savings account (ideally six month's worth of income) to cover expenses should you lose your job.

DEVELOP DREAMS AND GOALS
(Review Saving and Investing chapters.)

Dream about the future. Go for it! Dream big. What would you really love to do? What things would give you the biggest thrill and the most satisfaction?

Develop a plan. To realize your dreams, you must have a plan with specific, interim goals that you will need to achieve along the way. Write down these goals along with an estimate of the time and expense associated with achieving each one.

Create goals with different time spans. Create short-term goals (achievable in under a year, e.g., buying tech toys, clothes; going on a short trip); mid-term goals (achievable in 1-5 years, e.g., buying a car); and long-term goals (achievable in 5+ years, e.g., getting a college degree). It's smart to do this, because you won't be overwhelmed by trying to accomplish everything at once.

Plus, you'll have a sense of accomplishment every time you achieve a goal. The positive feelings you get from one success will give you energy to take on your next challenge.

SAVE MONEY FOR DREAMS AND GOALS
(Review Saving chapter.)

Pay yourself first and save regularly. It's smart to start saving as soon as you can. Even before paying for necessities, make a habit of putting 10-20% of your earnings in a savings and/or investment account. You are less likely to spend this money on nonessentials if it is safely stashed away. Some banks allow you to create subaccounts within your savings account that are tailored to different goals (e.g., emergencies, car, college, travel, entertainment, etc.)

Put your savings on autopilot. When you have a job, ask your employer to deposit part of every paycheck directly into your savings account.

Ask your parents/grandparents to match your savings. Your relatives may be willing to match a percentage of your savings in order to encourage you to develop good saving habits.

Save money by minimizing fees. Avoid overdraft fees on your bank account. When you have to pay an overdraft fee, you've lost money that could have gone into your savings account. Also, to minimize ATM fees, use ATMs associated with your bank account which charge low fees or none at all. And watch out for fees on various money card transactions.

> *"Twenty years from now you will be more disappointed by the things that you didn't do than by the ones you did do. So throw off the bowlines. Sail away from the safe harbor. Catch the trade winds in your sails. Explore. Dream. Discover."*
>
> — Mark Twain

BE A SMART SPENDER
(Review the Smart Spending, Loans and Debt chapters.)

Distinguish between needs and wants. You may want to buy something right now, but ask yourself: "Do I really need this?" Be sure you spend your money on needs before wants.

Don't give in to peer pressure. Your friends may urge you to buy stuff you don't need or even want. Ignore nudges who encourage you to do this.

Resist the impulse to buy. A TV commercial, sale sign or product display may tempt you to buy something you don't need. Resist the urge to buy.

Save your money for later. Before making a purchase, consider whether you might do better saving your money for something you may need or want later.

Can you afford this purchase? It's not enough to have decided that you really need something. You also must determine whether you have enough money to buy it right now. If not, keep saving until you can pay the full price comfortably.

Take time to think about a big purchase. Do research. Comparison shop for price, quality, features and warranty. Wait for sales.

Don't borrow money unless absolutely necessary. If you must borrow money, shop around for the lowest interest rate on a loan. Look for low-interest loans at credit unions and banks. Avoid high-interest loans – payday loans, rent-to-own arrangements, car title loans and pawnshop loans.

Charge only what you can pay back. You may experience a rare emergency and need to charge a large amount to your credit card. But as a rule, you shouldn't charge any more than you will be able to pay back completely when your next bill arrives. Always keep tabs on what you still owe on your credit card.

DEVELOP A THRIFTY LIFESTYLE
(Review Saving chapter.)

The more frugal your lifestyle, the more money you will be able to to set aside for college, a small business startup, retirement savings and other truly meaningful things.

Cut expenses wherever possible. Believe it or not, most millionaires are very frugal. They are vigilant about their expenditures; they try to live simply and avoid waste as much as possible. (If you don't believe this, read *The Millionaire Next Door* by Thomas J. Stanley and William D. Danko.)

So, pay attention to the small amounts of money you spend, that over time, can add up. For example, keep snack purchases to a minimum. Drink tap water and carry your own water bottle when away from home instead of buying soda or bottled water.

Be a frugal shopper. Thrift stores, flea markets and the Internet are great places to find inexpensive secondhand books, DVDs and all kinds of things you may need or want.

Learn how to cook. A good home-cooked meal is usually cheaper, tastier and healthier than food purchased from a fast-food joint, restaurant or the deli counter at a grocery store.

Live at home. If your parents are agreeable, live at home for a while after you start working. This will allow you to save money and cut living expenses even while you pay rent to your parents. (Of course, this doesn't mean you should go out and blow the money you've saved on frivolous things.)

Share living expenses with friends. Share an apartment with your friends. Share rides.

Delay getting married and having kids. Raising a family is very expensive these days, so it's a good idea to wait until you have completed your formal education and are earning a good salary.

BE A GOOD MONEY MANAGER
(Review Expenses, Bills and Budgets chapter.)

Think of a budget as a cool tool. It will help you save for things you might think of as beyond your reach (e.g., a tech toy, a clothing item, a car, a trip, a college degree, etc.).

Use electronic and online money management tools. You can do almost all your banking and bill paying online. There are many digital money management tools available for your PC, tablet and smartphone that can help you keep track of your money and your budget. But be careful. Don't do online banking when you're in public places like libraries and cafes.

For many young people, the first time they're really living on their own is when they go off to college. Here are some websites that can help you with budgeting personal and living expenses:

- tinyurl.com/lkfdmrm
- tinyurl.com/moyatly
- collegescholarships.org/student-living/save-money.htm
- collegetips.com/college-money/save-money-college.php
- collegeanswer.com/manage-your-money/

Create a budget. Include the amount of income you expect to receive during a given time period (e.g., a month or a year) and how much you expect to spend during that period. It won't be an exact picture of the future, but it will serve as starting point for managing your money. The more often you create a budget, the more skilled you will become at managing your money and planning for your financial future.

Track your income and expenses. This will allow you to see how closely you are adhering to your budget and whether you are keeping your head above water financially. You need to make sure your expenses are less than your income. If you find that more money is going out than coming in, it's time to increase your income, decrease your expenses, or both. Otherwise, you could start sliding into a debt trap.

Go paperless. You'll be better organized, and it'll be good for the environment. Sign up for electronic delivery of bills and financial statements. Use note-taking apps on phones, tablets and PCs. Use DMAchoice and the National Do Not Mail List to help you get rid of unsolicited commercial mail.

USE MONEY CARDS WITH CAUTION
(Review Prepaid Cards, Credit and Credit Cards chapters.)

Learn about the pros and cons of different cards. There are many different types of cards – debit (bank) cards, credit cards, gift cards and prepaid debit cards. Each has its own particular set of terms, conditions and fees and some are more advantageous for consumers than others.

Watch for hidden tricks. Read the fine print on card agreements.

Don't start using credit cards if you're not ready. If money tends to "burn a hole in your pocket," it's best not to own a credit card. Credit cards make it too easy to spend more money than you should, which leads to escalating fees and interest charges that can drag you into serious debt.

BUILD A GOOD CREDIT SCORE
(Review Credit chapters.)

Build the best credit history and credit score you can. Your credit history is a report that contains a lot of information about your finances and your ability to repay money you have borrowed. Your credit score is an actual number that expresses your creditworthiness based on your history of repaying debts. Credit scores are often referred to as FICO (Fair Isaac and Company) scores. A good credit history and credit score will serve you well when dealing with potential lenders, employers, landlords and service providers.

Pay on time and in full. Pay your credit card bills and loan installments on time. Try to pay your full credit card bill (or most of it) every month. Never pay only the minimum amount!

Check your credit report and credit score. Get a free copy of your credit report at least once a year at annualcreditreport.com. Review it for errors. Check your credit score at myfico.com.

GUARD AGAINST FRAUD AND IDENTITY THEFT
(Review Fraud chapter.)

Don't share your personal information. Only share your personal information with a professional whom you trust**.** Don't share personal information (e.g., passwords) with friends or strangers via email, text messaging or on the phone. Don't post personal information on social networking sites or unsecured websites. Don't leave papers with personal information lying around. If you don't need these documents, shred them. Losing your identity to a thief is one of the most unsettling things that can happen to you.

Protect your computer. Install the latest software updates on your personal computer, including antivirus software, antispyware and a firewall. Use "do not track" privacy settings on your PC browser. Block spam email. Beware of email/text messages asking you to click on links; these can be scams that thieves use to install "malware" on your computer and gain access to your bank account. Use Internet passwords that would be difficult to guess. Purchase things only from secure websites, that begin with "https" (note the "s" at the end).

Keep track of checkbooks and money cards. Contact your bank or credit card provider immediately to report a lost or stolen credit card, debit card or checkbook. The credit card provider or bank will then freeze your accounts so you won't be liable for unauthorized transactions.

Monitor activity in your credit card and bank accounts. Regularly monitor transaction records and review credit card bills and bank statements as soon as you receive them, so you can report any suspicious activity promptly. It's up to you to spot fraudulent charges or incorrect fees attributed to your credit and bank accounts.

Watch out for scams. Don't fall for offers that seem too good to be true. Look for tricks and traps embedded in the fine print of loan and credit card agreements. If you don't understand the fine print, find someone who does.

MINIMIZE RISK
(Review Risk, Insurance and Gambling chapters.)

Stay healthy physically and financially. Get enough sleep, eat right, maintain a healthy weight, move and keep fit. These things don't need to be burdensome; they should be a natural and enjoyable part of your everyday life. In maintaining your physical health, you will also be maintaining your financial health. Health problems can lead to expensive health care costs, job loss and even bankruptcy.

Don't take dangerous physical risks. Activities such as extreme sports can result in pain, injury or even death. Always wear safety gear – seatbelts, helmets, life jackets.

Make sure you have health insurance. Having no health insurance is a much greater financial risk than almost anything else. If your parents have health insurance, you may be eligible for coverage under their plan until age 26.

Buy insurance. Make sure you have adequate insurance for your car and belongings.

Don't indulge in gambling. If you feel compelled to gamble, you may be addicted. Don't wait. Seek the help of people who understand your problem. Call a gambling helpline or visit gamblersanonymous.org. There is no shame in admitting you have an addiction. You are not alone. Many people have struggled with, but then overcome, these problems.

DEVELOP YOUR HUMAN CAPITAL
(Review: Loan chapter.)

Your long-term financial security is highly dependent on your human capital – the education, skills, knowledge, and experience you possess that employers value in today's global economy.

Get your high school diploma and go on for a postsecondary school degree. A college graduate earns about 70% more than a worker who has only a high school diploma.

Arrange for a "529" college savings or prepaid tuition plan. Ask your parents or grandparents to consider setting up one of these plans with you as the designated beneficiary.

Pursue your interests and develop your talents. While still in high school pay close attention to what really interests you and where your talents lie. Getting to know yourself in this way is an important step in identifying a future career.

Study your post-high school options in depth. Trying to choose your next step after high school can seem daunting – there are so many possibilities. Take your time. Talk to people about careers and the training needed to pursue them. Take advantage of the many information resources available online and in libraries. Visit colleges. Don't decide to go to "Ivy Hall College" just because your friend's brother went there. Look for a college or school that suits your own particular needs. Otherwise, you risk borrowing money for an expensive degree that doesn't open the door to what you really want to do. This would be a very poor investment!

Compare college costs. Look for information about costs on college and United States government websites. Visit the federal student aid website – studentaid.ed.gov.

Consider low-cost options. There are many options, including state schools, 2-year community college programs and trade courses. You may be able to start at a low-cost school, then transfer somewhere more expensive in your junior year, if this fits with your educational plan.

Take a year off. If you can't decide how to continue your education, take a year off. Find a job or internship in a field that interests you. Then review your education options again and decide what to do. Don't wait too long, though; it becomes harder and harder to resume a study routine the longer you're away from school. (An emerging trend is for colleges to offer support to new students for "gap years". Check this out with the American Gap Association at http://www.americangap.org/.)

THINK BEFORE BUYING A CAR
(Review Loans and Debt chapters.)

Consider alternatives to buying a car. Don't buy a car unless it's absolutely necessary. Ask yourself if you can meet your transportation needs by walking, biking, sharing rides with friends or using public transit. If you need a car only occasionally, rent one.

Be aware of all the costs of car ownership. Over and above the purchase price, a car is expensive to own and drive. You may have loan installments to pay. There's gas, regular maintenance, insurance and an auto club membership for emergency roadside assistance if your car breaks down or won't start.

Can you afford to take out a car loan? If you have to borrow money to buy a car, determine whether you can afford the loan. Do you have the funds for a down payment? Can you keep up with the monthly loan payments (which include interest charges)? Shop around for the best loan with the lowest interest rate. Compare APRs (annual percentage rates).

Finance your car purchase with savings. Instead of borrowing money to buy a car, try paying for it the old-fashioned way, i.e., with savings. Make regular deposits in a car fund until you have saved up enough money to pay the full cost of a reliable used car. After buying a car, keep making payments into your car fund so you'll have money available to make repairs or buy the next car.

Shop around for car insurance. Whether you own, lease or rent a car, you need to buy auto insurance. As costs vary, compare what different insurance companies would charge. You can reduce the cost of insurance by taking a driver training course and/or buying a used car.

DEVELOP A RETIREMENT PLAN
(Review Investing chapter.)

If you want a comfortable and secure lifestyle in your senior years, you need to start planning for retirement when you're young. There's a lot of economic uncertainty these days. You will probably need to save more money for your later years than your parents or grandparents did. Also, you may need to work for more years than they did before you can comfortably retire. Time will go by a lot faster than you think. The longer you wait to start saving and investing, the harder it will be for you to build up enough funds to pursue your retirement dreams.

Start saving and investing as soon as you earn money. In addition to putting money in a savings account for rainy days, set up automatic contributions to a retirement savings plan (e.g., a Roth IRA). Invest money in low-expense-ratio index funds. Then you can actually enjoy the excitement of watching the stock market go up and down, knowing that, over the long term, your investment will grow in value.

Pay attention to new avenues of endeavor. By the time you reach 60, or even earlier, you may have had enough of your chosen career. It's good to dream about what you might like to pursue next – ideally something you will find exciting and emotionally satisfying, whether it earns you money or not.

> *"I learned a deep respect for one of Goethe's couplets: Whatever you can do, or dream you can do, begin it. Boldness has genius, power, and magic in it!"*
>
> — W.H. Murray (Scottish mountaineer and author)

GIVE BACK TO YOUR COMMUNITY

People who give generously of their time and money receive tremendous amounts of satisfaction in return and have a better appreciation of how fortunate they really are.

Volunteer your time and energy to help other people. There are many things you can do to make a difference. You could participate in a long-distance run to help raise money for a good cause, tutor disadvantaged children, or offer to do chores for an ill or elderly neighbor. You could accompany your parents or other family members when they volunteer at a community event.

Donate money to charities. Set aside part of your allowance or gift money for a charity you admire. Every little bit helps.

Donate used goods. Don't throw away things that are still in good condition. Someone else could use and enjoy your old computer or video game. Take the time to deliver such things to a nonprofit organization that collects goods for people in need. If you are making enough money to pay taxes, the value of your donations can be subtracted from your tax liability.

Money Tips For Parents

"I already know about the birds and the bees.
Now tell me about money cards and fees."

Almost all of us wish we'd had more "money smarts" at an earlier age. If we'd been better equipped with sound information about money, positive attitudes and good habits, we could have avoided a lot of problems and perhaps been better off today. In most cases, it wasn't that we didn't listen to our parents; it's just that they didn't know much about money either. Plus, the topic of money brings up all kinds of emotions, and for this reason, adults often have trouble discussing money with each other, much less with their kids. But given the complex financial world we live in today, it's imperative that we overcome our discomfort and start discussing money openly.

A LEGACY WORTH MILLIONS

You don't have to be a financial whiz to teach your kids about money. The lessons of your own life – what has shaped your personal approach to finances – are a great starting point. Then, to augment what you already know, consult this book and other resources – you'll find a lot of help is available.

Even if you don't expect to be able to leave your kids or grandkids a big inheritance, you can still impart the legacy of money smarts. You can give them the wherewithal to avoid common financial mistakes and set them on the road to saving and investing at an early age.

With the knowledge you pass on, your kids will certainly be happier and might even become wealthy as well. Without such a legacy, even the young beneficiary of a large inheritance could quickly squander, gamble or fritter away a fortune.

PROMOTE HEALTHY ATTITUDES AND VALUES

As a parent, you are the primary money mentor to your kids and you have a critical role to play in passing on healthy attitudes and values.

Spend time with your kids. You've heard it before – the most valuable thing you can give your kids is your time. All the expensive toys in the world won't add up to anything compared to the quality time you spend with your kids.

Reduce stress about money. Speak freely and frequently about family finances. Kids pick up on your vibes, so it's important that you become comfortable yourself with the matter of money. (If you don't have a financial advisor, you may want to find one to help you with this.) Be open about your own financial situation, the mistakes you've made and what you've learned from them. Find ways to have fun with your kids when you talk about money (see the Money Life$aver Quiz Games chapter in this book). By doing these things, you will help your kids develop a sense of ease around the topic.

Be aware of your actions. Your children learn by watching you. It's critical for you to set an example worth emulating. If you're telling your teens about the importance of saving, be sure they know what you're doing to save money.

Dispel the notion that money is inherently bad or evil. Help your kids understand that money is simply a tool. It can be used for bad purposes, of course, but also for many good purposes.

Sell education as one of the best uses of money. A good education helps us to fully develop our talents and enables us to live our lives free of serious financial worries.

Share your good fortune with others. Generosity may or may not come naturally to your kids; but when they see you volunteering your time or donating money, they may be more inclined to follow your example. Invite your kids to share in your community activities and encourage them to volunteer and donate to their favorite causes.

INTRODUCE THE MECHANICS OF MONEY
(Review Expenses, Bills and Budgets chapter.)

Use day-to-day activities as teachable moments. Kids learn best from observation, interaction and practice. Grocery shopping is an excellent teaching opportunity. Engage your kids in creating a shopping list. At the store, have them compare costs and use a calculator to total the cost of all your selected items. Afterwards, have them review the receipt for accuracy. When they've become sufficiently skilled and mature, they may even be able to do the shopping for you!

Include teens in estimating/setting a family budget. Call a short family finance meeting once a week or once a month. Share your household budget with your kids, introduce spreadsheets, talk a little bit about income taxes (at tax time) and review financial statements, like credit card bills and bank statements. Try to make it fun – over pizza, perhaps – and be sure not to dominate the discussion. Let the kids ask questions and share their ideas.

BUILD FINANCIAL CONFIDENCE AND INDEPENDENCE

As a parent, one of your major goals is to send your children out into the world as financially confident and independent young adults. When it comes to money, some kids believe in a "money fairy" who's always there when they want something or get into financial trouble.

Such magical thinking results when parents regularly succumb to their kid's demands or bail them out each time they make a mistake. When parents do this, their child may develop an entitlement mentality that will be very hard to shake. Not a good situation for anyone! In a worst case scenario, a kid may stay financially immature long into adulthood. So:

Learn to say "No!" We've all been there in a store when a kid needles a parent to buy a candy bar or the latest toy. And many of us have some emotional baggage of our own that inclines us to exceed our limits and give in to demands. We may feel that our kids will love us more if we surrender. But, as we all know, kids need limits. In addition, giving in too often to a child's demands could jeopardize one's own financial situation in the long run.

Don't overindulge your kids with money or stuff. Even if your kid is not overly demanding, you may be inclined to spoil them with material things out of sense of misplaced love or guilt.

Hold teens responsible for their financial choices. Let your teen experience the consequences of not following through on financial obligations. Don't help them out every time they screw up. But do let them know that it's OK to make mistakes – everyone does. This is one way people learn to better manage money.

Gradually transfer money management responsibility. As your teen becomes more mature, provide them with a larger allowance (see below, "Provide a Regular Allowance") and give them more and more responsibility for handling payment of their basic expenses, e.g., school-related items, clothing, transportation, entertainment.

PROVIDE A REGULAR ALLOWANCE

There is a great ongoing debate about the pros and cons of giving kids an allowance. The nays say it's a welfare-like handout that undermines the work-for-money ethic and leads to a sense of entitlement. The yeas counter that a regular, well-administered allowance is a great way for kids to gain hands-on, practical experience in managing money and setting spending priorities.

This book favors giving allowances. With a steady amount of income, kids can make their own choices. This means they don't have to beg whenever they want something (and parents don't have to deal with incessant demands either). Of course, giving allowances to kids also means parents may have to stand aside when their kids make mistakes. But they should feel confident knowing that, with proper mentoring, their children will be learning what it takes to be financially responsible adults. Moreover, their children will be gaining a greater sense of accomplishment, self-worth and independence.

Discuss the "family contract" and make expectations clear.

Explain to your teen that as a member of the family, they are expected to contribute to the day-to-day workings of the family and to pull their own weight. The family unit is governed by this unwritten social and economic contract.

Parents, of course, need to specify to their kids what is expected of them under the contract, namely to complete their schoolwork, pick up after themselves and help with specific household chores. Kids should also understand that, like everyone else in the family, they will be asked from time to time to do extra, unspecified tasks.

Here's where things can start to get tricky. Kids are likely from time to time to challenge their parents' authority. They may refuse to do their chores unless they are paid for them. Giving in to such demands, however, goes against the idea of the family contract, namely that every member of the family is simply expected to pull their own weight. A parent may need to remind the child about this contract by withholding something. However, to maintain the idea that an allowance is a learning tool and not payment for work, as in an employer-employee relationship, it's best to withhold a privilege (e.g., playing a video game) rather than the allowance.

Use an allowance as a learning tool. Kids don't naturally understand how to manage money. They need guidance from you. Don't just hand them money; talk with them regularly about how they're spending it, what their long term goals are and whether they're budgeting to achieve these goals. An allowance is intended to help kids learn that money is a valuable but finite resource that must be managed. They can use money to buy things, but unless they know how to resist temptation and set priorities, it can soon run out.

Match the allowance to the responsibilities. The amount of an allowance should equate to the amount of financial responsibility your teen is shouldering. As a child becomes more mature about managing money, parents may decide that it's time for the child to start paying for more things – clothing, some food, entertainment. At this point, parents will probably need to consider granting a larger allowance proportionate to the teen's added responsibilities.

EMPHASIZE THE LINK BETWEEN WORK AND MONEY
(Review the Employment and Income chapter.)

Until your teen starts working for money, they may not have a realistic view of where money comes from. They may assume it's free and just pops out of a parent's wallet or an ATM machine. They need to understand that when mom and dad go off to work, they are earning money for the family. When a teen starts working for money, they really start to see the connection.

Offer kids opportunities to work. Before your kid steps out of the house to seek work, you can introduce the concept of earning money by paying for certain discrete tasks they do over and above what is expected as part of their regular family responsibilities. They might mow the lawn or, like Huck Finn, paint a fence or put in a vegetable garden.

Encourage kids to find work outside your home. There really is no end of work to be done. Kids just need to look around. Neighbors may need someone to babysit or wash their windows. Kids may also find part-time jobs at local businesses.

Support your teen's entrepreneurial aspirations. When you encourage your teen's business ideas, you will be fueling their creativity and building self-reliance. Look into programs like those offered by Junior Achievement (juniorachievement.org) that are designed to help kids develop the practical and inventive skills they will need for work and entrepreneurial pursuits.

Be sure your teen always takes some time off just to have fun. "All work and no play makes Jack a dull boy." Without time off from work, a person becomes both bored and boring.

DISTINGUISH BETWEEN NEEDS AND WANTS
(Review the Needs and Wants chapter.)

Discuss the difference between needs and wants. Young people often have trouble distinguishing between needs and wants. To them a glass of water and an ice-cream cone may both seem like needs. Help them understand why one is, in fact, a need and the other, a want, i,e, water is critical to their survival, a sugary frozen dessert is not. It's essential that they grasp the difference.

Emphasize the importance of spending money on needs before wants. Help your teen see that when they spend money on wants before needs, they may run out of money to pay for all their basic needs.

Encourage your teen to resist peer pressure from friends. As we all know, teens are very susceptible to peer pressure – they want to be like their friends and will readily spend money on things they don't really need or even want. Advise them that when a friend suggests spending money on something, they need to stop and think first instead of acting on impulse. Prime them to ask questions such as: "Is this something I need right now?"; "Can I afford to buy this?"; "Are there better ways of spending this money?" Help them to build their self-confidence so that when they're pressured to spend money unwisely, they have the courage to resist going along with the crowd.

Point out how advertisers manipulate consumer emotions. Discuss the tricks advertisers use to entice people to buy things they may not need or want. In words or images, advertisers are always trying to persuade people to buy their products by pandering to their emotions with phrases such as: "You are special," "You deserve it," "You'll impress your friends," "Everyone is buying this fantastic product," "You'll be as pretty as this model (or as strong as this pro football player)," etc.

EXTOL THE BENEFITS OF A THRIFTY LIFESTYLE
(Review the Thrifty Lifestyle section in the Money Tips For Teens chapter.)

America is in love with big, glitzy, novel stuff and lots of it – big houses, Big Macs, shiny new cars, lavish weddings, the latest electronics, and on and on. But there's a problem here. Often, these things add up to big expenditures, big debts and a lot of stress on us and our planet.

The "think small" philosophy has arisen in response to our hyper-consumerism. It says that what we actually need more of now is less. The aim is not, however, that we all become monks and adopt a lifestyle of extreme self-denial. It simply means that by acquiring less extraneous stuff, we can use our money for really meaningful activities and things.

Set an example of thrift. Show your kids how you try to cut expenses when you do your budget, shop and plan your activities. Talk about what you find truly satisfying and how you are saving so you will be able to enjoy these things.

Encourage your kids to adopt a "think small" philosophy. It's not easy for kids to maintain their thrifty habits. Every day they'll come up against pressure from peers and advertisers to buy and buy some more. Challenge them to resist these forces. Encourage them to talk about what really matters to them and how they can use their money to do what they really want to do in life. In this way, they will be on their way to leading a fulfilling life and helping protect our planet as well.

Help them understand that frugality is not poverty. In fact, the more simple your lifestyle, the richer and more meaningful your life may be.

MODEL SMART SPENDING
(Review the Smart Spending and Loans chapters.)

Teach your teens to think before spending. Encourage your teens to ask themselves questions before they buy something. "Do I really need this?" "Will this item really enhance my life?" "Can I afford it?" "Is there a better way to use this money?" "Is this the best price, value, product?" "Should I wait for a sale?"

Point out that every spending decision is a trade-off. Kids need to learn that money is a scarce resource. As very few people ever have enough money to buy everything they want, almost everyone has to set spending priorities. We may have to forego a purchase altogether, or at least, wait until we've saved up enough to buy it.

Whenever we spend our money on one thing, we always lose the opportunity to spend it on another thing (opportunity cost). Kids need to understand that spending too much money now on snacks, electronics, clothes, entertainment, etc., may limit their freedom to spend money on more worthwhile things (e.g., college education) later.

Help your teen learn the value of money. We have to work to earn money to pay for our needs and wants. As the time and energy we can devote to work is limited, we need to value our efforts and not fritter away the fruits of our labor. When your teen wants to purchase an expensive item, ask them to determine: (1) how many hours they would have had to work to earn enough money for that purchase; (2) whether buying that item is worth working that much and (3) whether they should reserve their hard-earned money for a more suitable purchase.

Discuss and practice various consumer strategies. These include: comparative shopping, waiting for sales and discounts, buying used and trading with friends and relatives. Engage your teen in your decision-making process when you shop. Ask them to consider low-cost alternatives, collect coupons, look for sales in the newspaper, do product research and go on a treasure hunt to find the best value in terms of quality, value, price and warranty.

Warn your teen about loans and the dangers of borrowing. It's always best to avoid borrowing money. Of course, in some situations, like buying a house, most of us need help in the form of a loan. The most risky and burdensome loans are: payday, rent-to-own, car title and pawnshop loans.

FOSTER DREAMS AND GOALS

We can all get caught up in the day-to-day effort of living, but what is life all about if we don't take the time to dream a little?

Encourage your kids to dream about their future. It's important for kids to feel that some of their dreams really can come true, but they need to understand that realizing their dreams is a process that takes time.

Help kids convert dreams into attainable goals. Vaguely conceived dreams rarely come to fruition. "Goals are dreams with deadlines," says author Diana Scharf-Hunt. Ask your teens to write down specific goals along with estimates of time and costs associated with each one. Urge them to develop goals with different time spans: short-term goals (achievable in under a year, e.g., buying tech toys or clothes, taking a short trip); mid-term goals (achievable in 1-5 years, e.g., buying a car); long-term goals (achievable in 5+ years, e.g., college). With a plan for realizing their dreams, your teen will have a much better chance of success and success builds self-confidence.

EXPLAIN THE IMPORTANCE OF SAVING MONEY
(Review the Saving chapter.)

Promote saving money as an important habit. Money is essential to realizing dreams, so the sooner your teen develops this habit, the better.

Help your teen set up a savings account. Explain that, even if they put in only a small amount of money, their money will earn interest. In addition, with their money stashed in a savings account, they will be less likely to lose it or spend it on frivolous things. Many banks offer savings and checking accounts tailored for young children and teens. Of course, be sure that the bank or credit union is FDIC-insured.

Explain the powerful concept of compound interest. When interest earned on an original deposit (the principal) is added to that deposit, the new (increased) sum becomes the basis on, which even more interest is calculated etc. This is the process of compounding. Explain to your teen that the sooner he/she starts saving, the more time they will have to take advantage of this powerful money-making tool. Reviewing the chart on page 157 will help your teen understand compound interest.

Promote the "pay yourself first" principle. This sounds like bad advice. Don't responsible people pay their bills first? But the truth is, if you always pay your bills first, you'll never have much (if anything) left over for savings. This is unfortunate, because all it takes is a small amount of money saved on regular basis to build up a nest egg for the future. Encourage your teen to develop the habit of saving a fixed amount or percentage (10 to 20%) of their income on a regular schedule (weekly or monthly). One of the easiest ways to save is to automate the process by asking a willing employer to directly deposit a portion of every paycheck in a savings account.

Stress the importance of a "rainy day" fund. No one can foretell what the future will hold – a job loss, a health emergency, or a car breakdown. Maintaining a rainy day fund (e.g., money in a savings account) allows one to pay for these unanticipated expenditures without having to borrow money.

Encourage the habit of saving by matching what they save. For example, you could add a quarter to every dollar they save.

Help your teen distinguish between saving and hoarding. Hoarding is the act of accumulating money or other things just for the sake of accumulation. It is a compulsive behavior that can damage a person's well-being, whereas saving – the act of setting aside money for specific and sensible goals – can enhance one's life.

INTRODUCE BANKING
(Review Saving and Banking chapters.)

Help your teen open a checking account. Look for a bank that offers the services your teen needs at the best rates. Many banks offer accounts geared to teens and students that demand less money to open, require no minimum balance and charge low fees. A good time to open an account is when your teen has started to earn money and needs to pay some bills. At this point, you can introduce them to: making deposits and withdrawals; using an ATM; monitoring the bank account balance; writing checks; maintaining a check register; reviewing bank statements; and balancing their checkbook.

Introduce online banking. Once your teen understands the basics of banking using traditional tools, you can start explaining how to use a computer or smart phone to manage accounts.

Scrutinize your teen's accounts weekly or monthly. Typically, with teen bank accounts, the parent is co-owner and has full access to the account. Viewing teen accounts online is the easiest way for parents to monitor usage.

INTRODUCE MONEY CARDS
(Review Prepaid Cards, Credit Cards and Banking chapters.)

Discuss the different types of money cards. There are pay-before cards (gift cards and prepaid debit cards), pay-now cards (bank debit cards) and pay-later cards (credit cards). No money card is totally without risk, but because money cards are so prevalent these days, most teens will need to learn how to use them and to avoid their many pitfalls.

Start your teen with a prepaid (pay-before) card. Your kids are likely to receive gift cards from family and friends. You could also set them up with a basic prepaid debit card. Note that gift cards and prepaid debit cards differ. Most gift cards are not reloadable; prepaid debit cards are. Prepaid debit cards, unlike gift cards, are linked to an electronic payment network, like Visa. This makes them much more useful. But prepaid debit cards often have more fees associated with them than do gift cards.

You can think of pay-before cards as "credit cards with training wheels", because kids can use the card without the risk of falling into debt. They can practice monitoring the balance on their card (so they will always know how much money is left). They can also look into the fees, terms and conditions associated with their card and research other cards to see how they compare. Remind your kids that even pay-before cards are risky to some degree – if they lose a prepaid card, they may not be able to replace its cash value.

Help your teen obtain a bank debit (pay-now) card. Once your teen has a checking account, help them start using a bank debit card that is associated with their account. This card allows them to withdraw money instantly from the account. Your teen can use the card to make purchases and get cash from an ATM.

But there are dangers with bank debit cards. Caution your teen against using the card on the phone or Internet, as this may expose them to fraudsters. Also, stress the importance of monitoring the balance in their checking account to avoid incurring overdraft fees.

INTRODUCE CREDIT CARDS
(Review the Tips For Teens, Credit Cards and Credit chapters.)

Warn your teen(s) about the dangers of credit card debt. Teens need to develop a healthy fear of falling into a debt hole by misusing a credit card. Credit card debt can result in: paying a lot more for goods than necessary; lowering your credit score; limiting your future credit options; and suffering from unnecessary worry, stress and depression.

Emphasize the value of building a good credit history and credit score. This is critical, because one's credit history and credit score impact so many aspects of life. Potential creditors/lenders (e.g., banks, credit card companies) will review your teen's credit history and credit score when deciding whether or not to provide them with new loans or credit cards. A good credit history may also be an advantage when they go to rent an apartment, open utility accounts, seek a good rate on car insurance, or look for a job (potential employers may review their credit history). Conversely, a poor credit history can be a major hindrance in their everyday life and take years to repair.

Don't give credit cards to irresponsible teens. Signs of immaturity include: constantly losing important personal items such as car keys, cellphones, wallets; a poor work ethic and lack of interest in earning money; impulse buying; poor math skills.

Consider making your teen an authorized user. Kids under 18 are not allowed to open a credit card account on their own; but you can add them to your own credit card as an authorized user. Consider doing this only if you have a good credit score (700+). The big win here would be that by being an authorized user, your teen would start to build their own credit history just by piggybacking on yours. This would happen even if you decided not to allow them to a or might actually use the card.

If you do allow your teen to use your credit card, you should closely monitor their spending activities and give them advice as needed. Set clear limits on how they can use the card – "yes" on school-related expenses, "no" on extravagances – because their actions could affect your credit score. Involve them in reviewing the monthly statement.

Introduce your teen to good credit card habits. These include: checking credit card statements regularly; reporting irregularities immediately; never exceeding the credit limit; paying the full balance on time to avoid finance charges; avoiding the minimum payment trap; never getting cash advances; and taking steps to protect cards from loss or theft.

Consider being a cosigner on your teen's credit card. Kids over 18 may apply for their own credit card, but creditors could deny their application if the young person is not earning enough money. Alternatively a creditor could require parents to be cosigners and might provide only a small line of credit to the young person.

Parents should agree to be cosigners only if they believe their teen is mature enough to use credit responsibly. This is because the parent, as a cosigner, has equal responsibility for paying the credit card bills. If their kid misuses the card, both the parent and the kid will suffer the consequences, i.e., negative information in their credit reports and lower credit scores.

Consider a "secured credit card" for your teen. If you don't have a good credit score, it might be better to get your teen a secured credit card (see page 221). You will have to make a deposit to cover the card's charge limit and this should be no more than $500. Make sure the card has the lowest possible fees and that the payment history is reported to at least one credit bureau so your teen will start to build a credit history.

WARN TEENS ABOUT IDENTITY THEFT AND FRAUD
(Review the Fraud and Money Tips for Teens chapters.)

Emphasize the right to privacy. Make sure your teen knows that they have an absolute right to keep their personal information private. It is up to each one of us to decide who can obtain or use this information.

Warn your teen that there are many fraudulent schemes. The list goes on and on: identify theft, bogus goods, bait-and-switch tactics, skimming, telemarketing fraud, phishing on the Internet, etc. Kids are especially vulnerable to online fraud, so tell them to: buy only from secure websites (those with URLs that begin with "https"); create unique passwords for online accounts; keep their computers protected with up-to-date security software; block spam emails; avoid using computers in public places to do online banking; and never provide personal information in an email or on social media sites.

Stress the need to protect money cards. Different cards have different levels of protection. Your teen should know what protections each card issuer provides. They should understand the urgency of reporting a loss or theft immediately and be ready with all the necessary information (issuer's phone number or website, their account number, their social security number, etc.)

Help your teen manage important papers in a safe way. Make sure your teen knows: what papers to keep and for how long; how to safely and efficiently store important papers; and how to dispose of documents that thieves could use to link your child's name with other personal information and thereby gain access to their bank accounts and credit cards.

EXPLAIN PHYSICAL AND FINANCIAL RISKS
(Review the Risk chapter.)

The world is a dangerous place. The potential for damage to one's body and/or wallet is always present. But there are ways to reduce these risks.

Help your teen stay physically fit and healthy. Your teen needs to get enough sleep, eat right, maintain a healthy weight, move and keep fit. Otherwise, health problems could lead to financial problems. Provide a good model by taking good care of yourself.

Discourage your teen from taking dangerous physical risks. This is a tough one. Many kids get a thrill from taking physical risks and think they're invincible. The problem is they don't appreciate the real risks involved and the possible negative consequences. In any case, make sure they have good training for potentially dangerous sports activities and use the proper safety equipment.

Show through example how you try to protect yourself around the house by using the proper tools in the proper way, etc. Talk about the consequences of not being careful (i.e., injury, big bills, death).

Make sure your teen has health insurance. There are myriad options for health insurance coverage; do everything in your power to make sure your teen has adequate health insurance.

Discuss the various types of insurance your teen may need. These may include renter's insurance, car insurance, travel insurance, home-owner's insurance (one day in the future), umbrella insurance and more.

HELP YOUR TEEN MAKE EDUCATION CHOICES
(Review the Loans and Money Tips for Teens chapters.)

Start a 529 college savings or a prepaid tuition plan. Look into this as soon as you put this book down. Ideally you would have done this the day your child was born, but there's no time like today. College savings plans differ from state to state and have certain advantages and disadvantages, so do some research before you make your choice. (If the designated recipient doesn't use the money, it can be transferred to another sibling.)

Talk at length with your teen about their interests, talents and career possibilities. At every opportunity, engage your teen in talking about the future. Expect them to change ideas many times – this week a veterinarian, next week an astrophysicist. Only a small number of kids know exactly what they want to do.

Work with your teen to identify colleges and other schools that suit their particular needs. The array of postsecondary educational options can seem daunting. You and your teen can't make a choice in a weekend; it's a process. Start early and go slow. Look for helpful resources on college and government websites. Consider low-cost options that might suit your teen's needs. Consult with school guidance counselors. Take your teen to visit potential schools. Ask a lot of questions.

Look into your teen's eligibility for grants and scholarships. Investigate this avenue with your teen before turning to loans. This is money that won't need to be paid back.

Consider federal loans first. If you and your teen need to borrow money, apply first for federal loans, which have lower interest rates. Avoid high-cost alternatives, like credit card loans. Visit the federal student aid website – studentaid.ed.gov.

Calculate how much your teen needs to borrow. These days young people carry heavy debt loads for their educational expenses. It's not easy to determine up front whether they will be able to afford the monthly payments on their college loans once they graduate. Advise them to try to limit their total college debt to their anticipated annual salary for the first year out of school. Ideally, annual student loan payments should not exceed ten percent of their annual pretax income.

If your teen is really unsure about what they want to do, let them to take a year off. Paying for an inappropriate education could be a big waste of money. An emerging trend is for colleges to offer support to new students for "gap years". To learn more about gap year opportunities, go to americangap.org., idealist.org and globalcitizenyear.org. Alternatively, your indecisive teen could stay at home, help around the house and work in a field that interests them. During this time, they could take tours of work sites and interview practitioners in fields of interest. They could also volunteer, doing something that might be relevant to a possible career. This research and experience would give them more insight into the type of education they might need. A year is probably sufficient for this. As soon as possible, encourage your teen to make a decision about their postsecondary education. The longer one stays away from school, the harder it becomes to resume a study routine.

HELP WITH CAR OWNERSHIP DECISIONS

Discuss car ownership with your teen. For many teens, owning a car is one of their biggest dreams, but cars are expensive (not to mention potentially dangerous). When your teen starts thinking about owning a car, it's important to talk with them about why they want to make this commitment.

Do they really require a car to reach their desired destination or would the car be just a status symbol? Are there alternative ways of getting around – walking, biking, sharing rides, occasional rentals, public transportation? Can they finance a car themselves? If not, can you afford to help them finance a car? Can they afford to pay the car loan payments? Can they afford to pay for gas, maintenance and insurance? Would it be better to save their hard-earned money for something more important?

Talk about saving to purchase a car. If you and your teen decide that getting a car is desirable, the next step is to start saving for it. It's best to have saved enough money to pay the full price of the car, but if this is not possible, make as big a down payment as possible. Even if you have decided to help your teen pay for a car, they should make a significant contribution towards its purchase. The process of saving for a car can be a great learning opportunity. With the car as a carrot, your teen will be inspired to put aside money and will gain a deeper understanding of the connection between work, saving money and achieving goals.

Shop for the best car to serve your teen's needs. This is not the time to think about the latest model, high-end sports car. Look for a reliable, good-quality car. A lightly used, secondhand car might be the best choice.

Shop for the best deal. If your teen (and you) can't buy a car outright, then you'll need to take out a loan. Look for the lowest annual percentage rate (APR) on a loan with manageable monthly payments and a reasonable payback period. Be sure, when calculating the cost of the car, that you determine the total cost – base price plus interest on a loan of a certain duration. Don't be distracted by what seems like a low monthly loan payment. It might be easy to think you're getting a good deal when, in fact, you're setting yourself up to pay more in total for the car than necessary. Discuss with your teen the pitfalls of failing to make the monthly loan payments, e.g., repossession of the car, impact on credit rating.

Shop around for car insurance. Rates and policies vary, so compare different providers. A driver safety course can also help reduce the cost of insurance.

INTRODUCE INVESTING
(Review the Investing chapter.)

Investing is a way of growing your money, putting your money to work for you so that inflation does not have such a big impact on the value of your savings. You may or may not be comfortable yourself with the complexities of investing, and you may have some concerns about drawing your teen into this sometimes tumultuous sphere. But common wisdom still promotes investing as the best way to build retirement savings and hedge against inflation. Collaborating with you is the best way for your teen to gain experience safely.

Introduce frequently used investment terms. Make sure your teen knows the meaning of important terms and concepts including stocks, bonds, mutual funds, index funds, dividends, volatility, risk-return trade-off, the time value of money, compound interest, Rule of 72, dollar-cost averaging, diversification, and IRAs.

Encourage your teen to learn about the stock market. The SIFMA Foundation's Stock Market Game™ (SMG) gives students the chance to learn about the stock market and investing. Starting with a virtual cash account of $100,000, students strive to create the best-performing portfolio using a live trading simulation. To find out more, go to: smgww.org

Help your teen buy some stock. Owning some real stock is another good way for your teen to learn about investing. Start building a portfolio with your teen as soon as you think they are ready – it takes time to see how the market really works, how values rise and fall, how investments can grow in value over time.

At first, keep most of your teen's portfolio in a low-expense-ratio index fund. Buy enough shares to make the experience meaningful. The next step might be to help them pick a few relatively "safe", individual stocks to "play" with. Over time, consider buying more stock from other companies, as well as some bonds, so your teen can start to see the value of diversification.

Stress that investing differs from gambling. Investing is similar to gambling in that both involve taking risks with money. But gamblers take foolhardy risks, seeking the thrill of instant rewards. Investors, on the other hand, try to take reasonable risks. They do research and think carefully before making investments. They understand that making money often takes time.

Point out that investing differs from saving. As noted earlier, the first thing to do with the money you earn is simply to save some of it. Investing comes later. It's best if you can do both.

WARN ABOUT THE DANGERS OF GAMBLING
(Review the Gambling chapter.)

Explain that when you gamble, you risk: being short of money for everyday needs; squandering money that should have been reserved for long-term goals; going into serious debt and perhaps bankruptcy; wasting time and neglecting family, friends, school, etc.; and developing a gambling addiction that could ruin your life.

HELP TEENS PREPARE FOR RETIREMENT

No doubt, you've been thinking about your own retirement dreams. Share some of them with your kids to stimulate their thinking about the future, too.

Encourage your kids to develop their own long-term dreams. For your kids, retirement may seem unreal and light years away. Nonetheless, ask them to imagine a time when they wouldn't need to worry about money and could do whatever they find exciting and satisfying – a second career or an avocation that might not earn them any money at all.

Reiterate to your kids the need to save and invest for their later years. Our kids are growing up in a world of great economic uncertainty. The situation is this: wealth generated by home ownership is declining, student loan debt is higher, salaries are not keeping up with inflation, people are living longer and company pension plans are skimpy or nonexistent. With all this stacked up against them, young people need to start putting money into a retirement savings plan (e.g., a Roth IRA) and other investments as soon as they can. Saving and investing even a little money now will create a firmer base from which to pursue their dreams later on.

REVIEW THE MONEY TIPS FOR TEENS CHAPTER

The Money Tips For Teens chapter in this book has a lot of helpful financial advice for teens. Read the chapter yourself, then try to coax your teen(s) into reading it too. You can follow up the reading with a discussion. Ask your teen(s) if there are any tips they don't agree with or don't fully understand.

USE THE "MONEY AS YOU GROW" GUIDE
(moneyasyougrow.org)

Money As You Grow: 20 Things Kids Need to Know to Live Financially Smart Lives, developed by the President's Advisory Council on Financial Capability, is an excellent resource for parents.

Families can use this online guide as a basis for discussing money with their teens and helping them learn important lessons on saving, making choices and avoiding debt.

The guide "provides 20 essential, age-appropriate financial lessons – with corresponding activities – that kids need to know as they grow. Written in down-to-earth language for children and their families, *Money as You Grow* will help equip kids with the knowledge they need to live fiscally fit lives. The lessons in *Money As You Grow* are based on more than a year of research and are drawn from dozens of standards, curricula and academic studies."

Money As You Grow: 20 Things Kids Need to Know to Live Financially Smart Lives is available as a printable booklet along with other financial literacy resources at: donwfbell.com

Index

A

advertising, 66
allowance, 413
Annual percentage rate (APR), 210, 212

B

balance, 7, 72, 98, 102, 104, 106, 226
balance transfer, 226
Banking, 91-136, 416
   account, 96
   ATM (Automated Teller Machine), 116, 118, 120, 128
   bad check lingo, 110
   balance, 98, 102, 104, 106, 118
   balancing checkbook, 106
   bank account, 96, 391
   bank account management, 132
   bank debit card, 122
     advantages, 126
     disadvantages, 129
     safeguarding, 130
   banking services, 94
   bank statement, 106
   check, 96, 97
   checkbook register, 98, 104
   checking account, 96-112
     advantages, 110
     balance, 118
     diagram, 136
     disadvantages, 112

checking account - continued
   overdrawing, 110
   writing checks, 96
   check writing, 96
credit union, 94
debit card, 122, 126, 129
deposit, 100, 102, 118
direct deposit, 100
Electronic Funds Transfer (EFT), 134
Federal Deposit Insurance Corporation (FDIC), 113
financial services, 94
liquidity, 108
mobile banking, 133
money management basics, 124
non-sufficient funds, 110
online banking, 132
opening a bank account, 96
pay now card, 122
PIN, 116, 120
savings account, 112, 114
withdrawal, 102, 128
bankruptcy, 260
Bankruptcy Abuse Prevention and Consumer Protection Act, 260
barter, 24
base interest rate, 332
beneficiary, 286
bill, 166
bonds, 346
bonus, 44

431

Index

budgets, 160, 167, 172, 174, 176, 178, 180, 182, 396
Business, 315-320
  business ethics, 317
  business plan, 317
  contract, 317
  entrepreneur, 320
  inventions created by kids, 320
  profit, 320
  starting a small business, 316

C

capital gains, 354
capitalism, 323
capital losses, 354
Cars, 424
  buying a car, 242, 402
  car title loans, 244
  upside-down car loan, 241
cartel, 326
Cash
  cash flow, 168, 170
  cash income is taxable, 378
  getting cash from an ATM, 102
Certificate of Deposit (CD), 154
checkbook register, 104
coins, 28
collection agency, 256
commission, 44
competition, 326
complaint letter, 90
compound interest, 157, 412

Consumer Financial Protection Bureau (CFPB), 89
Consumer Price Index (CPI), 334
consumer protection laws, 90
counterfeit money, 36
Credit, 203, 206
  Annual percentage rate (APR), 210
  credit history, 208
  credit report, 207, 399
  credit score, 210, 398
  creditworthiness, 209
  interest, 206
  open-end credit, 206
  revolving/open-end credit, 206
Credit CARD Act of 2009, 218
Credit Cards, 213-236, 420
  acquiring a credit card, 220
  advantages/disadvantages, 236
  alerts, 227
  authorized user, 221, 421
  balance, 226
  cash advance, 228
  consumer protection, 218
  cosigner, 220, 421
  credit card options, 221
  credit cards - diagram, 215
  credit card statement, 222-224
  credit limit, 228
  federal protections, 218
  finance charges, 230

Index

fine print, 220
grace period, 226
late fees/penalties, 230
minimum payment, 232
pay later card, 216
principal, 226
read the fine print first, 220
safeguarding cards, 234
secured credit card, 221
verifying information, 226
credit counseling, 255
credit union, 94
currency, 34

D

debit card. *See* Banking
Debt, 247-260, 250
bankruptcy, 260
collection agency, 256
debt advice, 260
default, 254, 256
dumb debt habits, 250
Fair Debt Collection Practices Act, 256
garnishment, 258
good debt advice, 260
good debt vs. bad debt, 252
lender pressure tactics, 256
liability, 252
protected assets, 260
repossession, 258
when to borrow, 252
default, 254, 256
deficit, 178, 332
delayed gratification, 84
depression (economic), 330
donate, 404
Dow Jones Industrial Average (DJIA), 344
dreams and goals, 392, 411, 429

E

Economics, 321-336
balance of trade, 328
base interest rate, 332
capitalism, 323
cartel, 326
competition, 326
consumer price index, 334
deficit, 332
deflation, 334
demand, 326
depression (economic), 330
economy, 324
exchange rate, 333
free trade, 328
globalization, 328
government debt, 332
Gross Domestic Product (GDP), 334
human capital, 322
inflation, 334
invisible hand, 336
market/marketplace, 324

433

Index

Economics - continued
  monopoly, 326
  recession, 330
  supply, 326
  tariff, 328
  tragedy of the commons, 336
conomy, 324
Education, 424
  529 College Savings Plan, 382, 401
  education and income, 52
  education and unemployment, 40
  lifelong learning, 40
  student expenses, 396
  student loans, 245
Electronic Funds Transfer (EFT), 134
Employer-Sponsored Retirement Savings Plans, 364
Employment and Income, 39-52, 415
  bonus, 44
  career, 52
  commission, 44
  discretionary income, 48
  disposable income, 48
  earned/unearned income, 46, 378
  earning capacity, 52
  education and income, 52
  education and unemployment, 40
  employee, 42
  employee benefits, 50
  employee compensation, 48
  gross pay, 46
  interest income, 46
  part-time work, 50
  salary, 40, 44
  take-home pay, 48, 384
  unemployment rates, 40
  wage, 42
Equal Credit Opportunity Act, 218
equity, 361
estate, 285
exchange rate, 333
Expenses, Bills & Budgets, 159-182
  apartment lease, 164
  bill, 166
  budgets. *See* budgets
  cash flow flowchart, 168
  cash flow journal, 170
  deficit (personal), 178
  expenses - fixed & variable, 162
  lease, 164
  mortgage, 164
  payment methods, 166
  rent, 164
  surplus, 178
  utilities, 162

Index

F

Fair and Accurate Credit Transactions Act (FACT Act), 218
Fair Credit and Charge Card Disclosure Act, 218
Fair Credit Billing Act, 218
Fair Credit Reporting Act, 218
Fair Debt Collection Practices Act, 256
Federal Deposit Insurance Corporation (FDIC), 113
Federal Reserve, 332
Federal Trade Commission (consumer protection laws), 90
fiat money, 34
finance charges, 230
financial advisers, 368
financial emergencies. *See* rainy day fund
financial goals, 368
financial literacy, v, 2
fine print, 201, 220, 246, 250, 260
Fraud, 295-314, 395, 422
   card loss/theft, 306
   foiling thieves, 302
   fraud - avoiding, 302, 304, 312
   fraud - examples, 297, 298
   fraud on social networks, 313, 314
   identity theft, 300, 302

Fraud - continued
   phishing, 310
   proving your identity, 300
   safeguard your social security number, 311
   scam, 298
   skimming, 304
   telemarketing/phone fraud, 308
   work-at-home schemes, 310

G

Gambling, 287-294, 400, 429
   addiction - getting help, 294
   casino, 292
   gambling - examples, 290
   help for addiction, 294
   high-risk investments, 290
   lottery, 292
   odds/probabilities, 290, 292, 294
   risks of gambling, 294
   teen gambling, 290
   tricks and strategies, 294
garnishment, 258
gift cards, 188
goals (financial), 368
government debt, 332
Gross Domestic Product (GDP), 334
gross income, 378
gross pay, 46

Index

H
happiness economy, 4
health care directive, 280
health care proxy, 280
healthy attitudes & values, 406
healthy lifestyle rewards, 265
hoarding, 156
human capital, 401

I
identity theft. See Fraud
impulse buying, 80
income. See Employment and Income
income taxes, 376
index fund, 348
Individual Retirement Account (IRA), 364
inflation, 334
Insurance, 269-286
  auto insurance, 270, 276
  beneficiary, 286
  benefits, 274
  claim, 274
  comprehensive auto, 278
  coverage, 274
  deductible, 272
  disability insurance, 278
  exclusions, 274
  health insurance, 278
  homeowners insurance, 282
  insurance coverage, 274
  liability insurance, 284
  life insurance, 286
  limits to insurance, 272
  long term care insurance, 280
  Medicaid health insurance, 280
  Medicare health insurance, 280
  premium, 272
  renters insurance, 282
  umbrella insurance, 284
Interest, 206
  compound and simple, 157
Internal Revenue Service (IRS), 376
Investing, 337-372, 427
  active/passive investing, 348
  bonds, 346
  capital gains, 354
  capital losses, 354
  cash flow flowchart, 168
  diversification, 362
  dividends, 352
  dollar-cost averaging, 362
  Dow Jones Industrial Average (DJIA), 344
  employer-sponsored retirement savings plans, 364
  equity, 361
  financial advisers, 368
  financial goal, 368
  Individual Retirement Accounts (IRAs), 364
  invest for the long term, 362

Index

Investing - continnued
    investing vs. gambling, 338, 342
    investing vs. saving, 342
    investment performance, 354
    investment risk, 356
    investment strategies, 362
    investments - types, 340
    mutual fund, 348
    net worth, 368, 369, 370, 371
    Pension Protection Act, 366
    personal financial plan, 372
    portfolio, 352
    principal, 344
    prospectus, 350
    retirement, 363
    risk-return trade-off, 358
    risk tolerance, 356
    Roth IRA, 364
    Rule of 72, 360
    securities, 344
    stock market/exchange, 350
    stocks, 344, 352
    time value of money, 358
    U.S. Savings Bonds, 346
    volatility, 350
    yield, 354
    yield or rate of return, 354
IOU (I owe you), 96

L
late fees/penalties, 230
layaway, 68
legacy worth millions, 406
liability, 252
lifelong learning, 9, 40
liquidity, 108
living will, 280
Loans, 237-246
    car loans, 242
    car title loans, 244
    closed-end vs. open-end, 242
    deposit advance loans, 244
    easy access credit loans, 244
    fine print traps, 246
    loaning money, 240
    loan sharks, 244
    mortgage loans, 242
    negotiating a loan, 240
    pawnshop loans, 244
    payday loans, 244
    rent-to-own loans, 244
    student loans, 245, 246
    upside-down car loan, 241

M
macroeconomics, 324
market/marketplace, 324
Medicaid, 280
Medicare, 280
microeconomics, 324
mint.com, 174
Money
    banknotes, 30
    bills of exchange, 30

437

Index

Money - continued
  bitcoins, 34
  coins, 28
  commodity money, 26
  counterfeit money, 36
  currency, 34
  dollar - origin of word, 22
  dollar sign ($) - origin, 22
  electronic money, 38
  fiat money, 34
  history, 21-38
  letters of credit, 30, 32
  managing money, 372, 396
  mechanics of money, 408
  money cards, 398
  money over the centuries, 38
  money words, 22
  pay now card, 122
  representative money, 30
  virtual currencies, 34
  virtual wallets, 36
Money Advice
  Money As You Grow, 430
  Money Tips For Parents, 405
  Money Tips For Teens, 389
money cards, 419
Money Life$aver Quiz Games, 11-20
money management basics, 124
money order, 112
monopoly, 326
mortgage, 164

mutual fund, 348

N

National Foundation for Credit Counseling (NFCC), 255
National Standards in K-12 Personal Finance Education, 10
Needs and Wants, 53-60, 410
  job-related needs, 56
  need for employment, 56
  needs, 56
  needs come first, 58, 178
  needs vs. wants, 54
  opportunity cost, 60
  safety-related needs, 56
  wants, 56, 58
nest egg, 158
net income, 384
net worth, 368-371

O

opportunity cost/trade-offs, 60

P

pawnshop loans, 244
payday loans, 244
pay later card, 216
payment card network, 187, 190
payment methods, 166
pay yourself first. *See* Saving
peer pressure, 78
Pension Protection Act, 366

Index

personal finance, v
personal financial plan, 372
phishing, 310
piggy bank origin, 145
PIN, 116, 120
Point of sale (POS), 78
portfolio, 352
power of attorney, 280
Prepaid Cards, 183-202
  adding money, 196
  balance, 198
  cards for teens and students, 201
  fees, 191, 196
  gift cards, 188
    open loop, 188
    closed loop, 190
  prepaid cards - diagram, 184
  prepaid debit cards, 192, 193, 194
    adding money, 196
    holds, 198
    pros and cons, 202
    protecting, 200
    returning purchases, 197
    spending rules, 199
principal, 226, 344
privacy, 300
profit, 320
property taxes, 388
prospectus, 350

R

rainy day fund, 124, 150, 168, 178, 268, 392, 412
recession, 330
refund, 386
rent, 164
rent-to-own loans, 244
repossession, 258
retirement, 363, 403, 430
return or total return, 354
Risk, 261-268, 400, 423
  dangerous activities, 266
  health insurance risk, 268
  physical & financial risks, 265, 266, 268
  range of risk, 264
  risk management, 264
  risk-return trade-off, 358
  risk tolerance, 356
Roth IRA, 364
Rule of 72, 360

S

safe deposit box, 94
salary, 44
Saving, 137-158, 393, 411
  10% saving rule, 146
  buy without borrowing, 148
  Certificate of Deposit (CD), 154
  excuses for not saving, 142
  hoarding, 156

Index

Saving - continued
  nest egg, 158
  pay yourself first, 144, 412
  piggy bank - origin, 145
  rainy days. *See* rainy day fund
  safe deposit box, 94
  saving at sales, 146
  savings, 154
  savings account, 112, 114, 154
  savings goals, 148
  saving small amounts, 146
  tips on saving, 58, 393
  top three priorities, 150
  why save, 140
  windfall, 152
savings, 158
securities, 344
shopping binges, 86
skimming, 304
Smart Spending, 61-90, 394, 417
  advertising awareness, 66
  bulk buying, 74
  buying used/refurbished products, 67
  comparison shopping, 68
  complaint letter, 90
  compulsive shopping, 84
  consumer protection, 90
  credit card vs. cash, 72
  delayed gratification, 84
  extended warranties, 71
  false consumer notions, 70

Smart Spending - continued
  high pressure sales pitches, 76
  impulse buying, 80, 82
  making a big purchase, 66
  payment types, 70
  peer pressure, 78
  purchases
    after making a purchase, 88
    before making a purchase, 64
    saving for a big purchase, 68
    when making a purchase, 70
  return policies, 88
  sales, 73, 74, 76
  shopping binges, 86
  shortchanging yourself, 76
  spending priorities, 64
  product information, 66
  unit prices, 74
  used/refurbished products, 67
  ways to pay, 70
social networks, 313, 314
Social Security, 362
spendthrift, 86
standard of living, 180
stock market/exchange, 350
stocks, 344
supply, 326
surplus, 178

T

Taxes, 373-388
  529 college savings plan, 382
  cash income is taxable, 378

Index

Taxes - continued
   deductions, 380
   earned income, 378
   filing a return, 386
   gross income, 378
   income taxes, 376
   Internal Revenue Service (IRS), 376
   net income, 384
   payroll deductions, 384
   progressive income tax, 376
   property taxes, 388
   recordkeeping, 388
   sales tax, 388
   taxable income, 378, 380
   tax code, 376
   tax credit, 380
   tax deferral, 382
   taxes on interest earned, 114
   tax evasion, 386
   tax exemptions, 380
   tax refund, 386
   tip income, 378
   transfer payment, 385
   unearned income, 378
   what taxes pay for, 373
   withholding, 384
thrifty lifestyle, 395, 416
time value of money, 358
trust, 284
Truth in Lending Act, 242
Truth in Savings Act, 138

U

U.S. Savings Bonds, 346
utilities, 162

V

values, 6
virtual currencies, 34
volatility, 350
volunteer, 404

W

wage, 44
warranty, 68
Warren Buffet, 288, 357
wealth, 352, 368
welfare programs, 385
will, 285
windfall, 152
wire transfer, 134

Y

yield, 354

About the Author

Don Bell has over 30 years of experience working in education, media and technology. He has worked as a special education teacher, computer trainer, educational software marketeer and most recently as a web learning consultant at Rensselaer Polytechnic Institute. In the early 1990s he started working on developing games to teach kids about personal finance. In 2011 he developed a money quiz card game based on the Jump$tart Coalition's National Standards for K-12 Personal Finance Education. In 2012-2014 he converted the game into a book format. His aim is to provide parents, grandparents, home school educators, teachers, tutors and mentors with fun ways to teach teens financial literacy. He lives in Troy, NY, with his wife and editor, Diane.
Contact: donwfbell@gmail.com, donwfbell.com.

About the Cartoonist/Illustrator - Randy Rumpf is a cartoonist, illustrator and graphic designer. He has over 35 years of experience in the visual arts field. He was a designer and illustrator for Rensselaer Polytechnic Institute in Troy, NY, for 15 years and started his own studio, The Design Works, in 1989. His projects have covered a wide spectrum of creative visuals in that expanse of time. Randy has illustrated everything from children's books to corporate and not-for-profit publications. He has done stage set design and implementation for several Young Actors Guild musical presentations. He has never lost his love for the creative process. One of the biggest excitements in his life remains a blank sheet of good drawing paper. You can view his online portfolio at randyrumpf.com.